D1527822

The Salvadoran Crucible

The Salvadoran Crucible

The Failure of US Counterinsurgency in

El Salvador, 1979–1992

Brian D'Haeseleer

UNIVERSITY PRESS OF KANSAS

Published by the University Press of Kansas (Lawrence, Kansas 66045), which was
organized by the Kansas Board of Regents and is operated and funded by Emporia
State University, Fort Hays State University, Kansas State University, Pittsburg State
University, the University of Kansas, and Wichita State University.

Library of Congress Cataloging-in-Publication Data

Names: D'Haeseleer, Brian, author.
Title: The Salvadoran crucible : the failure of US counterinsurgency in El
    Salvador, 1979–1992 / Brian D'Haeseleer.
Description: Lawrence, Kansas : University Press of Kansas, 2017.
    | Series: Modern war studies | Includes bibliographical references and index.
Identifiers: LCCN 2017038271 | ISBN 9780700625123 (cloth : alk. paper)
    | ISBN 9780700625130 (ebook)
Subjects: LCSH: United States—Foreign relations—El Salvador.
    | El Salvador—Foreign relations—United States. | Military assistance,
    American—El Salvador. | Counterinsurgency—United States—History—20th
    century. | Counterinsurgency—El Salvador—History—20th century.
    | El Salvador—History—1979–1992.
Classification: LCC E184.S15 D48 2017 | DDC 327.7307284/0904—dc23
LC record available at https://lccn.loc.gov/2017038271.

British Library Cataloguing-in-Publication Data is available.

Printed in the United States of America

10 9 8 7 6 5 4 3 2 1

To

Claire, Eli, and Jackson

CONTENTS

ACKNOWLEDGMENTS

I, like practically every other writer, have received immeasurable help over the years from family, friends, and various institutions. The past year has been especially difficult for my family. I cannot even begin to express my sincere gratitude toward my wife, Claire, for all her help. She married an academic historian without fully appreciating the commitment and costs it entails. Without her, I would have been unable to finish my dissertation, this book, and many other things. I am also indebted to my parents, Walter and Jeannie, who probably would have preferred that I pursue a different career path. They have encouraged and supported me throughout my professional and scholarly adventures.

This book is the culmination of a process that began in London, England, in 2006. Max Paul Friedman, my graduate mentor, helped shape the manuscript and my transition from a graduate student to a historian. Chris White read multiple drafts and offered insightful comments. Aaron Bell, Ben Bennett, Andrew Birtle, Boris Chernaev, Josh Jones, Roger Peace, Arie Serota, and Harry Vanden commented on earlier versions of this project. David E. Spencer helped pave the way for a research trip to El Salvador. Herard von Santos facilitated interviews, transported me around El Salvador, and was a great host. Kyle Longley suggested that I submit the manuscript for publication. Louie Milojevic provided encouragement over the past few years. Chris Griffin charged me far less than the market value for indexing this book, and also did an excellent job.

I learned how to teach at Tallahassee Community College. David Proctor did his best to ensure that I was in front of a class every semester. Vince Mikkelsen gave advice about how to effectively run a class and interact with students. Ted Duggan offered a sympathetic ear about the various travails of higher education. Rita Dickey processed my daily interlibrary loans and helped me maintain access to current scholarship as a lowly adjunct.

Various institutions have also provided support. American University in Washington, DC, funded my research trips to El Salvador; Norman, Oklahoma; Palo Alto, California; and the Jimmy Carter and Ronald Reagan Presidential Libraries. Stephen Carney at Arlington National Cemetery provided me lunch, drinks, and extra leave time to craft early versions of the manuscript. The University Press of Kansas, including Joyce Harrison, Mike Kehoe, and Kelly Chrisman Jacques, has also been extremely helpful in shepherding this text through the publication process.

Portions of the "Pacification" subsection in Chapter 3 were published in *Diplomacy and Statecraft*. The article is located at www.tandfonline .com.

ACRONYMS

AIFLD	American Institute for Free Labor Development
ANDES-21	Asociación Nacional de Educadores Salvadoreños
ANEP	Asociación Nacional de la Empresa Privada
ANSESAL	Agencia Nacional de Seguridad de El Salvador
ARDE	Revolutionary Anticommunist Action for Extermination
ARENA	Alianza Republicana Nacionalista
BIRIs	Batallones (de Infantería) de Reacción Inmediata
BPR	Bloque Popular Revolucionario
BRAZ	Brígada Rafael Arce Zablah
CDs	civil defense units
CI	Counter-Insurgency (Special Group)
CIA	Central Intelligence Agency
CIDGs	Civilian Irregular Defense Groups
COIN	counterinsurgency
CONARA	National Commission for the Restoration of Areas
CORDS	Civil Operations and Rural Development Support
DIA	Defense Intelligence Agency
DRU	Unified Revolutionary Directorate
EDCOR	Economic Development Corps
ERP	Ejército Revolucionario del Pueblo
ESAF	Salvadoran Armed Forces
ESF	Economic Support Fund
FARN	Fuerzas Armadas de Resistencia Nacional
FDR	Frente Democrático Revolucionario
FENASTRAS	Federación Nacional Sindical de Trabajadores Salvadoreños
FES	Fuerzas Especiales Selectas
FID	Foreign Internal Defense
FINATA	Financiera Nacional de Tierras Agrícolas
FLN	Front de Libération Nationale
FMLN	Frente Farabundo Martí para la Liberación Nacional
FMS	Foreign Military Sales

FPL	Fuerzas Populares de Liberación
FUSADES	Fundación Salvadoreña para el Desarrollo Económico y Social
ICEX	Infrastructure Coordination and Exploitation
IDAD	Internal Defense and Development
IMET	International Military and Education Training
ISTA	Instituto Salvadoreño de Transformación Agraria
JRG	Revolutionary Junta Government
KISSSS	keep it simple, sustainable, small, and Salvadoran
LOC	Library of Congress
LP-28	Ligas Populares de 28 Febrero
MAP	Military Assistance Program
MEA	Municipios en Acción (Municipalities in Action)
MILGP	US Military Group
MTTs	Military Training Teams
NARA	National Archives and Records Administration
NCP	National Campaign Plan
NLF	National Liberation Front
NSA	National Security Agency
NSAM	National Security Action Memorandum
NSC	National Security Council
OIDP	Overseas Internal Defense Policy
OPAT	operational and planning assistance team
OPS	Office of Public Safety
ORDEN	Spanish word for order, adopted by the Organización Democrática Nacionalista
PCN	Partido de Conciliación Nacional
PCS	Partido Comunista de El Salvador
PDC	Partido Demócrata Cristiano
PPW	prolonged people's war
PRALs	Patrullas de Reconocimiento de Alcance Largo
PRTC	Partido Revolucionario de los Trabajadores Centroamericanos
PSYOPS	psychological operations
RF/PF	Regional Forces and Popular Forces
RN	Resistencia Nacional

SAS	Sections Administratives Spécialisées
SOA	School of the Americas
SOUTHCOM	Southern Command
UCA	Universidad Centroamericana
UCS	Unión Comunal Salvadoreña
UNTS	Unidad Nacional de Trabejadores Salvadoreños
UPR	Unidos Para Reconstruir
USAID	US Agency for International Development
VCI	Viet Cong Infrastructure

The Salvadoran Crucible

Introduction

The August 23, 2007, edition of *The Daily Show with Jon Stewart* featured an unusual guest: a uniformed military officer, Colonel John Nagl. Nagl's appearance on a show favored by young, liberal audiences represented a calculated political maneuver: promote the US Army and Marines' latest counterinsurgency manual, *Field Manual 3-24 (FM 3-24)*. During his segment, Nagl summarized the most recent variation of US counterinsurgency (COIN) doctrine: "Be polite, be professional, and be prepared to kill." Nagl's summation unnerved the crowd, but Stewart reassured his audience, noting that US soldiers had to "do what any Army has to do." That business, of course, is killing.[1]

Before the publication of *FM 3-24*, its authors spread the gospel of counterinsurgency through appearances on radio and the talk-show circuit. During the prepublication launch, they rarely discussed the necessity of lethal force. Instead they promoted the manual under the guise of respecting human rights and protecting civilians. To bolster the manual's humanitarian credentials, its authors touted the involvement of academic scholars, including anthropologists, Harvard's Carr Center for Human Rights, and input from Human Rights Watch. Despite the inclusion of academics and the necessity of respecting the rights of civilians, the manual does not represent a radical departure from past military doctrine. Indeed, many of the central premises of the manual can be traced back to Vietnam-era doctrine, especially the Internal Defense and Development (IDAD) program. *FM 3-24* is also informed by previous US and foreign interventions that prioritized the suppression of actors who challenged the existing status quo and US interests.

The latest version of US COIN is often synonymous with the phrase "hearts and minds," a term associated with the disastrous US war in Vietnam. Left to wither away in obscurity after Washington's defeat in Southeast Asia, US COIN enthusiasts waited for an opportunity to re-apply their principles and win. As Iraq unraveled in 2003 after the US in-vasion, they argued that the US military must embrace COIN to defeat the insurgency in Iraq. Instead of recommending Vietnam as a model, which was toxic politically, proponents suggested a lesser-known but equally important US intervention: El Salvador.

Throughout most of its history El Salvador avoided the power or reach of the "Colossus of the North" as its neighbors had experienced. In contrast to its treatment of much of Central America, the United States did not send US Marines to protect "American lives and prop-erty," chase "bandits," or occupy the country. El Salvador, a country famously compared in size to Massachusetts, had never been a major concern in either US domestic or foreign policy until 1979. However, this small nation then convulsed relations between the US Congress and the executive branch for eight years. As William LeoGrande inquired, "Why did such a small region loom so large in the American psyche dur-ing the 1980s?"[2] To fully answer that question, it is imperative to begin several decades earlier.

US cold war foreign policy in Latin America was designed to prevent communist expansion, maintain US hegemony, remove forces thought sympathetic to communism or its ideals, and ensure stability and order, especially for US investments. According to historian Stephen Rabe, US presidents from Harry Truman to George H. W. Bush believed they had to keep the region "secure" so that they could wage the cold war in other, more important parts of the world. Latin America was the "back-yard," and US leaders were determined to keep it tidy and orderly.[3] To accomplish these objectives, US policy makers implemented a COIN strategy that relied on US aid and military training to combat internal subversion in the Western Hemisphere.

During the cold war, the United States used Latin America as a testing ground for its COIN doctrine. The Pentagon deployed US Green Be-rets and other US Special Forces operatives and provided funds to help its allies either defeat or prevent the outbreak of insurgency throughout

Central and South America. The lessons learned from the various US COIN operations were not confined to other contingencies in the region. Instead, US strategists applied the knowledge gained from Latin America globally. Of all the various interventions, the most important occurred in tiny El Salvador. When the US government found itself confronted by a growing and intractable insurgency in Iraq in 2003, Pentagon officials leaned heavily on the US effort in El Salvador for solutions.

For almost twenty years after the Cuban Revolution, the United States prevented the emergence of another communist regime in Latin America. The overthrow of Anastasio Somoza in Nicaragua in July 1979 forced Washington to reevaluate its Central American strategy. That same year El Salvador teetered on the edge; in the 1960s, the country had been considered relatively stable. During the following decade, economic and political stability slowly deteriorated. Several months after the collapse of Somoza's regime, El Salvador was ripe for revolution. Massive political demonstrations and government-sanctioned violence had brought the country to the precipice. To forestall a revolutionary victory and prevent the same fate that befell Somoza's military, a group of reformist Salvadoran military officers overthrew the country's military dictatorship. Beginning with this coup, US interest in El Salvador expanded dramatically, marking the beginning of a massive and sustained intervention in that country's affairs.

The spread of revolutionary movements throughout Central America in the 1970s not only threatened to overthrow the socioeconomic systems nurtured by Washington but also fundamentally challenged the US view of progress and development. In 1981 the newly inaugurated US president, Ronald Reagan, elevated El Salvador from an irrelevant country into one whose fate was supposedly vital to US national security. This decision not only baffled but startled contemporary observers. President Reagan and his predecessor intervened in El Salvador based on its proximity to the United States and its location within the US imperial orbit. For decades Washington had used practically all means at its disposal to prevent any challenges to its commercial, political, and strategic interests in the hemisphere.

Instability in El Salvador allegedly posed a national security risk for the United States. Reagan policy makers, however, were not the first to use this rationale. A 1972 memorandum written by John Caldwell, a State Department official, expressed similar sentiments: "El Salvador is very small in terms of US interests," but "it is geographically and psychologically close and therein lies the importance of keeping it out of hostile hands."[4] The White House often reminded the US public that El Salvador was closer for some than the nation's capital. The country's location offered Washington the chance to intervene close to home in a place where it held the advantage over the Soviet Union. Of all the trouble spots in Central America besides Nicaragua, El Salvador seemed to be the most dire and in need of US assistance.

The US COIN effort in El Salvador also fits within a broader pattern of US interventions in the region and the global South that viewed challenges to the prerogatives of the US-supported elites as communist inspired. The Salvadoran insurgents' efforts to topple the government and socioeconomic system and redistribute the balance of power within the country threatened US interests in Central America. As in previous cases Washington resolved to confront the supposed challenge. Yet El Salvador represented a departure as well. Unlike in previous US experiences in Latin America, Washington did not have to contend with a leftist regime in El Salvador at any point. The United States did not deploy tens of thousands, or as in the case of Vietnam, half a million troops, to thwart the spread of communism. Rather, El Salvador became a supposed exemplar of a patient, nation-building experiment that defeated a communist insurgency by respecting human rights, spreading democracy, and fostering important socioeconomic reforms, all possible through generous and selfless US aid.

The US intervention also highlighted the political double standard Washington embraced throughout the cold war. Although the United States routinely condemned leftist violence, it rarely demonized the terror used by rightist US proxies across the globe, including in El Salvador, with the same vehemence. US policy makers refused to engage the moderate left in El Salvador before and during the war. Although embassy telegrams demonstrated that US officials were aware of differences between the various rebel groups, they did not take them seriously. Instead, they painted the entire left with a broad brush. Similarly, Washington preferred to work with the moderate Salvadoran right, including

INTRODUCTION [5]

the various business and commercial actors not tainted by death-squad abuses, at the expense of other forces. Additionally, the United States believed it could alter and modify the behavior of the moderate right forces in El Salvador. As with previous US experiences, controlling these actors proved far more difficult than officials imagined, and, quite often, they pursued their goals at the expense of US policy.

El Salvador also served as the lynchpin of a larger administration effort to contain communism and eventually "roll back" its spread in the Western Hemisphere. Although the primary focus was on Nicaragua, hardline cold war warriors envisioned that victory in the tiny Central American country could be achieved quickly and relatively cost free. Before the White House could turn its attention to Nicaragua, an obsession for many Reaganites, including the head of the Central Intelligence Agency (CIA), it had to contend with El Salvador. After US aid turned the corner, the administration could ratchet up its support for the Contras and destabilize the Sandinistas.

The US intervention in El Salvador was also part of a larger plan initiated by Reagan to restore Americans' confidence in their country by achieving a quick and relatively cost-free victory and ending the post-Vietnam malaise. Members of the administration believed that defeating revolutionary movements in Latin America would demonstrate their resolve to US adversaries and send a notice to the Soviet Union that they would not be restrained as were their predecessors. President Reagan also portrayed the conflict as part of a larger cold war struggle between the East and West, not an internal civil war fueled by historical, political, and socioeconomic grievances.

It was an ambitious effort. For the next twelve years the United States implemented an expensive and thorough COIN effort aimed at preventing a victory by either the extreme right or the insurgents. Instead, US policy makers sought to establish and promote a government and political system that occupied the middle ground between those two forces. These efforts aimed not only at ending the conflict but also at remodeling the country's socioeconomic system more along the lines of that of the United States. Washington's efforts in El Salvador represented the largest nation-building endeavor undertaken by the United States after South Vietnam until the invasion of Iraq in 2003.

This book focuses on US COIN strategy in El Salvador during its civil war, circa 1979 to 1992. It investigates the US policies, both political and military, used in the conflict to defeat the spread of "international communism." These included efforts implemented at the macro and micro levels. The book analyzes the various policies used by US strategists and offers an evaluation of their effectiveness and of the theories that supported them. In addition to assessing US policies, my research also places the intervention in the context of broader US foreign policy toward the region.

Within the fields of US diplomatic history and US–Latin American relations, interest or discussion of COIN has been either absent or negligible. Various aspects of US COIN policy have been discussed, such as counterterror, police training, and other closely related topics.[5] Nonetheless, a holistic study has yet to be undertaken that emphasizes the development of military and political efforts underlying US COIN doctrine. This study is intended to fill this gap and begin a process of unifying existing critiques of President Reagan's Salvadoran policy and synthesizing many of the larger issues surrounding US foreign policy toward Central America during the cold war.

Most studies of US involvement in the conflict are highly critical. In particular, they have emphasized the human rights abuses committed by the Salvadoran government and criticized the misguided nature of US policy toward El Salvador.[6] Former US participants and military writers, however, have portrayed the conflict as a successful application of COIN.[7] Most supporters argue that US aid established democracy, prevented the leftist rebels from overthrowing the Salvadoran government, professionalized the country's military, and curbed human rights abuses. Some have taken it a step further and proposed that the conflict presents a useful case model for suppressing insurgency.

Supporters of the US intervention have often viewed the end of the conflict as a success for the Salvadoran government and as a vindication of the US strategy. Although the government did not defeat the insurgents militarily, US aid denied the Frente Farabundo Martí para la Liberación Nacional (FMLN) a triumph on the battlefield. Military writers have been the most vocal in claiming victory for the government and Salvadoran forces.[8] Among the most important results of US aid was that the US advisory effort strengthened and improved the battlefield capacities of the El Salvadoran Armed Forces (ESAF). Moreover, military advocates argue that the introduction of Americans also improved the regime's terrible human rights record. Perhaps most importantly, the Americans learned an important "lesson" from Vietnam: the host nation had to fight its own war.[9] Instead of US soldiers fighting and dying, the small number of US advisers ensured that the Salvadorans bore the brunt of the fighting. Therefore, by relying on a well-supported proxy, the United States was able to avoid the introduction of US ground troops and thus another quagmire. Unlike in Vietnam, there was no "Americanization" of the conflict.

Proponents of the success narrative also cite the spread of democracy to El Salvador as an important result of the war. They note that during the conflict, a peaceful transition of power occurred without incident and point out the five successive postwar presidential elections. Many of these works, however, are silent on the role the United States played in meddling in the Salvadoran presidential election of 1984 to ensure José Napoleón Duarte's victory. Nevertheless, although there is some merit to these claims, they must be weighed against Greg Grandin's conclusion: "It took an unvanquished insurgency to force the kind of democratization that the United States had grudgingly supported as a means to defeat that insurgency in the first place."[10]

As Reagan policy makers learned rather quickly, the intervention in El Salvador was more complicated than they had envisioned. In spite of approximately $6 billion in US aid and the application of US COIN, the FMLN remained undefeated. Moreover, observers also questioned whether this aid allowed the United States to gain leverage over its Salvadoran allies. According to a former US adviser to the Salvadoran high command, its members begrudgingly accepted US advice when it was accompanied by promises of military aid, such as logistical or aviation support. Regarding operational advice, US advisers often walked away discouraged. Members of the Salvadoran high command believed their situation was unique and US operational advice did not apply.[11]

The FMLN created one of the region's most powerful guerrilla armies. Its war against the state forced the Salvadoran government to end its previous exclusionary policies and initiate the democratization of El Salvador. The issue of external support for the FMLN remains controversial. Offering a precise financial figure is even more difficult. David E. Spencer argues that without foreign assistance, especially from Nicaragua, the Salvadoran insurgents could not have continued the war.[12] For example, the shoulder-fired anti-air missiles they received from the Nicaraguan military helped create a stalemate because the government's aircraft became vulnerable to ground fire. Although the rebels received military supplies and weapons from abroad, they were also careful enough not to be completely reliant upon it. Washington's commitment to San Salvador, however, greatly overshadowed and most likely dwarfed the aid the FMLN received from its external allies.

Washington's history of flooding war-torn countries with US weapons has often backfired. The M-16s used by the FMLN generally came from two sources: Salvadoran soldiers and paramilitary forces that surrendered or dropped their weapons, or the arms stockpiles of former allies. The Vietnamese military shipped surplus US weapons from the Vietnam War to revolutionary movements in Latin America, including in El Salvador.[13] These weapons, captured after Saigon's collapse, came from the South Vietnamese Army. More recently, the Mexican cartels' firepower, especially their M-203s, grenade launchers often attached beneath M-16s, is derived from US military equipment supplied to the Mexican government.[14] Thus, US weapons often fall into the hands of US adversaries. Even when US military surplus or training is provided to our "allies," it can be turned against the United States, as events in Afghanistan have demonstrated. Washington would do well to consider such previous examples as it continues to weigh its support for Syrian rebels.

Relying largely upon the support of Salvadorans and their own means, the insurgents battled a well-funded US proxy to a stalemate. Their ability to remain undefeated is a rather remarkable achievement given El Salvador's size; the military could easily reach the most distant points of the country within several hours by helicopter. It is also a testament to their organizational skills, revolutionary ardor, and popular support from the masses. The US intervention should also serve as a reminder that if Washington could not defeat a poorly armed, peasant army in a

US sphere of influence, then it is no wonder more recent US contingencies have failed.

Overall, those who view the US experience in El Salvador positively believe it offers a series of lessons for counterinsurgency interventions. These include:

- Maintaining a small and minimal US presence, or "small footprint."
- Restricting the number of US trainers (because this forced the Salvadorans to prosecute the war themselves and avoided "Americanizing" the conflict).
- Holding elections in the midst of war because it furthers democratization.
- Using aid and threats as leverage because this can improve an ally's behavior and human rights record.

As this book will demonstrate, the various measures Washington devised were impractical for El Salvador as well as for more recent insurgencies, especially in Iraq. They also rested on a mistaken and flawed analysis of the contemporary and historical contexts in which the civil war erupted. US planners assumed that they could apply the Vietnam model to El Salvador without understanding its geography, culture, or history, not to mention its neighbors. Both the White House and Pentagon believed that the benefits of democracy were self-evident and did not require further explanation. Che Guevara could be accused of falling into a similar trap in Bolivia.[15] Interpreting the conflict through a narrow cold war lens as part of a global insurgency driven by Moscow obfuscated US policy makers' understanding of the conflict and how to resolve it. Simply reapplying "lessons" from previous experiences devastated El Salvador and inflicted a tremendous level of suffering on that generation of Salvadorans.

The "success" claim is mistaken and fails to hold up under careful scrutiny. When viewed from the narrow military perspective that the Salvadoran guerrillas did not take power or that US ground troops were not committed, it appears that the US intervention was highly successful. When the lens is widened, the argument that the conflict represents a triumphant application of COIN becomes problematic. To emphasize the positive outcome of the US efforts in El Salvador is especially curious because the war ended in stalemate and a negotiated settlement—which possibly could have been achieved several years earlier had recalcitrant forces, including the US government, Salvadoran military, and its right-wing allies, not fiercely resisted.

Contrary to what COIN advocates and promoters of the "success narrative" in El Salvador have argued, the end of the conflict was not the result of the application of US COIN or years of aid and support from Washington. Consequently, the establishment and strengthening of democracy that Washington policy makers and supporters of the US intervention in El Salvador have trumpeted did not occur as the result of US actions. Rather it was the consequence of a mixture of events, including some that happened far from El Salvador's borders as well as internally. For example, after 1989, Salvadoran society had grown weary of the war, and both sides wanted out. Moreover, as the civil war moved toward its conclusion, international and regional events also prohibited the continuation of the conflict.

Significant US funds and training helped prevent an insurgent triumph but at great cost to Salvadorans. The US intervention in El Salvador prolonged the war, devastated the country, and contributed to distortions in the country's socioeconomic landscape. US aid greatly enlarged the size of the Salvadoran military and its arsenal, kept El Salvador's economy from collapsing, and prevented the overthrow of Washington's preferred Salvadoran leader, Duarte. Beyond producing a stalemate, it inflicted tremendous suffering on the Salvadorans for a limited set of foreign policy gains. It also undermined a political opening by reinforcing a commitment to military victory.[16] In spite of all of the US advice and funds as well as the political subterfuge used by the White House to ensure the aid pipeline continued to flow, Washington and its ally never vanquished their enemy. Even more importantly, the various reforms enacted during the war failed to address the underlying issues that had caused the outbreak of war in the first place and continue to plague El Salvador.

Before delving into the US intervention in El Salvador, it is necessary to clarify a few key terms I will use throughout this book. Recent US military joint doctrine defines "insurgency" as an "organized movement aimed at the overthrow of a constituted government through the use of subversion and armed conflict."[17] However, this broad and vague definition fails to note the political aims of an insurgency. Insurgency can also be classified as a "struggle to control a contested political space, between a state (or a group of states or occupying powers) and one or more popularly based, non-state challengers."[18] An insurgency can be motivated by a variety of factors, including nationalism, repression, foreign occupation, ideology, or even socioeconomic justifications; in fact, there might be more than one explanation. Whether radical or conservative, insurgent movements are at their core political.

Conversely, the US military defines "counterinsurgency" as the military, paramilitary, political, economic, psychological, and civic actions taken by a government to defeat insurgency.[19] Expressing the term in this manner makes it very broad and malleable. Although establishing a precise definition eludes even the experts, for the purposes of this book, COIN will describe an integrated set of economic, political, social, and security measures intended to end or prevent the recurrence of armed violence; create and maintain stable political, economic, and social structures; and resolve the underlying causes of an insurgency.[20] In other words, COIN is not only designed to defeat an insurgency but also is meant to address the underlying causes of the outbreak.

Civic action uses development projects to demonstrate the central government's commitment to its citizens' well-being and establish its legitimacy. This tactic involves the military and civilian agencies. Several of the more commonly used efforts include building wells, repairing and building roads, constructing homes, and implementing sanitation projects. They can also include providing dental and medical care. Civic action programs were tested throughout the world, including in Latin America and South Vietnam. Although these projects sound noble, if they are driven by short-term political goals not sustainable in the long term or do not fundamentally solve popular grievances, at best they provide a temporary solution.

Civil defense provides security and time to allow development projects to continue. It also frees the country's military and security forces from guarding static locations, enabling them to focus on tracking and killing insurgents. Generally, members are recruited from villages; the underlining idea is that local residents are more committed to providing security than are professional soldiers. Civil defense units, however, have been plagued by inadequate resources, outdated weapons, lack of training, low pay, and distrust toward the government trying to win their affection. These forces are also vulnerable to well-armed and coordinated insurgent attacks and, in many instances, have become involved in corruption and human rights abuses. Civil defense forces throughout the world, including in El Salvador, routinely abused the very people they were supposed to protect. As such, they contributed very little to the overall COIN efforts.

Chapter Layout

This book will be broken up into five chapters and a coda. The first two establish the groundwork for the US intervention in El Salvador. Chapter 1 analyzes previous US experiences combating insurgency across the globe in the twentieth century. US strategists studied these contingencies to devise a list of "appropriate" tactics to defeat their enemies. Several of these measures were repeatedly used—including in El Salvador—such as the formation of long-range reconnaissance patrols and civic action programs. Equally important were foreign influences, especially British and French, whose efforts at defeating insurgency have been routinely analyzed and cited by US counterinsurgency practitioners.

Chapter 2 focuses on US efforts to establish a COIN strategy for El Salvador during the cold war, beginning with the "counterinsurgency ferment" in the 1960s. The election of President John F. Kennedy, who developed a keen interest in combating "Wars of National Liberation," initiated a surge of interest in the subject. Under Kennedy, US operatives used COIN to combat revolutionary movements across the globe. For the next several decades, albeit with some modifications, the US military relied on a COIN strategy in Latin America developed under President Kennedy. The chapter will conclude with a section focusing on the presidency of Jimmy Carter, who laid the groundwork for the escalation of the US intervention under his successor, Ronald Reagan.

Chapter 3 analyzes the war between 1981 and 1983, when US interest in the conflict and the violence was at its peak. During this phase of the war, the United States and its Salvadoran allies launched several of the more notable COIN campaigns, including implementing an important development program and holding constituent (parliamentary) and presidential elections. Although the Salvadoran government's prospects had been bleak initially, the momentum began to slowly shift in its favor beginning in 1984.

Chapter 4 discusses the "stalemate" phase of the conflict (1984–1988). Beginning in 1984, the Salvadoran government rebounded from its earlier poor showing and slowly regained the initiative. To prevent their own defeat and preserve their forces, the insurgents opted for a classical, guerrilla war strategy aimed at prolonging the conflict and eventually terminating US aid. Slowly but surely, the Salvadoran government's enemy laid the groundwork for launching one last offensive to alter the status of the war.

Chapter 5 begins in 1989 and continues until the end of the conflict. In early 1989 conventional wisdom in Washington assumed the war was progressing positively, albeit more slowly than US policy makers desired, and eventually the Salvadoran government would overwhelm its adversary. During 1989 several key events challenged prevailing assumptions about the war. In elections held in El Salvador and the United States, new leaders emerged who were not as committed to waging the conflict as their predecessors. Later that year, an insurgent offensive rocked San Salvador and shook existing conceptions about the conflict. The guerrillas' assault also demonstrated that years of significant US funding not only had failed to alter the mentality of the Salvadoran military but also had not weakened the rebels decisively either. Finally, as the cold war moved toward its denouement, the Salvadoran belligerents realized that they had more to gain from negotiations than constant conflict.

After the end of the Salvadoran Civil War, the United States did not participate in any large-scale COIN or nation-building efforts until 2003.[21] Shortly after the US-led invasion of Iraq in 2003, that country rapidly descended into chaos. Pentagon officials analyzed the past for clues or examples regarding how to deal with insurgency, including the US intervention in El Salvador. To counter the raging insurgency in Iraq, Donald Rumsfeld deployed Colonel James Steele, former head of the US military advisory mission in El Salvador, to train the fledgling Iraqi

Army in the art of COIN. Many journalists claimed that the George W. Bush administration used strategies derived from the Salvadoran Civil War, known as the "Salvadoran Option," in Iraq to defeat the insurgency. The Coda will assess these claims and their validity. The section will also offer an assessment of the US intervention and argue that its successes have been overstated.

Well before Reagan increased the US commitment to El Salvador, the United States had accumulated considerable experience combating insurgency. Over the course of the twentieth century, the US military established a counterinsurgency doctrine based on its previous interventions across the globe. Thus, when US operatives arrived in El Salvador, they had nearly a century of guidance from which they could draw. Before discussing the history of US COIN in El Salvador, this book will begin at the end of the War of 1898, when the United States found itself confronted by a nationalist revolution in the Philippines. To defeat this insurgency, the US military relied upon its former experiences combating Native Americans as well as devising new strategies. It was a formula Washington repeated many times throughout the remainder of the century.

Historical Antecedents

Many authors have emphasized that the United States has a vast amount of experience fighting unconventional wars. Despite this background, counterinsurgency enthusiasts, often dubbed "COINdinistas," have argued that the United States is generally unprepared and does not wage COIN campaigns effectively.[1] Nonetheless, the nation has been involved in many unconventional operations. During the twentieth century, the United States waged a variety of small wars across the globe, including in Latin America, Africa, and Southeast Asia.[2] The US military reused many of the same strategies and tactics over this period, including civic action, development, and military training. Although Washington may have defeated several insurgencies, its policies failed to produce lasting stability in numerous countries.

This chapter analyzes several of the counterinsurgency operations in which the United States participated during the twentieth century, including in the Philippines after the War of 1898 and later during the Huk Rebellion, the hunt for Augusto César Sandino's rebels in Nicaragua, and the fight against the National Liberation Front in Vietnam. The British experience in Malaya and French experience in Algeria, respectively, also merit discussion. Both of these cases are important for understanding US COIN operations during the twentieth century because of the historical comparisons often made between these conflicts and others, whether even accurate, and the tendency of US COINdinistas to draw lessons from the British and French experiences. In particular, this chapter focuses on change and continuity in US COIN practice. It will also address several closely related questions. What strategies did the United States use to defeat insurgency across the globe? Has Washington reused or reapplied techniques learned in one conflict to another? Were they successful? And finally, as this chapter and following ones will investigate, were any of these strategies used in El Salvador?

US-Filipino War

In the middle of the War of 1898, Commodore George Dewey sent one of his vessels to Hong Kong to bring exiled Filipino nationalist Emilio Aguinaldo back to his native country. In a meeting between the two men, Dewey supposedly informed Aguinaldo that the United States intended to grant the Philippines its independence. The Filipino nationalist, however, quickly realized the United States had other intentions. Over the course of the fall and winter, distrust and hostility between the former allies increased. It only deepened after President William McKinley issued his benevolent assimilation message, in January 1899, which announced the US intention to rule the archipelago.

As the US Senate debated the Treaty of Paris, the United States and Aguinaldo's troops exchanged fire. This event marked the opening salvo in the US-Filipino War (1899–1902). For the next several years the United States fought to suppress Filipino freedom and extend its control over the Philippines. The US-Filipino War also foreshadowed similar frustrations US troops experienced in future conflicts. For the next three years, turmoil in the Philippines embroiled the United States in a costly counterinsurgency operation that sapped any future interest in acquiring overseas colonies.

The US military relied on its previous experiences battling indigenous Americans to defeat the Filipino insurgents. As Walter Williams has observed, US Indian policy served as a "precedent for imperialist domination over the Philippines and other islands occupied during the Spanish-American War."[3] Out of the thirty generals who served in the Philippines, twenty-six participated in the various conflicts with Native Americans in the late nineteenth century.[4] Senior military officers drew upon one important lesson from their experiences on the Great Plains: to defeat "uncivilized savages," US forces must use brute and overwhelming force.

The US Army also used *General Orders 100*, written during the Civil War. *General Orders 100* attempted to strike a balance between moderation, reconciliation, and blunt force. Even though it acknowledged that military necessity "allows of all destruction of property" and "withholding of sustenance or any means of life from the enemy," US forces were required to avoid actions that alienated the enemy's population, especially during occupation duty.[5] Magnanimity was not extended to those who divested "themselves of the character or appearance of soldiers." These combatants, "if captured, are not entitled to the privileges of prisoners of war, but shall be treated summarily as highway robbers or pirates."[6] As the United States struggled to pacify the archipelago, senior military officials justified its harsh tactics based upon these regulations.

Under the policy of "benevolent assimilation," the United States proclaimed it was bringing civilization to the residents of the archipelago and tutoring them in the principles of democracy and other US institutions. Alternatively referred to as the "policies of attraction," they were designed to win the support of Filipinos, especially the *ilustrados,* the wealthiest members of society. This would not be a short-term process. William Howard Taft, as governor general of the Philippines, was critical of the Filipinos' capacity for self-government. Taft reported that "our little brown brothers" would need approximately "fifty or one hundred years" of close supervision to "develop anything resembling Anglo-Saxon political principles and skills."[7]

From the point of view of US policy makers, accommodation was cost effective because the conquered population participated in its own subordination by administering and policing itself. Keeping the country subdued in this way would theoretically allow the United States to reduce the number of US soldiers in the country, ease the burden on the US Treasury, and quiet the anti-imperialist press at home. By 1901 the McKinley administration had concluded a tacit bargain with prominent Filipinos that, although denying immediate independence, called for greater elite participation in running the archipelago's own affairs, with the promise of eventual independence.[8]

In November 1899 Aguinaldo launched a guerrilla war against the US occupation.[9] Aguinaldo's decision to adopt unconventional warfare annoyed and frustrated US soldiers and commanders. As Richard

Welch noted, US hatred for Filipinos clearly accelerated when the war moved into this stage.[10] People justifying US tactics have often placed the blame on the insurgents for violating prevailing concepts of warfare. H. L. Wells, a correspondent for the *New York Evening Post,* succinctly expressed many prevailing themes about nonwhite peoples in tropical environments when he claimed,

> There is no question that our men do "shoot niggers" somewhat in the sporting spirit, but that is because war and their environments have rubbed off the thin veneer of civilization. . . . Undoubtedly, they do not regard the shooting of Filipinos just as they would the shooting of white troops. This is partly because they are "only niggers" and partly because they despise them for their treacherous servility. . . . The soldiers feel that they are fighting with savages, not with soldiers.[11]

Classifying people as uncivilized served an important purpose: it dehumanized the insurgents and provided a rationalization for the increasingly harsh tactics used by US soldiers. Because the Filipinos allegedly lacked the trappings of civilization, they were not owed the restraints of war offered to civilized opponents. Faced with uncooperative Filipinos and a popular insurgency, in frustration, the military turned toward violence to compel the citizens to cooperate.

US troops employed reconcentration on a large scale in Batangas, at the southern end of Luzon, beginning in 1901. General J. Franklin Bell aimed to make life unbearable for the insurgents by depriving them of food and civilian support. US forces confiscated animals and crops, torched villages, and drove the civilians into disease-ridden camps. After being relocated, Bell's troops kept a vigilant watch over the population. Anything outside of the camps was destroyed—houses, livestock, food, and whatever other items could conceivably be used to support the insurgents. This practice contributed to the spread of malnutrition and disease in the camps and the countryside, particularly cholera, dysentery, and smallpox.

The purpose of these concentration centers was to separate the civilians from the insurgents and deny them access to foodstuffs, other essential items, and intelligence. This policy was employed on a large scale in Batangas. US military officers were well aware of the analogies between their practices and those employed under the Spanish General Valeriano Weyler.[12] The concentration centers isolated the guerrillas from the population and starved many of them into submission.[13] Although relocating Filipinos into concentration centers was arguably an effective counterinsurgency tactic, its cost in human suffering was unquestionably high. Despite efforts to alleviate conditions, people suffered from overcrowding, food shortages, and poor sanitation.[14] At least 11,000 on Batangas perished from a combination of disease, malnutrition, and other health problems.[15]

The idea that one can easily separate civilians from insurgents of concentration centers rests on the false assumption that there is a clear separation between insurgents and civilians, a curious assertion because insurgents emerge from the people. Nonetheless, this tactic has been used repeatedly by the United States and other powers in their efforts to crush insurgency. In conflicts after the Filipino War, relocation often created more rebels, not fewer.

In March 1901, a daring raid led by Frederick Funston resulted in the capture of Aguinaldo. However, his capture did not end the Filipino insurrection, nor did it induce large-scale surrender of his combatants. US tactics grew increasingly harsh after Aguinaldo's capture. The repression intensified especially after approximately fifty US soldiers were massacred in September 1901 at a US garrison in Balangiga, on the island of Samar. In response, the commanding US general in the Philippines, General Adna Chaffee, tasked General Jacob "Hell-Roaring Jake" Smith with pacifying the island. Smith promised swift retaliation. His orders included "kill everyone over the age of ten," and he promised to make the island a "howling wilderness." Smith's troops followed their superior's orders using all means, including torching villages; killing men, women, and children; and using the "water cure" to crush the rebellion on the island.

A little more than a year after Aguinaldo's capture, the US government felt the insurrection had been sufficiently pacified that it could end the war and focus on benevolent assimilation. On July 4, 1902, President Theodore Roosevelt gave an official speech declaring victory. The same day the president also issued Proclamation 483, granting "full and complete pardon and amnesty to all persons in the Philippine Archipelago who have participated in the insurrections."[16] When the war was officially declared over in 1902, the response was muted relief, and the nation's press mostly treated it perfunctorily.[17] Over the course of four years, the United States lost more than 4,000 soldiers. Approximately 200,000 Filipino civilians perished through a combination of disease, famine, and war. Ultimately, after the success in pacifying the Filipino resistance, the US Army and the US Marines relied on similar tactics to quell disorder and revolt across the globe, especially in the Western Hemisphere.

The Hunt for Sandino

Washington's priorities in the Western Hemisphere focused on ensuring stability and protecting US investments. In countries the United States occupied, such as the Dominican Republic and Haiti, Washington launched several public works programs including instituting sanitation, digging ditches, paving roads, and constructing schools. The main goal was to improve the country's infrastructure and employ men. The marines' reliance on forced labor to construct roads, especially in Haiti, backfired. Also known as the *corvée,* it was a form of unpaid labor instituted by France when Haiti was part of its empire.[18] Although the goals may have been commendable, their implementation helped fuel resentment against Washington, especially in Haiti.

The US military also created "constabulary forces" in the countries it occupied in Latin America (and in the Philippines) before the Great Depression. These forces were designed to maintain security and order within the countries, allowing the United States to terminate the occupation. Generally, these forces comprised military or paramilitary soldiers tasked with carrying out police functions. Constabulary forces were meant to resemble the US military; they were supposed to be nonpolitical. As historian Walter LaFeber has aptly noted, only later—too late—did these officials understand that in Central America such a force would not remain above politics but single-handedly determine them.[19] As one study noted, every Latin American country that received US training turned into a military dictatorship or faced intervention by the

United States or a proxy force.[20] As these forces grew repressive and remained associated with the United States, in Latin America they fueled growing anger toward this nation.

In 1926 the United States terminated its occupation of Nicaragua. However, after its departure, tensions between Nicaraguan liberals and conservatives led to the outbreak of another civil war. In response, the US government deployed the marines and tried to bring the warring parties to the negotiating table. Most Nicaraguan politicians and army officers supported the cease-fire and accepted its terms, with one notable exception: Sandino. Sandino and his followers waged a five-year guerrilla campaign against the government.[21] His patriotic anger was also representative of a broader ideological current of Latin American anti-imperialist and leftist nationalism sweeping the region.[22]

For the next several years, US Marines, along with the Nicaraguan Guardia Nacional, chased Sandino's band of guerrillas throughout the hills and countryside. Relying on previous practices used by the US Army in suppressing Native American rebellions and foreign revolutions, the marines recruited the Miskito Indians as allies to combat Sandino.[23] In a departure from previous campaigns, the US counterinsurgency operation in Nicaragua featured the usage of air power to combat insurgency.[24] Although supporters of the aerial campaign have praised its efficacy, it actually fueled the rebellion it was meant to suppress and became a lightning rod for anti-US protest.[25]

The effort to suppress Sandino has not been widely heralded in the COIN literature, if at all.[26] More importantly, Nicaragua also demonstrated that although defeating the US military was impossible, the strategic "center of gravity" was US political culture and its tendency to grow weary of protracted and unproductive warfare in distant regions.[27] When news reached the US public, including reports of dead or wounded marines, popular support waned. Consequently, US officials began to rely more heavily on the Guardia Nacional.[28] Decades later, the United States discovered in Vietnam that the longer a conflict continued, the more the chances for lasting political success decreased.

In 1933, the United States formally ended its occupation of Nicaragua, and the last marines departed. The reasons for the end of Sandino's rebellion had little to do with a successful counterinsurgency campaign.

Rather, the Great Depression and Japanese machinations in Manchuria aided Sandino's cause and lessened US interest in continuing the occupation.[29] The intervention was also criticized routinely both in Latin America and in the United States. The marines' poor performance in Nicaragua also had little impact on the formation of COIN doctrine, especially for the US Army.[30]

The Huk Rebellion

In 1946, after the United States had granted independence to its former colony, the Philippines erupted in revolt.[31] For the second time in fifty years, the United States was once again involved in suppressing an insurrection in the Philippines.[32] Almost eight years of war followed before the Filipino government, with US assistance, effectively suppressed it.

By 1950, the situation was serious enough that the United States became more actively involved. After the death of President Roxas in 1948, his successor, Elpidio Quirino, made a fateful decision. Quirino, under tremendous pressure from the US ambassador, selected Ramon Magsaysay as minister of defense. Magsaysay's selection has generally been heralded as the turning point in the conflict.[33] During his tenure, Magsaysay instituted many of the US suggestions, including reforming and reorganizing his security forces.[34] Although relying on force, Magsaysay also attempted to win the people over through kindness and responsiveness to their needs.[35]

Magsaysay had a very close working relationship with Lieutenant Colonel Edward Lansdale, a former advertising executive. In the Philippines and elsewhere, Lansdale used his advertising background to champion the ideas of consumption and "American progress" in Southeast Asia.[36] Lansdale and Magsaysay were almost inseparable; they ate, bunked, and traveled together and spent almost twenty hours every day in each other's company. Supposedly, the only time the two were not together until Magsaysay was indoctrinated was "when he went to bed with his wife."[37]

In addition to wielding the stick to smash the Huks, Magsaysay also attempted to address the social and economic grievances underlying the conflict by creating the Economic Development Corps (EDCOR). This program created rehabilitation colonies for captured insurgents by re-settling them and giving them land.[38] The main purpose behind EDCOR was to address the peasants' main grievance, the need for land reform, and undercut the Huks' slogan, "Land for the landless."[39] In spite of the importance of this issue, EDCOR's efforts were miniscule; fewer than 1,000 peasants were resettled, of which only 246 were former insurgents.[40] Overall, assessment of the program is mixed.[41]

US and Filipino counterinsurgency efforts featured the use of psychological operations (PSYOPS). Lansdale, who played an integral role, designed the PSYOPS mission with three goals in mind: influence the enemy, the public, and the armed forces.[42] The program included dirty tricks and other strategies such as offering bounties for the arrest of important Huk leaders, playing on villager fears of vampires, rewarding intelligence information, and distributing propaganda in areas where the insurgents routinely patrolled.[43]

US advisers assisted in creating "hunter-killer" teams: small, mobile units deployed to seek out the enemy aggressively. They operated in hostile territory and often took a no-holds-barred approach to the conflict. Also referred to as "Force X," these forces infiltrated enemy units by pretending to be insurgents.[44] Hunter-killer units targeted high-profile Huk leaders and terrorized the guerrillas and their supporters.[45] According to one former Filipino army officer, "When I was stationed in the Candaba area [in Pampanga], almost daily you could find bodies floating in the river, many of them victims of [Napoleon Diestro] Valeriano's Nenita Unit."[46]

Valeriano, although noting that these forces were accused of excesses, downplayed the number of killings but acknowledged that they increased support for the Huks.[47] He later defended these tactics, noting that although these measures created ill will from certain sectors of the population, they were "undeniably effective means of hitting active guerrillas" and were "essential to make the armed forces more effective in hitting them, and this could scarcely be done if techniques of proven utility were summarily abandoned."[48] US officials were aware of the excesses committed by Nenita. In private, Lansdale was critical

of the units' tactics, noting, "These Filipinos run around Central Luzon with skull and crossbones flags flying from their jeeps and scout
cars. . . . Cruelty and lust for murder are commonplace."[49] Later in the
twentieth century, in El Salvador, similar units were created and trained
by US advisers to track, capture, and kill insurgents.

The end of the conflict came in 1954, after the arrest of Huk leader
Luis Taruc. Despite his surrender, the rebellion continued with dwindling support until 1960. The reasons for the Huks' defeat vary, but
most authors argue that a combination of greater US involvement and
the reforms carried out by Magsaysay contributed to their defeat.[50] Several of these reforms included instituting a US-financed plan aimed at
rooting out corruption, improving the discipline of Filipino troops in
the field, and implementing EDCOR. Generally, the suppression of the
Huk Rebellion has been viewed as a vindication of US aid and tactics,
but not all writers agree.[51] The US intervention in the Philippines guided
its subsequent COIN operations, including the usage of PSYOPS, civil
defense, and the adoption of quasiguerrilla tactics. In hoping to replicate
the success of the Huks' defeat, the United States struggled to find "another Magsaysay" in its subsequent COIN operations.

The Malayan Emergency

For approximately twelve years, from 1950 to 1962, the British were
engaged in a costly counterinsurgency effort, battling a communist-
inspired insurgency in Malaya. The British response during the Malayan
Emergency is widely considered the first modern COIN effort and the
archetype of a successful operation.[52]

The British strategy in Malaya featured the usage of reconcentration
centers, or New Villages. These centers served two purposes: deny the
insurgents access to food, intelligence, information, shelter, and other
essential forms of support, and protect government supporters from insurgent intimidation.[53] Their inhabitants described them as "detention
camps with barbed wire and guards at every post. . . . No one was free
in a Chinese village."[54] Often, coercion and harsh measures, including
restricting food supplies and rations, were required to resettle civilians.

This program was thought so successful that one of the architects of the plan, Sir Robert Thompson, was deployed to South Vietnam to assist in drawing up a similar plan.

British officers also employed the "oil-spot" strategy, modeled on the approach created by French General Hubert Lyautey. Known in French as the *tache d'huile,* his strategy was first used by the French in the 1890s to subdue rebellion in their colonies.[55] Starting from a strong position, government forces then spread slowly into the periphery. While government forces expanded their reach, they simultaneously provided essential services to the beleaguered civilians and improved local security. As Thompson noted, this was central to the British success and hence crucial for resolving future conflicts.[56]

By 1960, the insurgency had largely petered out. The Malayan Emergency has been studied widely and cited as a successful application of COIN.[57] Andrew Mumford demurs, sarcastically noting, "A counter-insurgency campaign taking twelve years to eradicate an isolated group is not a glowing achievement and is hardly deserving of the academic salutations it has garnered."[58] The insurgents, ethnic Chinese, had failed to win much support from the majority of the population, yet managed to continue the struggle for more than a decade.[59] Even contemporary observers criticized the effort, especially as a model for Vietnam.

British COIN doctrine, especially its emphasis on "minimum force," has received a sympathetic reading and enjoys a privileged position in US literature.[60] Several recent studies have contrasted the British, French, and US approaches to COIN and have found the latter two lacking. In theory, the British concept of minimum force, along with their tactical flexibility and civil-military cooperation, allowed the British to avoid the excesses of the French in Algeria and the firepower-intensive approach of the United States in Vietnam.[61]

During the Malayan Emergency the British relied on their previous colonial conflicts for guidelines and strategies developed by the French decades earlier.[62] Thus, there is nothing necessarily, quintessentially "British" about them. In some cases, such as the oil-spot strategy, they replicated tactics the French had used to suppress rebellions in their colonies. Moreover, ideas about civil-military cooperation were also used by the French. Thus, when authors approvingly cite the British model, they are also drawing from doctrine practiced by France. Coercive force was a mainstay of British tactics in Malaya and in other British wars of decolonization. As military historian David French recently noted, British COIN experience was "nasty not nice."[63]

While the British were combating insurgency in Malaya, a rebellion broke out in another British colony in 1952. The Mau Mau Uprising erupted in the British colony of Kenya. One of the distinguishing features of this campaign was the construction of large penal colonies, or gulags.[64] Mass imprisonment, harsh interrogation practices, and relocation were commonplace.[65] Similar tactics were used in both Malaya and Kenya. What differentiated them was that the British employed them with a heavier hand in the latter. Consequently, the British defeated a larger insurgency there more quickly than in Malaya.[66] However, the insurgents were less unified and organized and lacked money and an adequate strategy.[67] Within the COIN literature, this operation has been curiously absent.[68]

L'ALGÉRIE FRANÇAISE

Unlike the British in Malaya, the French effort to suppress a revolution in Algeria between 1954 and 1962 is viewed negatively in the COIN literature. The reasons for this appraisal vary, but there are several commonalities in all accounts. Not only did the French lose but also their effort was marred by torture and human rights abuses. Further compounding these errors, the French military's actions alienated public support. A flyer advertising a 2005 Pentagon screening of Gillo Pontecorvo's film *The Battle of Algiers* portrayed the film as an example of "how to win a battle against terrorism and lose the war of ideas."[69] Paradoxically, in spite of Algerian independence, many of the French practices in the conflict have influenced US thinking, especially reflected in *FM 3-24,* including the emphasis on the centrality of the population, politico-military cooperation, and PSYOPS.[70]

In November 1954, the Front de Libération Nationale (FLN), a nationalist revolutionary movement, launched a rebellion against French rule in Algeria. Although the French-Algerian War (1954–1962) was part of the larger struggle of decolonization, Algeria was different from the previous cases because it was officially part of France, not simply a colony. The conflict would be characterized by brutality, including reprisal killings, torture, and wanton terror.

To defeat the FLN, the French military used *regroupement,* or resettling, to move entire villages to areas more accessible and controllable for the French Army.[71] Between 1957 and 1961, the army moved approximately 2 million civilians.[72] This strategy's ultimate aim, as in other COIN campaigns such as Malaya, was to control the population and convince it to support the counterinsurgents.

The French also carried out several civic action measures to maintain control of the countryside. Conducting a census was touted as an effective means of physically isolating the civilians from the insurgents because it allowed the Counter-Insurgency Special Group (CI) to restrict their movement and control their actions.[73] After establishing security in a particular area, the French deployed members of the Sections Administratives Spécialisées (SAS) to maintain security and carry out civic action programs. The activities included reforming local government, setting up medical services, and training local police and military forces.[74] Their main task was to effectively control the Muslim population. The SAS was not interested in understanding the Algerians; rather it wanted to turn them into docile collaborators and impose upon them French cultural, historical, and medical practices. These paternalistic practices were divisive and caused resentment.[75] Despite the efforts of the SAS, they played a small role in the overall COIN effort, and for some, they were deployed too late in the conflict to have a meaningful impact.[76]

To overcome the overwhelming disparity between France and the rebels, the FLN internationalized the conflict. The FLN leadership realized that confronting the French militarily would have been futile. Instead, it used international organizations such as the United Nations and friendly countries such as Egypt to disseminate its message and publicize French misconduct, including torture. As Matthew Connelly noted, "For weapons the Algerians employed human rights reports, press conferences, and youth congresses, fighting over world opinion and international law more than conventional military objectives." The conflict's most decisive battles occurred not in Algeria but in the international arena. By the end of the conflict, the FLN had rallied majorities against

France at the United Nations, won the accolades of international conferences, and received twenty-one-gun salutes across the globe.[77] Arguably, the FLN's "diplomatic revolution" was as important, maybe even more so, than French actions in the conflict.

If COIN studies have not discussed the Algerians' diplomatic efforts, they have discussed FLN terrorism, including the massacre of French civilians at Philippeville and attacks on destinations frequented by Europeans such as cafés or discotheques. Alistair Horne noted that although the FLN's attacks against Europeans dominated the headlines, Muslims in Algeria bore the brunt of the terror.[78] These attacks were designed not only to intimidate Algerians into supporting the FLN but also to provoke the French into overreacting. Revolutionaries also designed this approach to drive a wedge further between the two communities, creating even more hostility and suspicion. According to most accounts, the French reacted as the Algerian leadership hoped they would by torturing and using indiscriminate force.[79] Consequently, the French supposedly lost the battle of legitimacy and struggle for the hearts and minds of millions of Algerians.

The French-Algerian War lasted approximately six years and ended not with a military defeat but with a negotiated settlement. In March 1962, the French government signed the Evian Accords, formally ceasing France's control over Algeria. According to most accounts of the conflict, the French military had defeated the FLN militarily but lost the political battle both in Algeria and in France. The FLN's strategy of internationalizing the conflict played a prominent role in French withdrawal and Algerian independence. More importantly, the French throughout their colonial rule had not convinced the non-European inhabitants that remaining part of L'Algérie Française was better than independence. Despite the French defeat, the lessons from the conflict continue to offer case studies for future conflicts.

Killing Che Guevara

As Washington continued to escalate the war in South Vietnam, the US government discovered that international revolutionary Che Guevara had infiltrated Bolivia. Guevara hoped to unleash a revolution that would spread to neighboring countries and engulf the region. His primary enemy, though, was not the Bolivian government per se but the United States. Ultimately, Guevara wanted to create "another Vietnam" to destroy US imperialism in the hemisphere once and for all. In theory, the Bolivian military did not pose a formidable opponent. Widely ridiculed, its troops received the scorn both of its neighbors and of Washington. As Guevara quickly discovered, the conditions for creating another *foco* in Bolivia were less than ideal.

Unlike its effort in Southeast Asia, Washington preferred to maintain a light footprint in Bolivia. Instead of deploying combat troops, the US government sent the 8th Special Forces Group, the Green Berets, to train Bolivian soldiers. The Bolivian military argued with its US counterparts over the exact form of aid, preferring heavy US firepower to overwhelm and destroy Guevara's revolutionary forces. US officials balked, fearing that massive ordnance would produce civilian casualties, thus providing willing recruits for its enemies. Bolivian officers also proposed the creation of an elite commando unit similar to the hunter-killer teams established in the Philippines. US policy makers feared these forces would be used less to target Guevara and more as a palace guard.[80] President René Barrientos eventually agreed to allow the Green Berets to train a Ranger Battalion to hunt down the Argentine revolutionary.

US military aid to Bolivia contributed to Guevara's demise. Although most sources focus on the training of the Ranger Battalion, Washington completely rebuilt the Bolivian Army after 1952. Conventional Bolivian units played a crucial role in the defeat of Guevara's forces. The vaunted Ranger Battalion had not even been trained prior to the Argentine's infiltration. Although the unit eventually made it into the field—just in time—regular Bolivian troops discovered enemy caves, harassed Guevara's forces, and ultimately prevented the establishment of an insurgent stronghold.[81] Eventually, Guevara and the remainder of his followers were trapped in a ravine between several Bolivian military units. In the ensuing firefight, Guevara was wounded, captured, and taken to a small schoolhouse for interrogation. The precise details of his execution, including who ordered it, remain in dispute.

Guevara failed to replicate his feats in the Sierra Maestra in Bolivia. His target population, the *campesinos* (peasants), strongly supported the central government. They viewed the revolutionaries as outsiders and distrusted their intentions. Thus, the revolutionaries never found a receptive population. Guevara and his revolutionaries could not offer much, including land, to the region's peasants. As a critic of Guevara recounted, "What was Che going to offer . . . still more land they could not use?"[82] Guevara did not establish any links with the most radical sector of Bolivian society, the miners. If the Cuban and Bolivian insurgents had established their headquarters closer to the country's mines, it would have potentially exposed his units to annihilation more quickly.[83] Bolivia's Communist Party and other orthodox communist parties in the region and elsewhere also condemned Guevara's motives. Party leaders made it adamantly clear they were unwilling to participate in a revolution directed by a foreigner on their own soil.

After Guevara's demise in Bolivia, US military groups continued to create and train Ranger Battalions throughout the world. These units were considered among the most effective at eliminating insurgents. The largest effort occurred not in the Western Hemisphere but in Southeast Asia.

Vietnam

Of all the previous COIN campaigns, Vietnam has been the most analyzed. It is also the most contested; as one author noted, Vietnam is the "never-ending war."[84] Since the termination of the conflict, authors have debated why the United States lost.[85] In spite of the US failure, the conflict continues to serve as a model for COIN strategy, including in the most recent US wars. Vietnam represented a testing ground at which US policy makers and strategists devised new techniques they applied elsewhere. General Maxwell Taylor, testifying before a House subcommittee in 1963, referred to the country in similar terms:

> We have recognized the importance of the area and have consciously used it as a laboratory. We have had teams out there looking at the equipment requirements of this kind of guerrilla warfare. We have rotated senior officers through there, spending several weeks just to talk to people and get the feel of the operation, so even though

not regularly assigned to Vietnam, they are carrying out [*sic*] their experience back to their own organizations.[86]

The US military faced a formidable opponent in Vietnam: the doctrine of prolonged people's war (PPW). Under the leadership of Võ Nguyen Giáp, the North Vietnamese used a combined military-political approach to wage a protracted war against South Vietnam and Washington. All elements, including diplomatic, ideological, military, and organizational were united into one common cause, *dau tranh*. By creating a committed group of revolutionaries derived from the people and supported by a significant portion of them, North Vietnam and its allies outlasted the United States and defeated a US-designed and -supported regime.

Revolutionary ideology provided the antidote to US technology and firepower. Many US troops lacked the traits their enemy possessed: dedication, determination, and will to succeed. As the US experience in Vietnam demonstrated, superior technology cannot compensate for a flawed strategy or be the means to defeat a well-committed and dedicated group of revolutionaries. It is a lesson with which US policy makers and strategists continue to grapple. Throughout the conflict, senior US military leadership never devised a strategy to counter Giáp's approach successfully, even though Washington committed half a million troops and employed COIN tactics that were previously successful. Revolutionaries throughout the world, including Salvadoran rebels, studied the US experience in Vietnam to learn how a "raggedy-ass little fourth-rate power," to use President Lyndon Baines Johnson's charitable term, defeated a superpower.

During the US advisory mission (ca. 1954–1965), the South Vietnamese government implemented two large-scale population resettlement efforts aimed at separating the civilians from the insurgents and placing them in newly constructed and fortified villages. These programs also had another concern in mind: establishing control over the peasants. Ultimately, both of these programs did not fulfill their objectives.

In June 1959, Ngo Dinh Diem, the president of South Vietnam, who faced a growing insurgency in the countryside, launched a new initiative: the Agrovilles.[87] Diem's plan was designed to control villages, not aid their economic or social development.[88] These settlements served as a recruiting tool for the Viet Cong because of the concentration of masses of disaffected villagers who were poorly defended.[89] Even though the Agrovilles failed, their failure was not viewed as the result of deficient strategy or tactics. Rather, it was perceived as faulty implementation.

In 1962, inspired by British success in Malaya, the Diem regime unveiled the Strategic Hamlets program.[90] Robert Thompson, fresh from his exploits in Malaya, acted as an adviser to Diem. The plan eventually carried out was radically different from what Thompson advocated.[91] Diem's brother headed the program and envisioned it as a means of furthering Saigon's political control over the peasantry. Similar to its predecessor, Strategic Hamlets aimed at separating the civilians and insurgents and asserting control over the rural population.

The construction of Strategic Hamlets was supposed to be an orderly process, conforming to the oil-spot approach used by the British in Malaya. The program did not begin auspiciously. In March 1962, Operation Sunrise began with the first hamlet established in an enemy stronghold, the reverse of what Thompson advocated. The construction of hamlets proceeded rapidly, often without adequate security measures, and many were hastily built. South Vietnamese officials routinely pointed to the sheer number of buildings constructed as evidence of success. US officials were keenly aware of the numerical discrepancies and preferred a more methodical and slow approach. Despite the rapid expansion of the program, the numbers belied the results. In the process, rather than controlling or protecting the population, the Diem regime succeeded in further alienating rural South Vietnamese civilians.

There were several reasons for the program's failure. The corruption in Saigon and the pilfering of materials for sale on the black market did little to win the people's allegiance. In some cases, peasants were forced to buy barbed wire and pickets out of their own pockets.[92] This had important ramifications for the hamlets' security because they were also poorly defended and easily overrun by the National Liberation Front (NLF). More importantly, as Hannah Gurman has noted, the program embodied the central contradiction of the COIN effort in Vietnam: the population was protected from an insurgency many supported. The government protecting them was the same one whose corruption and contempt for rural villagers had fueled unrest in the first place.[93] Unlike in Malaya or Kenya, the NLF enjoyed more popular support than did its fellow revolutionary groups. Whereas the Mau Mau and Malayan insurgents represented one small ethnic group each, the NLF had broader representation from society. In other words, the NLF was inseparable from the people.

Perhaps the phrase most commonly associated with the conflict was the effort to "win hearts and minds." This was part of a campaign directed toward South Vietnamese civilians to demonstrate the legitimacy of the Saigon government and win their loyalty and popular support. Several US strategies used to woo South Vietnamese civilians included civic action programs and civil defense. Washington faced an uphill battle because of an increasingly apathetic South Vietnamese population, the ongoing fighting, a growing domestic protest movement, and war weariness in the United States. Compounding these issues were Saigon's endemic corruption and economic malaise.

Civic action programs in Vietnam aimed at winning the civilians' allegiance. Civilian agencies, especially the US Agency for International Development (USAID), played the dominant role in implementing these socioeconomic reforms. During the conflict, these efforts included building roads, constructing medical centers, and providing health and dental care. One of the more novel programs was village festivals, where cultural groups performed songs to woo villagers and demonstrate that a remote and indifferent central government was now committed to ameliorating their conditions. However, the main method to attract villagers relied on PSYOPS and civic action.[94] These programs were implemented after enemy forces had been removed from a particular district or village. Ultimately, Washington and Saigon never attracted a substantial portion of the South Vietnamese to their side.

The United States relied on several incarnations of civil defense, including the Regional Forces and Popular Forces (RF/PF) and Civilian Irregular Defense Groups (CIDG). These units provided village security, thus allowing the United States to implement its various civic action programs to reclaim momentum in the countryside. The programs were also designed to incorporate civilians into the pacification effort and act as a force multiplier, allowing US troops to avoid static defense duty and concentrate on fighting the North Vietnamese and the Viet Cong.

Despite the infusion of US ground troops in 1965, the overall situation—economic, military, and political—in Vietnam remained tenuous. In May 1967, President Johnson created a new organization, Civil Operations and Rural Development Support (CORDS), headed by Robert Komer, a civilian. Under CORDS, a single official managed the pacification effort in Vietnam. CORDS established "unity of effort": uniting the civilian and military under one leader, a practice the COIN literature associates with success. Recent US COIN doctrine emphasizes this agency's achievements despite the US loss in Vietnam.

To combat the control of US enemies over the South Vietnamese population, CORDS attempted to identify and destroy the Viet Cong Infrastructure (VCI). The VCI cadres were the building blocks of the revolution, the mechanism by which the Viet Cong spread its influence.[95] To combat the VCI, CORDS created a new agency, Infrastructure Coordination and Exploitation (ICEX). In December 1967, ICEX was renamed Phoenix; on the Vietnamese side the program was called Phung Hoang, after the mythical Vietnamese bird. Phoenix built on the work of the CIA-created network of the more than one hundred provincial and district intelligence operations committees in South Vietnam that collected and disseminated information on the VCI to police and paramilitary units.

The Phoenix Program produced lists of known and suspected VCI operatives. To disrupt the various enemy networks throughout South Vietnam, the Phoenix Program tried to capture and interrogate insurgents or kill them. Primarily, South Vietnamese units carried out these functions. If suspects were captured, they were taken back to the regional interrogation centers for questioning. However, suspects were often assassinated. Debates over the program's effectiveness and cruelty continue to rage within the literature.[96] As a more recent RAND study noted, the persistent political fallout from Phoenix had negative consequences for "information operations."[97] Simply put, criticism of the program harmed the battle for public opinion and support. Thus, programs such as Phoenix have to maintain a delicate balance. If they receive faulty information and kill innocents, or torture them, this approach will likely fill insurgent ranks.

As a result of the Paris Peace Accords in 1973, direct US military involvement in Vietnam came to an end. Reductions in the level of US

troops had started years before, under President Richard Nixon's policies of Vietnamization and the Nixon Doctrine. Less than two years after the ink in Paris had dried, Saigon officially ceased to exist. Although
COIN's star might have dimmed as a result of failure in the Vietnam
War, it retained a small coterie of adherents determined to implement
the lessons they had learned from the conflict.

Conclusion

Throughout the twentieth century the United States used counterinsurgency to achieve important foreign policy goals, especially in the
third world. All of these interventions were unique in their own regard,
and the US approach to combating the insurgencies differed in each
case, from relying on proxy forces to subdue the Huk Rebellion to the
introduction of US ground troops in Vietnam. Some of the common
denominators included civic action, civil defense, civilian and military
cooperation, relocation, and security force creation.

Of all the conflicts discussed above, arguably Vietnam has had the
most profound and continuing impact on US COIN strategy, especially
the most recent variant. This may seem striking because the conflict
ended in US defeat. Nevertheless, these policies are enduring. Current
US doctrine has relied on several of the measures and lessons drawn
from the pacification effort in the Vietnam War; however, they were
fluid, contested, and changeable.[98]

The major insight from an analysis of the conflicts discussed above
is that COIN strategy, whether American, British, or French, contains
variations within an overall common set of principles. Many of the tactics used by foreign armies have been used by the United States and
vice versa. The United States, Britain, and France also viewed revolution through a similar lens, believing that unrest in the third world was
communist inspired. Despite some analysts' championing of the British
use of minimum force and their approach to unconventional war in the
recent US-produced studies of COIN, official US doctrine also reflects
French military theory.

One of COIN's central goals is to establish and support the legitimacy of a government. Even if CIs are militarily successful, they can

lose if the government they support lacks legitimacy. In theory, legitimate governments are ethical, protect their citizens, and make them believe they have a stake in the new society. Yet practically none of the governments threatened by insurgency can be characterized as a liberal democracy. Indeed, the lack of political space available under a closed system often bred resentment, which led people toward solving their grievances through violence.[99] Arguably, the governments in many of the nations in which the United States has intervened had little, if any, legitimacy with their citizens. Washington has typically viewed insurgent movements—including the NLF in Vietnam and the insurgents in El Salvador—as illegitimate actors, despite their belonging to popular movements. Instead, the United States has sought to engineer or construct a government more palatable to its own citizens.

Constructing legitimacy cannot be completed in a short time frame. Anthropologists such as David Price have criticized COINdinistas for believing they can manufacture legitimacy quickly and sell it to the public.[100] Historically, constructing legitimacy has been a problem for foreign occupiers. In his study of insurgencies, William Polk has argued that foreign occupiers can never be viewed as legitimate. Thus, the "single absolutely necessary ingredient in counterinsurgency is extremely unlikely ever to be available to foreigners."[101]

When military force is used to provide security, it often results in killing innocent civilians and more devastation.[102] Population security makes civilians an object of competition between the belligerents and places them closer to danger and the threat of retribution. As David French and Gian Gentile argue, the hearts-and-minds approach is not only misinformed but also dangerous to civilians and troops. Thus, it accomplishes the opposite of what CIs intend: it creates more rebels. Whether it is the British experience in resettling people during the Anglo-Boer War, General Valeriano Weyler's reconcentration of Cuban insurgents, or the Strategic Hamlets program in Vietnam, the population has often suffered more, not less. In the cases where it has been successfully used, especially in Malaya and Kenya, the insurgents represented a small ethnic group that could be isolated easily. Population-centric policy is based on the questionable assumption that the people are separable from the insurgents.

Most of the COIN literature advocates a mixture of coercion and political reforms to defeat insurgency. One of the chief assumptions is that force is necessary but must be applied judiciously and selectively. Critics of COIN including French and Gentile disagree, arguing that coercion has played a significant role in defeating insurgencies, especially in establishing physical control over civilians. This approach can ultimately backfire; the historical record is replete with examples of failed attempts to suppress insurgencies by using overwhelming force and counterterror, including the Soviet Union in Afghanistan, the Russians in Chechnya, and the French in Algeria.

In the cases analyzed above, political reforms played a very minor role in successful counterinsurgency operations. When authors have discussed reforms, they mostly analyze military measures, such as the introduction of COIN doctrine, not the establishment of good governance. Even if political reforms are discussed, they are very minor aspects of the overall argument. CIs succeeded in part because their opponents were isolated from internal and external support. There were several factors that contributed to their isolation, including their size, lack of broad representation from society, and in some cases poor strategy. Consequently, the government-backed forces exploited their weaknesses and crushed them. In cases in which insurgents had significant international backing or support from the people, the results were much different.

The odds are generally stacked against insurgents, especially because of disparities in military technology and wealth. For a variety of reasons, insurgencies have generally been defeated. Sometimes CIs have succeeded because of their overwhelming material, political, or technological advantages. Political, tactical, and strategic mistakes committed by insurgents have often doomed their struggles. Insurgencies that lack either cross-border sanctuaries or outside support, including financial, political, military, and moral, have suffered defeat.[103] As Edward Luttwak has observed, "Insurgents do not always win; actually they usually lose. But their defeats can rarely be attributed to counterinsurgency."[104] Simply put, when the insurgents lose, their defeat cannot always be attributed to a brilliantly executed COIN strategy.

After the US defeat in Vietnam, US practitioners who wanted another opportunity to wage a COIN campaign did not have to wait long.

This time the battlefield was no longer in Southeast Asia but in the US backyard. El Salvador presented the US Army its first counterinsurgency campaign opportunity in the post-Vietnam era. It was the largest irregular conflict in which the US military participated between the end of Vietnam and the second US-Iraq War. US COIN strategists looked to the past to devise policies to defeat revolution during the Salvadoran Civil War. In Greg Grandin's words, Latin America—including El Salvador—was a laboratory in which US policy makers tested policies they would later implement in Afghanistan and Iraq.[105] Before discussing the Salvadoran conflict, it will be necessary to briefly analyze the ferment of COIN during John F. Kennedy's presidency and how he and his successors used prevailing theories about the subject to prevent the outbreak of communist subversion and the establishment of "another Cuba" in El Salvador prior to 1979.

2

The Development and Implementation of US Counterinsurgency Strategy in El Salvador and Latin America, 1961–1979

In the wake of Cuban dictator Fulgencio Batista's overthrow, US policy makers were determined to avoid the establishment of "another Cuba" in the hemisphere. Washington used all means at its disposal, including CIA-sponsored regime change, US economic aid, the deployment of US troops, and combating internal enemies through the Foreign Internal Defense (FID) and Internal Defense and Development (IDAD) programs. By the end of the cold war, the United States had spent billions of dollars to prevent this occurrence. More often than not, the United States grossly exaggerated the danger. The red boogeyman was used to justify the militarization of the region, support right-wing dictators, and ensure the region was safe for US investments. However, US policy, interests, and goals in the region were fiercely contested throughout the cold war, including in El Salvador between 1979 and 1992.

This chapter provides an overview of the various counterinsurgency initiatives and programs used by Washington to prevent and defeat revolutionary challenges in El Salvador from the end of World War II until the presidency of Ronald Reagan. During John F. Kennedy's presidency, the United States supplied lavish economic and military aid to El Salvador despite any existential threat. Many of the essential features of US military policy initiated under Kennedy continued through the Reagan administration. Until its demise, the Office of Public Safety (OPS) trained Salvadoran police officers and security forces, and the Pentagon deployed Special Forces operatives to train the country's military and intelligence units. Salvadoran officers also attended the various US military academies across the region. Thus, by the outbreak of the Salvadoran Civil War, many of El Salvador's military commanders had been exposed to the fundamental tenets of US counterinsurgency doctrine. The question is, did they find the strategy appropriate and would they employ it?

US policy makers implemented a counterinsurgency strategy throughout the region that prioritized military training and economic aid to thwart the spread of communism in the Western Hemisphere. The main assumption behind COIN was that it would defeat communist intrigues and stabilize, reform, and modernize the target country's infrastructure and institutions. In theory, increased levels of US aid and military training professionalized the region's militaries and improved human rights.

Moderate officers within the Salvadoran military embraced these ideas and promoted socioeconomic development programs to combat the spread of revolutionary agitation and the gross inequalities, such as the lack of land and poverty, facing their compatriots. Beginning in the 1960s, reformist officers and civilians from the Partido de Conciliación Nacional (PCN) supported state-driven modernization programs to improve El Salvador's socioeconomic landscape. From their perspective, the country's elite, especially the large landowners, had selfishly pursued their own agenda at the expense of the majority of Salvadorans. Their greed had created fertile ground for the spread of communism in El Salvador.[1]

These modest reforms provoked a backlash from the private sector and landowners who condemned any state intervention, especially when they believed it was dictated by the central government, as unwarranted intrusion into their sphere of interest. Hardliners in the military also disagreed with their moderate counterparts, who viewed opening El Salvador's economic and political space as potentially threatening. As frustrations mounted in the late 1960s and early 1970s, reformist officers' loyalty to their institution and their fears over disorder and revolution led them to support the use of repression to silence the discontent. Although US training and the cold war shaped their ideological perspectives, their "fears were also conditioned on a long-standing distrust toward popular politics and foreign adversaries, both of whom posed a threat to internal stability."[2] Unfortunately, deteriorating economic conditions, concerns over civil society's radicalization, and loyalty to the army tempered any far-reaching internal reform efforts.

Under President Jimmy Carter the White House maintained many of the existing aid programs and the ideological assumptions behind them. The administration continued to view the left as hostile to US interests and refused to engage it. Even as chaos engulfed El Salvador, US policy makers supplied aid to the Salvadoran military that, although nonlethal, contributed to the repression. US officials also incorrectly assumed that providing aid and US training would professionalize their clients. US policy failed on all accounts. By the end of President Carter's term, the United States had increased the amount of aid and deepened US involvement in El Salvador. Arguably, Carter paved the way for his successor, who accelerated the US commitment.

Recent Salvadoran history is also integral to this story. Internal strife in El Salvador, combined with a rigid socioeconomic system and mobilization among the students, peasants, and the Catholic church, pushed the country to the brink. This period also featured the fragmentation of the Salvadoran left and the creation of radical splinter groups that formed armed wings in the 1970s. Eventually, these groups united in 1980 and for approximately twelve years contested US and Salvadoran initiatives aimed at defeating them. Although US counterinsurgency policy aimed at preventing formidable challenges to allied regimes, the succession of unsavory and repressive Salvadoran governments and the institutionalized socioeconomic and political systems that granted exclusive participatory rights to the El Salvador elite served to radicalize significant portions of the country's population.

Kennedy and the "Counterinsurgency Era"

As a presidential candidate in 1960, John F. Kennedy lambasted President Dwight D. Eisenhower, arguing that his administration had allowed the Soviet Union to narrow the missile gap between the two countries. During the campaign, Kennedy criticized President Eisenhower for his "willingness to place fiscal security ahead of national security."[3]

Although critical of the New Look Policy, JFK also maintained several features of Eisenhower's national security ideations, including National Security Council Action No. 1290d, which established US internal security assistance strategy. This policy aimed at preventing disorder and communist subversion and employed US advisers to professionalize security forces across the globe. Administration officials viewed this program as vital because "many countries threatened with communist subversion [had] neither the knowledge, training, nor means to defend themselves successfully [against communism]."[4]

Under Kennedy, the United States implemented a COIN strategy to accomplish essential US foreign policy goals in the third world, including combating "wars of national liberation," launching development projects, reforming the political and socioeconomic systems of Washington's allies, and, of course, preventing the spread of communism. These initiatives included training internal security forces, carrying out political and agrarian reform, and using military power to defeat subversion and insurgency. Kennedy viewed "guerrilla warfare" as a new and different form of warfare.[5] The president used his influence and the powers of the executive office to convince others of the seriousness of this threat and the need to establish new capabilities to confront it.

Shortly after his inauguration, JFK asked Secretary of Defense Robert McNamara to examine the means for placing more emphasis on the development of "counter-guerrilla forces."[6] Kennedy also inquired about the various active training programs the US military conducted within Latin America. Of particular concern were programs aimed at "controlling mobs" and guerrillas. National Security Action Memorandum (NSAM) 124 created the CIs in January 1962 to consider how to implement the president's emphasis on confronting insurgency across the globe. The CI group approved a policy for countering subversion known as Overseas Internal Defense Policy (OIDP). Promulgated in NSAM 182, it argued,

A most pressing U.S. national security problem now, and for the foreseeable future, is the continuing threat presented by communist inspired, supported, or directed insurgency, defined as subversive insurgency. Many years of experience with the techniques of subversion and insurgency have provided the communists with a comprehensive, tested doctrine for conquest from within. Our task is to fashion on an urgent basis an effective plan of action to combat this critical communist threat.[7]

OIDP emphasized the need for development, interagency coordination, and minimization of US direct involvement in certain instances.[8] Maintaining a light US footprint concealed US involvement and would, the administration hoped, fully prevent criticism of Washington's policy at home and abroad. Host-nation governments were also anxious to downplay direct US assistance as well, fearing a loss of their own political legitimacy. Although Kennedy's plan shared similar features with Eisenhower's internal defense strategy, the young president expanded its police-training component and the Pentagon's relationship with the region's militaries.

After World War II, the Pentagon expanded its intelligence, military, and police partnerships within the Western Hemisphere, including in El Salvador. Initially, a frosty relationship existed between the US and Salvadoran militaries. Although the latter wanted US materiel and grants, it resented the high prices and arrogant US mission chiefs. Washington's failure to establish the equivalent of a command and general staff school in El Salvador further irritated senior Salvadoran officers. They reached out to the Chileans, who sent a five-man team to establish an academy. Consequently, El Salvador became the only Central American country to welcome a non-US military mission after World War II. Chilean officers also imparted an early version of the National Security Doctrine to their pupils that urged complete restructuring of the country's economic, military, political, and spiritual resources to better prepare for total war.[9] The continuing existence of a Chilean military mission concerned Ambassador Thomas C. Mann, who feared that country had gained the upper hand in El Salvador. The ambassador did not have to be concerned for too long, however. A countercoup launched by the Salvadoran military in 1961 appeared to usher in a new era in relations between the two.[10]

Over the next two decades, the US military strengthened its cooperation with its Salvadoran client through a variety of initiatives including aid programs, participation in service academies, and training efforts. Salvadoran officers used the lessons learned from their encounters and interactions with US officials to repress their citizens and maintain their institutional prerogatives. Until the late 1970s, Washington supported their efforts and continued to believe that US military aid had made a positive impact. Although the Salvadoran military might have prevented a revolution in the short term, its tactics backfired and spawned the growth of several revolutionary popular movements in El Salvador.

Military aid programs served US goals, including the Military Assistance Program (MAP), the International Military and Education Training (IMET) program, and the Foreign Military Sales (FMS) program. Washington also frequently deployed Military Training Teams (MTT), which often consisted of soldiers from the Special Forces.[11] The types of weapons, supplies, and training curricula provided by the United States varied from one region to another. In Latin America after the Cuban Revolution, the principal items donated to the region's militaries included helicopters, cross-country vehicles, and surveillance gear. These were considered among the most important items for counterinsurgency operations. As McNamara explained in 1967, the MAP in Latin America "will provide no tanks, artillery, fighter aircraft, or combat ships. The emphasis is on vehicles and helicopters for internal mobility [and] communications equipment for better coordination of in-country security efforts."[12]

US Southern Command (SOUTHCOM), the US military command responsible for Latin America, and US military intelligence worked to create Latin American intelligence units proficient in psychological warfare, counterguerrilla tactics, and interrogation to combat internal subversion.[13] Many of those who received training often used it for repressive purposes in their own countries, including torturing citizens, overthrowing governments, corroding democratic governance, and carrying out assassinations.[14] Among those frequently targeted included students, intellectuals, union organizers, and religious workers. Although US counterinsurgency doctrine did not specifically condone such behavior, US military assistance did not prevent such abuses.

Many Latin American officers received training at the infamous US School of the Americas (SOA), commonly referred to as the "School of the Golpes," or "School of the Dictators." The school was established under Kennedy and designed to give its cadets training in US COIN doctrine. Classes at SOA were originally held in the Panama Canal Zone but were transferred to Fort Benning, Georgia, in 1984. Between 1950 and 1972 more than 1,000 Salvadoran soldiers received training in the Panama Canal Zone.[15] Salvadoran officers who attended SOA included ten graduates who participated in the notorious El Mozote massacre in 1981.[16] Even more egregious, two-thirds of those accused of committing human rights abuses during the war attended the school.[17]

US counterinsurgency strategy also promoted the usage of civic action.[18] Its purpose is to build legitimacy between the government and its citizens by demonstrating that the former cares about the well-being of its populace. Put another way, civic action seeks to facilitate "an identification of governmental programs with the aspirations of the people."[19] Civic action programs were tested throughout the world, including in Latin America, but also in South Vietnam. Several of the more popular civic action projects included repairing and building roads, instituting sanitation, and constructing homes.[20] As the coordinator of both military and economic assistance, USAID performed the vital role of managing US economic assistance and civic action projects.

The Kennedy administration hoped that civic action would improve the image of Latin American militaries by incorporating them into development projects that served the people's needs.[21] US military officials labored under the illusion that they could create a "responsible and non-political military establishment" through their participation in civic action programs.[22] The funds dedicated to civic action in Latin America were not commensurate with its lofty goals. According to Cole Blasier, between 1961 and 1970 only 0.3 percent of military aid was directed toward civic action.[23]

Increased involvement by previous generations of Latin American militaries in such projects, such as in the Dominican Republic and Haiti, had failed to produce the cherished apolitical force. Unfortunately, these programs implicitly encouraged the military to enter the political arena by linking security to development and allowing this expanded role to permeate other sectors of society to defeat or forestall any challenges to the status quo.[24] Rather than enhancing their image with the people, Latin

American militaries used their power to destabilize governments with which they disagreed and crush internal dissent or reform movements.

Other federal agencies supported the Kennedy administration's counterinsurgency effort, especially USAID. AID played a significant role in US COIN efforts, especially its police-training program. The organization established the OPS in November 1962 to coordinate its efforts across the globe. Police officers were often considered the "first line of defense" against insurgency. As David Bell, a former AID administrator, remarked in 1965, "The police are a most sensitive point of contact between government and the people, close to the focal points of unrest, and . . . better trained and equipped than the military to deal with minor forms of violence, conspiracy, and subversion."[25]

OPS established programs in crucial and peripheral regions including El Salvador, Iran, and South Korea.[26] The organization trained personnel for every conceivable role in law enforcement, ranging from traffic control to paramilitary combat operations.[27] OPS provided necessary material such as shotguns and riot-control gear, offered advanced training to foreign police agencies, and promoted greater links with these forces.[28]

The aim of OPS was to establish and maintain law, order, and internal security. An additional responsibility was creating a climate conducive to sound economic, social, and political development. As Jeremy Kuzmarov noted, these programs fulfilled a less explicit agenda in securing the power base of local elites amenable to US interests. As the same author noted, this often backfired politically, breeding anti-US sentiment and resentment and fueling vicious cycles of violence.[29]

By 1968, its peak year, OPS fielded 458 advisers in thirty-four countries, with a budget of $55.1 million. In Latin America, more technicians worked in the program than in sanitation and health.[30] From its inception in November 1962 to its demise in 1975, the program trained some 7,500 senior officers in US facilities and anywhere from 500,000 to more than 1 million foreign police overseas.[31]

In El Salvador between 1957 and 1974, the United States spent approximately $2.1 million to train 448 Salvadoran police officers and provide arms, communication equipment, riot-control gear, and transport vehicles.[32] OPS agents also built a national police school and communications centers that housed computerized databanks of supposed subversives and provided weaponry and riot-control training. The agency's phase-out report in 1974 claimed that under US tutelage, El Salvador's police force had advanced from a "non-descript group of poorly trained men to a well-disciplined and respected uniformed corps with good riot control and investigative capabilities, good records, and fair communications and mobility."[33]

El Salvador under the Alliance for Progress

Kennedy's successors maintained many of the counterinsurgency initiatives launched by the fallen president. US military assistance programs in El Salvador, and in Latin America in general, emphasized the threat of internal subversion. Nevertheless, the Salvadoran military also continued to focus on external issues, primarily during the 1960s, as tensions with Honduras increased. During the 1960s, El Salvador was one of Central America's most stable republics, especially compared with its neighbor Guatemala. No real security concerns posed a risk to its stability. Nevertheless, US military aid and assistance programs not only continued but were greatly expanded.

Under the Alliance for Progress, El Salvador became the largest recipient of US aid in Central America. Between 1962 and 1965, the country received $63 million worth of aid.[34] During the same decade Washington as well as the World Bank and Inter-American Development Bank offered approximately $100 million in nonmilitary aid. This money financed school construction, food distribution, and telecommunications upgrades.[35] Military aid included but was not limited to radios, jeeps, gas masks, binoculars, gas grenades, and ammunition. The OPS trained the National Guard, the National Police, and the Treasury Police, all implicated in serious human rights abuses. The leader of OPS, Byron Engle, believed that the program improved the capabilities of these organizations.[36] Despite Engle's positive assertion, these units routinely violated human rights in El Salvador before and during the Salvadoran Civil War.

US military aid emphasized the threat posed by internal enemies, not only communists but also those critical of the regime, and aimed to keep them from gaining power. Anticommunist rhetoric disseminated in US service academies established a negative image of actors critical of US-supported regimes and those who demanded reforms as synonymous with enemies of the state. The heavy indoctrination cadets received in US military schools increased their distrust of groups pursuing political reforms and reinforced conservatism within the military.[37] In El Salvador, as in the rest of Latin America, the term "communist" was a catchall phrase for anyone opposed to the government, from students to labor organizers to religious workers. Individuals deemed hostile to the Salvadoran state often paid a heavy price, including their lives. The US military presence not only contributed to the shift in the Salvadoran military's ideological stance on behalf of anticommunist policy with international ramifications but also consolidated a long association between the Pentagon and the Salvadoran military high command.[38]

Arguably, the most notorious Salvadoran unit created during this juncture was the Organización Democrática Nacionalista (ORDEN; the Spanish word for "order"), a rural paramilitary group founded by Colonel José Alberto "Chele" Medrano, responsible for maintaining security in the countryside and fighting communists. Its purpose was to "indoctrinate the peasants regarding the advantages of the democratic system and the disadvantages of the communist system."[39] Its methods of persuasion varied, but when verbal persuasion failed, it resorted to other means, including kidnapping, torturing, and killing supposedly subversive *campesinos*. The Green Berets helped Medrano plan the structure and ideology of ORDEN and trained its leaders, including Colonel Nicolás Carranza and Domingo Monterossa, who would go on to play prominent roles in the civil war.[40]

Medrano also created the Agencia Nacional de Seguridad de El Salvador (ANSESAL).[41] Its goal was to create a network of *orejas* (ears, or informants) to provide the regime information on individuals or activities considered threatening or unfavorable to the state.[42] *Las orejas* were part of a larger network of informers who spied on peasants and other individuals with suspect motives or loyalties.[43] Predictably, this arrangement was often used to settle old scores or vendettas. ANSESAL assessed information received from ORDEN and passed it along to the president, who also made the important decision of how to act upon the intelligence. According to journalist Allan Nairn, US military operatives provided technical expertise and intelligence advisers to ANSESAL and supplied the organization intelligence and surveillance later used against individuals assassinated by "death squads."[44]

Between 1962 and 1965, the 8th Special Forces Group—the Special Action Force for Latin America—deployed 234 MTTs to seventeen different countries, including El Salvador. During this span, El Salvador received eleven teams, including missions that focused on counterinsurgency, civic action, PSYOPS, engineering, ordnance, forestry, airborne operations, and infantry tactics.[45] This time span also corresponded with the highest rate of US military advisers deployed to Latin America. Throughout the mid-1960s, the United States had approximately 1,300 military personnel stationed in the region, compared with 800 in 1959.[46]

During President José María Lemus's (1956–1960) reign, El Salvador was considered an island of stability. However, the changing political landscape in Latin America—Venezuelan dictator Marcos Pérez Jiménez's ousting and Fidel Castro's rise to power—inspired a new wave of political mobilization in El Salvador.[47] State Department officials, although consistently noting the small size of the Partido Comunista de El Salvador (PCS), also worried about Lemus's efforts to combat communism.[48] In his request for US aid, Lemus played upon the Cuban Revolution and the Domino Theory. As the president of El Salvador remarked to the US ambassador, "Central America is like an exposed hemisphere geological backbone. Break one of the vertebrae, a single country, and the whole hemisphere crumbles politically. Let El Salvador fall to communism, and the neighboring countries will be automatic."[49]

After initiating a crackdown at the National University in San Salvador, Lemus was overthrown and replaced by a civil-military junta. Despite having a more reliable government in power, the US Embassy in San Salvador continued to keep a close watch on the PCS. Embassy officials fretted over the likelihood of exiled leaders carrying out attacks outside of the country as well as the influence of the Cuban Revolution.[50] In the initial aftermath of the president's removal, the threat from insurgency abated. As one official noted, however, "The subversive organizations of Castro/Communist orientation, while temporarily handicapped by the exiling of many of their more capable leaders, continue to exist, and they retain a sizeable following."[51] To argue that the tiny PCS—a party that lacked popular support—threatened either the Salvadoran Army or the stability of El Salvador was untrue. It would not be the first or the last time an embassy official stretched credulity to the breaking point.

A study conducted by the Department of Defense in 1963 offered a different assessment, noting the small size of the PCS and the success of the government's vigorous anticommunist campaign.[52] By the end of 1963, the threat posed by communist elements to the government of El Salvador sharply declined. According to the CIA in 1964, it was "one of the hemisphere's most stable, progressive republics."[53] By the early 1970s, El Salvador had state intelligence repressive capacities that might have seemed beyond any reasonable calculus of need, even considering the possibility of war with its neighbors.

In 1965 the Salvadoran military spent approximately $10 million on defense, a figure accounting for over 8 percent of all government expenditures.[54] El Salvador ranked only behind Guatemala in military spending in Central America, which faced a much more formidable insurgency. Indeed, the state was prepared and predisposed to confront an enemy that did not exist.[55] More importantly, given El Salvador's intractable issues such as poverty, illiteracy, malnourishment, and lack of arable land, the government's decision to commit such a large sum to military expenditures prevented it from addressing the very issues that posed an existential threat to its survival.

Revolutionary Ferment

From 1932 until 1979, an alliance between the elite and the military governed El Salvador. The former, commonly referred to as *los catorce* (the fourteen families), owned practically all of the arable land in El Salvador and thoroughly dominated its economy. In reality the oligarchy comprised about forty wealthy families connected through marriage and a common goal of preserving their interests. William Stanley has characterized this relationship as the "protection racket state." In exchange for ruling and allowing its officers to enrich themselves through ownership in companies such as ANTEL, the state-owned telecommunications company, the Salvadoran Army protected the oligarchy's power. The military also wielded political power in El Salvador, and its senior officers served as the country's presidents. It was not always a smooth relationship. There were often disagreements, especially between the oligarchy and those military officers more oriented toward reform. These tensions boiled over in October 1979.[56]

Tranquility often came at an appalling price. In 1932, the government brutally suppressed a peasant rebellion in the western portion of El Salvador involving approximately 60,000 people. The La Matanza massacre, orchestrated by President Maximiliano Hernández Martínez and his security forces, killed an estimated 10,000–30,000 Salvadorans.[57] The precise number will probably never be known. Beyond producing a massive death toll, the violence also gravely weakened indigenous culture, which culminated in a form of genocide.[58] The massacre not only represented a watershed event in modern Salvadoran history but also proved formative in the construction of the ruling elite's ideology.[59]

The Salvadoran security apparatus prevented the emergence of another massive uprising for several decades by instilling a climate of fear across the country. Ostensibly, this strategy worked; yet, beneath the surface, Salvadoran actors resisted by creating local grassroots organizations. The country's elite viewed indigenous peoples and *campesinos* as potential subversives and second-class citizens who had to be "kept in their place by whatever means necessary."[60] In the countryside, state terror targeted the "local grassroots opinion leaders" who mobilized, organized, and provided political education to the majority of the population.[61] The Salvadoran elites also used fraud and intimidation to silence reformers, including the negation of José Napoleón Duarte's election in 1972.

Occasionally, reformist Salvadoran military officers tolerated brief periods of reform, which allowed the creation of several important civic organizations, including the Asociación Nacional de Educadores Salvadoreños (ANDES-21). ANDES-21 organized Salvadoran teachers, agitated for improved pay, and eventually led a nationwide strike that was brutally suppressed. Although these reform efforts did not greatly alter the country's socioeconomic landscape, they created larger political awareness, which would be harnessed in the 1970s.[62]

Reformist Salvadoran army officers also experimented with state-directed modernization, including restructuring the agrarian sector. The number of Salvadorans without land had skyrocketed since the end of the brief Soccer War with Honduras in 1969. Years later, in 1973, President Arturo Armando Molina organized a National Seminar on Agrarian Reform for military officers, who learned about the principles underlining the program and how the military could participate.[63] The need for access to land had become acute. In 1975 up to 40 percent of Salvadorans were classified as landless.[64] Molina's government introduced a land reform bill to address the growing crisis. His legislation ruptured the relationship between the government and its allies in the private sector. Although the amount of land affected would have been marginal, the right responded with outrage, especially the Asociación Nacional de la Empresa Privada (ANEP) and the Frente Agrario de la Región Oriental. Eventually, the government backtracked and sidelined the program.[65] The fiasco also hardened the feelings of reformist military officers toward their conservative counterparts in the elite. Future agrarian reform efforts confronted the same problem: rightist opposition forced the government to either remove or stall the implementation of key sections of the program.

Throughout the 1970s several important events undermined the Salvadoran political and economic systems.[66] After the fraudulent presidential election in 1972, El Salvador became increasingly polarized. The country descended into further chaos under the victorious candidate, Molina. His rule radicalized Salvadoran society and sparked the growth of popular organizations.[67] These groups formed the nucleus of a growing insurgency in El Salvador. Although in the early 1970s they could have been considered inconsequential, by the end of the decade they represented a growing threat to the prevailing social order in the country.

Threats to stability and order also emerged from the political right. Prominent individuals and organizations from the private sector pressured President Carlos Humberto Romero, Molina's successor, to use all means at his disposal to combat the growing protest movement. Agricultural and industrial elites also used their own measures—paramilitary forces and death squads—to punish the Catholic church and popular movements for supporting a variety of subversive ideas, including land reform. The state responded by passing the Law for the Defense and Guarantee of Public Order in November 1977. The legislation criminalized political opposition, violated basic civil liberties, and in the words of the late political scientist Enrique Baloyra "was practically a license to kill."[68] It also failed to produce the desired results. Increasingly, the Salvadoran right and its allies in the military responded to the popular agitation through state terror. The unabated violence undermined the Salvadoran state, created more sympathy for the popular fronts, and forced Washington to take a more sustained interest in the country's affairs.

As Salvadoran society unraveled, the Salvadoran left fragmented. The viability and necessity of adopting armed struggle represented a major fault line. In 1970, Salvador Cayetano Carpio and his followers split off from the PCS to form the Fuerzas Populares de Liberación (FPL) in 1972. Around the same time, a group of students led by Joaquín Villalobos and Rafael Arce Zablah departed from the FPL and formed their own organization, the Ejército Revolucionario del Pueblo (ERP). After the murder of Roque Dalton, a Salvadoran intellectual and one of Latin America's most renowned poets, and intense ideological debates, the ERP further fragmented, leading to the creation of the Fuerzas Armadas de Resistencia Nacional (FARN). Finally, there was the independent Partido Revolucionario de los Trabajadores Centroamericanos (PRTC). By the end of the 1970s, there were numerous insurgent groups in El Salvador that had differing aims, strategies, and goals.[69] What united them was a common desire to overthrow the existing government and a shared perception of the PCS as a revisionist party that had profoundly deviated from Marxist-Leninist doctrine.[70]

Tiempos de Locura

US interest in El Salvador dramatically increased after the overthrow of President Anastasio Somoza Debayle in July 1979.[71] Officials in Washington feared Somoza's removal could potentially trigger similar revolutions throughout the hemisphere. That same month, the US Embassy in San Salvador concluded, "If confronted with a Nicaragua-type situation the El Salvadoran military establishment could easily collapse in four to six weeks."[72] Recognizing the gravity of the situation, US policy makers developed a series of contingency plans. According to one of the options, should President Romero step down and transfer power to a transitional government, the United States would "firmly come to the support" of El Salvador, providing its government military aid and technical assistance to help the Salvadoran Army "better cope with the guerrillas." As the contingency plan noted, "This might require US advice for counterinsurgency."[73]

Within El Salvador, Somoza's overthrow had a profound effect on many Salvadoran army officers, many of whom could envision the same fate befalling them. The Nicaraguan revolution, more than any other single event, galvanized the feeling of a group of young reformist military officers that there was a need for change.[74] This group, the Juventud Militar, wanting to avoid a repetition of the fate that befell Nicaragua, decided to depose President Romero in October 1979. The coup deepened US involvement in El Salvador and paved the way for the acceleration of aid under Carter's successor, Reagan.

The Revolutionary Junta Government (JRG) replaced President Romero after his deposition. The first junta included three civilians and two colonels. Strong internal contradictions within the group eventually became untenable. After recognizing the JRG, government officials debated US policy toward the new regime. Ambassador Frank Devine argued that the new Salvadoran regime represented the last chance "of staving off a takeover by the extreme left."[75] Washington also fretted about the possibility of hardliners in the private sector and the military launching a countercoup and unleashing even more violence. From a US policy standpoint, the immediate problem in El Salvador was the inability of the Christian Democrats and reformist military officers to reach an agreement on a new cabinet or the direction of the new government.[76] In spite of these issues, the Carter administration moved quickly toward supporting the junta and preventing the dominoes from tumbling in El Salvador.

For the remainder of Carter's presidency, US political objectives in El Salvador consisted of bolstering the JRG and preventing its collapse. Washington supported the creation of a democratic government committed to the promotion of human rights. In order to divide and weaken El Salvador's left, one Carter official called for opening a dialogue with key Salvadoran actors, such as the archbishop of El Salvador, Óscar Arnulfo Romero, in hopes of convincing them to cease cooperating with supposed extremist elements and support the JRG.[77] The other actors considered most likely to topple the junta were hardline military officers and their allies in the oligarchy. Carter administration officials reasoned that US aid was essential for these goals to succeed.[78]

The Salvadoran government preferred for US assistance to be part of a multilateral effort. The JRG was keen to minimize any possible public perception that it was especially beholden to the United States for military aid, lest it become a political liability and "a battle cry of the extreme left."[79] Robert Pastor, National Security Council adviser for Latin America, agreed, arguing, "One of the biggest problems that the junta had to wrestle with is that it is perceived as a US creation without any political base of its own. In short, we have the right approach to the problem, and it would be a mistake to abandon it when it is working."[80]

On March 3, 1980, the head of the second junta resigned, plunging the country into another crisis. Several days later, on March 9, José Napoleón Duarte, former mayor of San Salvador and leader of the Partido Demócrata Cristiano (PDC), returned to El Salvador and assumed control of the government. This new governing coalition attempted to make radical reforms to Salvadoran society and prevent further violence against civilians by outlawing ORDEN and ANSESAL. Unfortunately, the government presided over a period of violence in which the Salvadoran security forces murdered approximately 1,000 civilians a month. The junta also attempted to address land reform, one of the most glaring issues in El Salvador.

Three days later, the JRG promulgated agrarian reform in a program supported and encouraged by the Carter administration. In the words of Colonel Adolfo Majano Ramos, the leading progressive military officer in the junta, "The law will take the land out of a few hands and give it to many. . . . Up till now, the masses of people have lived on the marginal edge of the nation's economy. We're going to take the land away from the very few and give it to the many so they can control their own destiny."[81] In El Salvador, the ownership of land was one of the most unequal in all of Latin America. The country had both the highest ratio of landless families out of the total population of any country in Latin America and the highest ratio of tenant farmers to total population. Approximately 40 percent of peasants either lacked land or enough income to adequately provide subsistence for their families.[82] Although the Carter administration had given the land reform its blessing, several officials, especially the new ambassador, Edmund Muskie, were concerned about its implementation.[83] Carrying out land reform was essential to restructuring the exploitative social structure that fueled the Salvadoran insurgency.

The oligarchy did not respond favorably to the agrarian reform. Many among those privileged ranks viewed it as a threat to their livelihood. Some members opted for exile in Honduras or Miami, where they pursued their opposition to land reform, including the formation of death squads. The existence of these death squads and their connection to these affluent expatriates was open knowledge to officials in Washington, who dubbed the exiled members of the oligarchy the "Miami Six."[84] Others openly resorted to violence. On January 4, 1981, two Americans, Michael Hammer and Mark Pearlman, along with head of the Unión Comunal Salvadoreña (UCS) Rodolfo Viera, were murdered at the Sheraton Hotel in San Salvador. Viera, like many others who met their ends at the hands of death squads, had been publicly threatened prior to his assassination. The land reform workers' murders were most likely a calculated political statement, especially because they were carried out by members of the National Guard who had ties to Hans Christ, a prominent Salvadoran business owner.[85]

Almost as soon as the reforms were decreed, peasants began to be evicted by their disgruntled landowners. The number of evictees is hotly disputed. The UCS claims it was as high as 9,000, whereas the Financiera Nacional de Tierras Agrícolas (FINATA) claims it was significantly less, at around 3,822.[86] Violence plagued agrarian reform throughout the course of the Salvadoran Civil War. Both government forces and the FMLN attacked vestiges of the program. Most sources, however, including the American Institute for Free Labor Development (AIFLD), attributed most of the violence to Salvadoran government forces.[87]

President Carter's Salvadoran policy attempted a rather delicate balancing act: providing military and security aid and training to a repressive force while improving its professionalization. James Cheek, a US diplomat, believed this policy would allow Washington to wage a "clean counterinsurgency" effort.[88] For such a scenario to occur, US strategists had to marginalize the extremist elements responsible for human rights abuses. Washington's policy was predicated on the presumption that generous aid would provide the United States leverage over the Salvadoran military by tying US support to improvements in human rights.

Administration policy makers debated sending a variety of MTTs, including teams specializing in helicopter repair and training, guerrilla warfare, and civic action. These units were deployed to train the Salvadoran Army, not the other security forces. According to one supporter, this would help the United States strengthen the hands of the Salvadorans trying to curb the repression. There was another reason as well: to make it clear to both the military officers within the JRG and the extreme right that the "purpose is to train the army to deal with extremists on both sides by 'using the minimum lethal force.'"[89] Using a divide-and-conquer strategy, the MTTs would "wean" the moderate elements in the military away from the oligarchy.[90] Officials within the PDC concurred. As one US policy maker noted, the PDC viewed the MTTs as a way of demonstrating US support for reforms and as a means to increase its leverage (through the United States) over the military.[91] It was not a unique formula; Carter's successor followed a similar strategy.

Several officials within Carter's administration believed that a continuation of aid to El Salvador's military, a thoroughly unpopular Salvadoran actor, damaged US prestige and its goals in the country. Ambassador Robert White argued that the "MTTs will be interpreted by all [Salvadoran] sectors as support for the armed forces as currently constituted and as approval for the campaign of repression."[92] William Bowdler also expressed his skepticism by observing, "We deceive ourselves if we think that we will save the situation by putting these MTTs in." Should the United States decide to proceed and the Salvadoran military continue the same tactics, the United States would find itself "in a position of receiving the blame for what they're doing."[93]

Several prominent Salvadorans opposed US military aid, including a former member of the JRG, Hector Dada Hirezi, and Archbishop Romero. Dada Hirezi, a member of the second junta who resigned in March 1980, complained that sending US advisers would cause further violence, not prevent it. Dada Hirezi also argued that additional US "counterinsurgency advisers" would lead to another dirty war.[94] In February 1980, Archbishop Romero composed a letter to President

Carter. Romero argued that providing weapons to the regime instead of "promoting greater peace and justice in El Salvador would undoubtedly serve to make more acute the injustices and repression against those groups who have often strived to obtain respect for their fundamental rights."[95]

Secretary of State Cyrus Vance wrote the response to Romero's letter. As Vance declared in his letter, the Carter administration viewed the JRG as offering the "best prospect for peaceful change toward a more just society" and declared that the bulk of the aid was economic. The secretary of state also promised that if any of the aid were used to repress human rights, the United States would reassess the situation, implying the termination of US aid.[96] Unfortunately, Romero's view proved more prescient. On March 24, 1980, a few weeks after the launch of agrarian reform, Archbishop Romero was assassinated while performing mass. His murderers were linked to Roberto D'Aubuisson. In a country already increasingly polarized, the archbishop's murder pushed El Salvador past the breaking point. Although the death squads and military had attacked, harassed, and murdered priests in the past, Romero's death marked a departure, plunging the country into further chaos. Arguably, the archbishop's murder marked the beginning of El Salvador's civil war in earnest.

Romero's death did not alter US policy toward El Salvador. US aid continued to flow despite growing concern in the United States over US support for a government incapable of keeping the violence within its borders in check. In June, Ambassador White, who harbored reservations about US policy, outlined the justifications for supporting the regime:

The U.S. main interest is in fostering the creation of a stable, progressive, popularly supported, democratic government, capable of finding peaceful solutions to the social and economic problems that have troubled this country for decades, thereby introducing domestic stability, which in turn will contribute substantially to the peace and stability of the whole region. The security assistance program is intended to remove major obstacles standing in the way of that interest, principally domestic terrorism and subversion from, both left and right with assistance from abroad.[97]

US aid and influence failed to halt the bloodshed. Instead, the Carter administration continued to allow the supply pipeline to flow. In August 1980, the United States provided El Salvador $6 million in credits for the purchase of basic transportation, communications, and riot-control equipment. Congress had rejected the last item the year before because of the deteriorating human rights situation.[98] Ambassador White's predecessor argued that US riot-control training had allowed the Salvadoran government to deal effectively with demonstrations and occupations of factories and farms without "resorting to their traditional method of maximum force with guns and bullets."[99] As Warren Christopher noted, the administration would not continue assisting the country if it used US aid for repressive purposes.[100] Christopher also argued that US aid could increase the professionalization of the Salvadoran military and "enhance orders not to abuse human rights."[101]

As El Salvador moved toward civil war, the various insurgent groups continued to bicker.[102] Uniting the disparate guerrilla factions proved challenging. While the groups quarreled, Fidel Castro pledged to withhold his support if they could not put aside their differences and form a unified front.[103] In October 1980, with Castro's patronage, the disparate insurgent organizations combined, forming the FMLN. This facade of unity masked deep ideological and strategic divides that separated the various factions. Nevertheless, the FMLN proved a formidable enemy.

The murder of six leaders from the Frente Democrático Revolucionario (FDR) on November 27, 1980, prompted several US policy makers, including Christopher and Patricia Derian, assistant secretary for human rights and humanitarian affairs, to reconsider their support for Carter's approach. Derian argued that US policy had failed because it had been applied inconsistently and was beset by contradictions. Consequently, elements hostile to US interests controlled the Salvadoran military.[104] Christopher, Derian, and White argued to discontinue military aid and training. They also viewed this as an opportunity to promote US goals in the country by using the event to pressure the JRG to reform the military.[105]

Events only further deteriorated. Weeks before Reagan's inauguration, on December 4, 1980, the bodies of four US churchwomen were exhumed outside of San Salvador. The women had been arrested, raped, and killed by members of the Salvadoran National Guard for being alleged subversives.[106] In response to the death of the churchwomen, the Carter administration suspended aid to El Salvador on December 4, 1980. Less than two weeks later, another event led the White House and US policy makers to reconsider the ban.

On January 10, 1981, the FMLN launched its Final Offensive. The offensive aimed at both toppling the existing junta and presenting the Reagan administration a fait accompli. According to the Defense Intelligence Agency (DIA), the insurgents believed that the Reagan administration would pursue a more active policy, threatening their goals and plans.[107] As guerrilla commander Fermán Cienfuegos declared, "The situation in El Salvador will be red hot by the time Mr. Reagan arrives. I think Mr. Reagan will find an irreversible situation in El Salvador by the time he reaches the presidency."[108] The FMLN was emboldened by the recent Sandinista success and because the Salvadoran Army was weak and divided.[109] It was a formula the FMLN would try again, in 1989, with slightly better results.

When the Final Offensive began, the Salvadoran security forces, despite being weak and poorly trained, successfully anticipated the attack. They also defeated the offensive through overwhelming force. Within a week, the offensive had faltered, and the rebels were forced to retreat back to the countryside. The popular uprising the FMLN hoped for never materialized. It also failed to trigger any large-scale desertions from the Salvadoran military. Two major issues hampered the Salvadoran rebels' efforts: despite being unified, the groups were not completely in sync, and they lacked the proper military capacity to take power, including arms and ammunition.[110] Even after suffering a setback, one FPL insurgent noted that the offensive had provided the firsthand battle experience to FMLN troops that attacking isolated army guard outposts could not.[111]

The rebels analyzed the offensive to try to learn from their mistakes. According to an internal study, "The FMLN recognizes that, except for the attack on the central base of the air force, it did not manage to strike the forceful military blows in the capital that were needed to sustain the full development of the strike" and ignite a popular insurrection. The FMLN also justified its withdrawal not as a defeat but as part of its strategy.[112] Yet, the failure of a popular uprising to materialize must also have been disconcerting for the guerrillas given the widespread support for the popular front groups in the late 1970s. In a private interview with one senior FMLN comandante, the official noted, "If the enemy had been well prepared, efficient, and coordinated, we would have been annihilated."[113] Even though the rebels avoided annihilation, the state terror unleashed by the military and security forces disrupted their urban networks and forced many to flee to the countryside or go dormant. The rebels used their time wisely over the next few months to build military schools to train their new combatants and concentrate their forces.[114]

The Salvadoran military launched a counteroffensive immediately after the offensive to hunt down the fleeing guerrillas and destroy them. Despite the army's best efforts, the soldiers failed to encircle and defeat their enemy. Instead, the rebels managed to avoid the large sweeps and lived to fight another day. The military, however, terrorized the countryside by unleashing a vicious scorched-earth campaign culminating in the infamous massacre at El Mozote. These rampages increased opposition to the state and contributed to the rise in support for the FMLN in *el campo* (the countryside).

Following the launch of the Final Offensive, Carter's advisers pressed for immediate resumption of aid to the increasingly embattled JRG. Supporters claimed that it was in the US national interest to support the JRG, arguing that failure to resume military assistance could weaken and unravel the government.[115] Carter's hawkish national security adviser, Zbigniew Brzezinski, eyeing long-term ramifications and the administration's legacy, justified the resumption of aid: "It would be extremely damaging not only to our national interest but to the historical record of this administration to leave office unwilling to take the hard decision to provide lethal assistance to an essentially middle of the road government, beleaguered by revolutionaries almost openly assisted by the Cubans via Nicaragua."[116]

Ambassador White agreed, stating that in "having to choose between guerrilla terrorists of the far left and a badly flawed but decent government working to control rightist excesses, the people have definitely turned their backs on the far left and refused it any active encouragement."[117] According to one unidentified State Department official, the decision was based on "substantive merits." As the official explained,

"The guerrillas and their external supporters were taking advantage of our forbearance and were moving fast, so as to be one step ahead of the new administration. We would have appeared naïve at best had we not reversed our policy prior to the Reagan inauguration. This was among other things, a test of our own professionalism."[118] Shortly before leaving office, Carter authorized additional military and economic aid to El Salvador, including rifles, helicopters, ammunition, grenade launchers, and flak vests.

By the time Carter departed the White House, according to official counting, there were twenty-three US military personnel in El Salvador, including helicopter maintenance crews, an Operations and Planning Team working with the Salvadoran high command, and the permanent military group (MILGP), all stationed in San Salvador. Nevertheless, there were discussions about increasing the number of advisers in El Salvador by thirty-three. This expansion would be accompanied by a broadening of their roles to include naval interdiction training, counterguerrilla initiatives, and airmobile operations. As the briefing paper cautioned, this increase would bring Americans closer to attacks by hostile forces by increasing US visibility and could potentially bring the US administration within the terms of the War Powers Resolution, meaning that Congress would have to authorize these actions.[119]

As President Carter left office, he was still plagued by the unresolved Iranian hostage crisis, Soviet intervention in Afghanistan, and a Soviet Union purportedly gaining strength and looking to take advantage of US vulnerability across the world, including in the Western Hemisphere. After winning the presidential election in 1980, Reagan soon made it clear that he would stake his reputation and define his foreign policy by making progress against the Soviet Union in Latin America. One of the countries where he thought his administration could score a quick victory against the Soviet Union was El Salvador. In the process, the president elevated the country to an important position in his administration's policy making not commensurate with its strategic significance to the United States. Perhaps more importantly, it was not as easy or cost free as the new president and his policy makers imagined.

3

The Reagan Administration Enters the Maelstrom, 1981–1984

On February 2, 1982, the atmosphere on Capitol Hill was heated. On that day, the Reagan administration was set to certify that El Salvador had made significant progress on human rights in the previous six months. Receiving a congressional stamp of approval was required to continue providing aid to the beleaguered US ally. Congress enacted this measure to ensure for itself a hand in shaping US foreign policy toward El Salvador despite the fact that members (as well as the US public) had serious doubts about the wisdom of continuing to provide aid to a country so beset by government corruption, violence, and human rights abuses.

Assistant Secretary of State for Inter-American Affairs Thomas O. Enders testified that although progress was slow, there were encouraging signs in El Salvador, including on human rights, agrarian reform, and a commitment to holding elections. On this basis, Enders argued that Congress should continue funding the Salvadoran government. In response to his testimony, US Representative Gerry Studs (D-MA) could barely conceal his disdain. Studs, evoking Orwellian language, thundered:

> I think someone has done the president a great disservice. Someone somewhere has obviously prevailed upon him to sign his name to that certification document. If there is anything left of the English language in this city after your assault by your immediate superior, it is now gone because the President has just certified that up is down and in is out and black is white. I anticipate his telling us that war is peace at any moment. . . . You take empty rhetoric and call

it reform. You accept promises without having demanded action. You look at a 14-month gap between a murder and the application of a lie detector test and call it an investigation.[1]

Enders's testimony and Studs's incredulous response encapsulate the intensity and emotion the Salvadoran conflict elicited in the United States. Although the names and faces might have changed, throughout the next several years the message remained the same. When testifying in front of Congress, White House officials and government policy makers routinely asserted that the United States was making progress in El Salvador. It had to do so. Its Salvadoran ally was almost completely dependent on US support to survive. Severing that country's lifeline would have left the Salvadoran government gravely weakened and potentially on the edge of collapse.

This chapter focuses on US involvement and COIN strategy during the height of the Salvadoran Civil War (1981–1983). US interest in El Salvador peaked during these years. Continuing human rights violations, insurgent victories, and deepening US involvement generated a contentious national debate over the administration's Salvadoran policy. Newspapers frequently reported grisly accounts of massacres, human rights violations, and insurgent victories, all of which the Reagan administration disavowed. For the first two years of his administration, the president spent a considerable amount of time and political capital pursuing US goals in the country; Reagan's Salvadoran policy, however, aroused significant opposition in US society and Congress. These years also coincided with an intensification of the cold war on all fronts in which the Reagan administration attempted to reverse Soviet gains across the globe.

One of the primary aims of this chapter is to analyze and discuss the various US-supported and -funded COIN programs designed to defeat the FMLN, reform El Salvador's political and social system, and maintain the US-backed regime. Using US government and Salvadoran sources, this chapter will analyze and trace the development of these programs. Many of the ambitious policies developed to achieve US goals were practiced during this time, including launching the National Campaign Plan (NCP), continuing agrarian reform, professionalizing the military, and holding elections to build a centrist, stable, and pro–United States Salvadoran government. Several of these policies had been used in previous conflicts, such as in the Philippines and Vietnam. Although these efforts might not have been exact replicas, former US COIN experiences informed US strategy in El Salvador. For the next several years the US government helped its Salvadoran ally stave off defeat. Nevertheless, although US aid and assistance might have prevented a FMLN victory, its partner came no closer to victory during this period than it was at the start of the Reagan administration.

This chapter will also incorporate the FMLN and its evolving strategy. For the next few years, the insurgents employed a combination of conventional and unconventional tactics in their attempt to overthrow the Salvadoran government. Using interviews with former insurgents and captured guerrilla documents, I will discuss the origins of the FMLN strategy and how its members combated both the Salvadoran and US COIN efforts. This is important because most studies of COIN neglect a very important aspect: the insurgents get their own vote.

"Win One for the Gipper"

Although President Jimmy Carter had paved the way for increased US aid to the beleaguered ally, his successor quickly amplified it. For the first two years of Reagan's presidency, the administration expended considerable time and attention on the Salvadoran Civil War. Preventing a revolutionary triumph in El Salvador served the White House's larger interests in the region. Even though Central America's smallest country was also the most vulnerable, Reaganites eventually hoped to turn their attention toward their most pressing concern, the Sandinistas. After stabilizing El Salvador, hardline officials could begin destabilizing and terrorizing Nicaragua through their proxy army, the Contras.

The White House offered numerous rationales for the massive intervention. According to official pronouncements, the United States confronted a dire threat to its national security in Central America. Reagan characterized the threat posed by a FMLN takeover as imperiling the United States. As the president noted, "San Salvador is closer to Dallas than Dallas is to Washington, D.C. . . . It is at our doorstep and it's become the stage for a bold attempt by the Soviet Union, Cuba, and Nicaragua to install communism by force throughout the hemisphere."[2] Reagan's policy makers believed that a failure to confront communism and defend US regional allies would trigger a domino effect. As President Lyndon Baines Johnson rhetorically asked his audience decades earlier, "If this little nation goes down the drain and can't maintain her independence, ask yourself, what's going to happen to all the other little nations?"[3] Administration officials justified US involvement in the Salvadoran Civil War with similar ideations. Even though Reagan wanted to "roll back" communist gains in the region, his administration belatedly discovered there were limits to US options.

The Reagan administration also depicted the Salvadoran conflict as another cold war confrontation between the East and West.[4] It largely ignored the socioeconomic context and focused on the "irrational" behavior of the insurgents and their ties to Cuba, Nicaragua, and the Soviet Union. Even when they did address popular grievances, including the lack of political space, US officials offered a narrowly defined vision of reform. The White House repeatedly argued that Moscow and Havana's machinations were responsible for the upsurge of revolutionary activity and violence in the region. Reagan described his administration's policy in El Salvador as designed to stop the advance of communism and support moderate anticommunist governments that produced political change, social reform, and economic growth peacefully and incrementally.[5]

El Salvador's importance to the Reagan administration did not lie in its economic resources. US investments in Central America constituted less than 10 percent of total US assets abroad in the early 1980s.[6] Rather, the country's proximity to the United States and especially its location within the US imperial orbit meant that it had to be kept out of "enemy" hands. Throughout the twentieth century, the United States expanded and attempted to retain its hegemony over the region. Keeping Central America and the Western Hemisphere "secure" would also allow Washington to wage the cold war in other, more important parts of the world and ensure stability and order so that US investments could thrive. Increasingly, US business interests viewed El Salvador, and the rest of Central America, as a vital region for enhancing their competitiveness through low production costs and proximity to the United

States. Politicians on both sides of the aisle as well as US manufacturers and financial institutions were unwilling to tolerate any actors deemed hostile to US commercial interests.[7]

For Secretary of State Alexander Haig, the Salvadoran conflict was "winnable."[8] In the minds of Reagan and his inner circle, success in El Salvador was key to the administration's goal of restoring the credibility of the United States after years of erosion and excising the "Vietnam syndrome" from the country's psyche. Burying the ghosts of Vietnam was an important part of both Reagan and US conservatives' attempts at confronting the Soviet Union and winning the cold war. Before taking office, Reagan stated, "It is time we purged ourselves of the Vietnam syndrome. If the US cannot respond to a threat near our borders, why should Europeans and Asians believe that we're seriously concerned about threats to them?"[9] To challenge the "Evil Empire," Reagan expanded and rebuilt the US military. Reagan, like previous US leaders, believed that once again, US credibility was at stake. The administration "wanted to send a message to others in the world that there was a new management in the White House."[10] As countries in the region quickly realized, the Reagan administration was not afraid to flex US military muscle.

The Reagan administration's goal in El Salvador was to defeat the FMLN both militarily and politically. Viewing the Salvadoran conflict as a Soviet incursion into Washington's sphere of influence, the administration believed that a political settlement was inadequate. The president-elect declared, "You do not try to fight a civil war and institute reforms at the same time." Rather, "Get rid of the war. Then go forward with the reforms."[11] Reagan also reminded his advisers of the stakes: "We can't afford a defeat. El Salvador is the place for victory."[12] As Undersecretary of Defense for Policy Fred Iklé remarked, "We do not seek a military defeat. We do not seek a military stalemate. . . . We seek victory."[13] It proved to be a long, difficult task.

The Foundations of US Military Strategy in El Salvador

US COIN strategy in El Salvador rested on several pillars. To prevent the further spread of communism and increase domestic and international support for the Salvadoran regime, carrying out important political and economic reforms was essential. These efforts aimed at redressing socioeconomic imbalances fueling discontent, along with establishing the Salvadoran government's credibility and legitimacy. Among the most important milestones was holding Constituent Assembly elections scheduled for 1982. These elections were considered important not only for the government's legitimacy within El Salvador but also for its reputation abroad. The military aspect of the equation focused not only on defeating the FMLN by adopting US COIN strategies but also on re-educating and professionalizing the Salvadoran Army to prevent further human rights abuses and to support the political process. Closely related were efforts to win Salvadoran civilians' hearts and minds through a series of civic action programs.

From the early 1980s, US COIN strategy in El Salvador can be described best as adhering to the policy known as "KISSSS": keep it simple, sustainable, small, and Salvadoran.[14] The US operated in El Salvador under the principle of supplying the besieged ally weapons, ammunition, and economic aid while preserving the principle that the war was theirs to lose.[15] Instead of ground troops, the United States deployed Special Forces advisers to train the Salvadoran military using COIN techniques to defeat the insurgency.[16]

The remainder of 1981 was not an auspicious year for the US COIN effort in El Salvador. In spite of the failure of the FMLN Final Offensive, the government's position remained tenuous. As Ambassador Deane Hinton noted in June 1981, not only was the situation "bad" but "matters may be going against the army." In Morazán and Chalatenango—two insurgent strongholds—the situation "is worse today than ever."[17] Concern existed among Salvadoran officers that if the insurgents could not be dislodged from Morazán, then the country could conceivably be split in two.[18] Roger Fontaine, director of the Latin America Affairs Directorate of the National Security Council (NSC), also captured the bleak situation, noting that the FMLN had made progress on wearing down Salvadoran troops, consolidating liberated zones, increasing its followers, and regaining international legitimacy. Although noting that insurgent gains would not force the government of El Salvador (GOES) to capitulate, a stalemate did not favor US interests.[19]

Both US and Salvadoran officers realized that the army suffered from several deficiencies, including an inappropriate and incoherent strategy, and failed to grasp how to respond to the enemy.[20] One of the primary goals of the US COIN effort was to improve the Salvadoran military's operational performance. As one US adviser noted, "We were on our last legs. We had to reform or we were going to lose. And it wasn't because the guerrillas were so good; it was because the Army was so bad."[21] As early as 1981, the CIA considered the war a stalemate.[22] Haig agreed but also worried that the country might collapse because the cumulative economic losses might demoralize the people and discredit the government.[23]

By February 1981, approximately twenty-five US personnel were stationed in El Salvador, including helicopter pilots, maintenance MTTs, OPAT, and MILGP. The NSC had also approved an additional six-person MTT, increasing the number of Americans to more than thirty. All of these individuals were stationed in San Salvador or in its immediate environs. The Reagan administration, as well as Salvadoran president José Napoleón Duarte, preferred to increase the number, preferably to fifty-four, and expand their presence outside of the capital.[24] US military personnel in El Salvador were slated to perform a variety of roles deemed essential to carrying out US strategic goals, especially interdicting weapons sent from overseas and halting the infiltration of foreign fighters.[25]

Administration officials were also aware of the dangers this expansion entailed, including placing Americans closer to combat and thus potentially provoking Congress into using the War Powers Resolution.[26] Reagan's policy makers also recognized the need to "blur the distinction between 'adviser' and 'trainer.'"[27] The term "adviser," although ostensibly neutral, was indelibly linked to Vietnam. During congressional testimony, John Bushnell, a State Department official, addressed the term "advisers" and their role in El Salvador: "I think we get a little tied up here in terms of the words we use. I resist the word 'adviser' because it covers an awful lot of things. We don't have anyone in El Salvador that is going out on missions with Salvadoran forces. All the people that we have are technicians or trainers who are doing a backup job, teaching them to use helicopters, repair helicopters, make plans, this sort of thing."[28] Despite Bushnell's assurances, advisers were occasionally involved in combat. In a particularly embarrassing incident, US advisers were filmed by a television crew carrying their M-16s.[29] Consequently, the soldiers were flown out of the country to avoid any further discussion of the matter.

In February 1981, Reagan authorized the first of several large aid shipments to El Salvador, including $25 million in aid, the majority of which came from discretionary funds that allowed it to circumvent congressional approval. Later that month, the administration increased the number of military personnel in El Salvador from twenty-eight to fifty-four.[30] Reagan's moves immediately provoked controversy, especially in Congress. His use of discretionary funds represented the first of many battles over Salvadoran policy between the executive and legislative branches.

The continued poor performance by the Salvadoran Army against the FMLN led US officials to rethink their overall war strategy. In November 1981, General Fred Woerner was dispatched to El Salvador as head of the MILGP to study the Salvadoran Army and write a report based on the group's observations. The group's primary mission was to draft a strategy compatible with US national security objectives and interests and receive the endorsement of the Salvadoran military.[31] It had other tasks, such as designing a force structure within El Salvador's resource capabilities, strategically assessing the military situation, and imparting upon the Salvadoran high command the importance of strategic planning.[32] Ultimately, the general and his staff spent approximately eight weeks analyzing the country's military and addressing its weaknesses. Woerner's report pessimistically stated that the Salvadorans "couldn't win the war with what they were doing."[33]

Woerner painted a picture of an incompetent military led by officers who had no grasp of how to confront the insurgency they faced. For example, the D-2, the military intelligence officer, was characterized as "incompetent, stupid, and lazy." The Salvadorans' counterinsurgency capabilities were nonexistent. Civic action was considered unnecessary because the Salvadoran military believed "the people are with them and thus see no requirement." However, virtually no data existed to back up these claims except a public opinion poll conducted in San Salvador months before the team arrived.[34] Perhaps more importantly, civic action was "primarily a function of the interest of local commanders, which is quite minimal, if not zero."[35] Although strategy called for population-control measures, no national registration system existed that could catalogue people's identities or survey them.[36] PSYOPS were also frowned upon because Ambassador Hinton considered them "black propaganda" and believed that the "best way to proceed is to tell the truth."[37] Despite the deficiencies discussed, Woerner believed that they could be overcome.[38]

For policy recommendations, Woerner's report presented three courses of action. First, US officials could continue funding the Salvadoran military at current levels, which Woerner cautioned would result in failure because of economic and political collapse. The White House could also expand funding levels to approximately $277 million, which, although improving internal defense capabilities, would not produce a strategic victory. The last option came with a price tag of $402 million. This amount of funding would provide arms and the adequate training required while simultaneously providing "enhanced defense against Nicaragua."[39] The report recommended adopting this course of action, and US policy makers agreed.[40]

Woerner based his plans on a hypothetical five-year timeline (he did not explicitly define how long the campaign would take) and estimated that it would cost approximately $300 million.[41] Despite the official status of the mission, Woerner's report was never formally approved by the Department of Defense. Nevertheless, it established the foundation for US military assistance to El Salvador. According to Hugh Byrnes, the Woerner plan and the subsequent buildup and rearming of the Salvadoran Army not only prevented an FMLN victory in 1983 but also contributed to a change in guerrilla strategy the following year.[42]

Constructing an Aggressive Force

For many US COIN practitioners, the Salvadoran military required more than cosmetic changes. Supposedly, the Salvadoran Army maintained a "garrison" and nine-to-five mentality and refused to take the fight to the insurgents. According to US COIN strategists, the Salvadoran Army lacked the essential training to successfully implement US pacification efforts. For those familiar with US military aid programs to the region during the cold war, this was a curious assertion. The Salvadoran military had received decades of US schooling provided at the SOA and US military academies, military hardware, and collaboration between the Green Berets and Salvadoran intelligence agencies such as the ANSESAL. As one adviser acknowledged, the problem was not lack of US COIN training, it was "getting them to actually use these tactics."[43] Critics of US policy in El Salvador viewed the matter quite differently: because the Salvadoran military had been practicing US COIN strategy for decades, it was responsible for the devastation of the country.

In 1980, the US Army created the first of several aggressive Salvadoran units designed to hunt down and destroy the insurgents, Los Batallones (de Infantería) de Reacción Inmediata (BIRI). These units were capable of quickly deploying across the country and conducting the small-unit and long-range reconnaissance patrols at the foundation of COIN strategy. The US military had created similar units in earlier conflicts, including the "hunter-killer" teams in the Philippines after World War II. BIRIs received the best equipment available and were trained by the US military at a variety of locations, including in the United States and Panama. These units participated in several important battles throughout the conflict, including large-scale pacification initiatives. By the end of the conflict, there were five rapid-reaction battalions; however, all of them were disbanded at the behest of the FMLN after the signing of the Chapultepec Peace Accords in 1992.

The first and most important unit was the Atlacatl Battalion, a name derived from a mythical figure in Salvadoran history. The Atlacatl Battalion was considered the most professional and aggressive unit in the entire Salvadoran Army. According to a State Department telegram, it was unique because it was the "largets [*sic*]" unit in the army and comprised soldiers recruited from across the nation, not locally.[44] In a British diplomat's opinion, the battalion was unlike the rest of the army. As he noted, "They are different, they, like the IRA [Irish Republican Army], enjoy killing."[45] US advisers also noted the battalion's brutality and penchant for macabre war trophies; a US adviser witnessed an Atlacatl soldier transforming a human skull—reported to have belonged to a FMLN insurgent killed in action—into a desk lamp.[46] In the beginning,

US Special Forces trained 1,383 members. Two years later, only 250 of the original members still served in the unit.[47]

Despite being labeled the most elite and professional unit of the army, the Atlacatl Battalion was implicated in numerous human rights abuses throughout the conflict, including the massacre at El Mozote, in which approximately one thousand people were murdered. One of the more egregious examples occurred near the end of the war, when members of the unit assassinated six Jesuits and their housekeeper and her daughter at the Universidad Centroamericana in 1989; an act that would have severe ramifications for US aid.

US military operatives also formed *cazador*, or "hunter," battalions. These forces were smaller than their BIRI counterparts, containing about a third fewer soldiers. Most of these forces were trained in Honduras at the Regional Military Training Center. The United States hoped to build approximately fourteen of these units, each comprising 350 troops. Similar to the rapid-reaction battalions, these units were designed to attack the FMLN and perform small-unit and long-range reconnaissance missions. However, they operated within a specific theater and did not constitute a nationwide force that could rapidly deploy across El Salvador at a moment's notice.

In addition to creating more aggressive forces schooled in the art of US counterinsurgency, US military trainers focused on professionalizing the Salvadoran Army. This included persuading the Salvadoran military to adopt US tactics to fight insurgency and halt human rights abuses. Leigh Binford argues that the magnitude of this task should not be underestimated. "It consisted of nothing less than a total makeover of the military institution and its personnel, rather like insisting that an adult who had grown up speaking one language and acting according to one set of cultural assumptions internalize a completely different language and way of being—and rapidly, in a matter of months or at best a few years."[48] It also required a "large dose of imperial pretentiousness" to believe that the Salvadoran Officer Corps and its allies would adopt the US advisers' advice, especially when their livelihoods and property remained in the balance.[49] One could also presumably understand Salvadoran hesitancy to accept US COIN advice when one considers that the US military had used these same tactics in Vietnam and lost.

US military advisers did not have the luxury or time to create a new Salvadoran Army from scratch. Instead they had to remodel a flawed institution and convince its senior leadership to respect the sanctity of human life. For US military trainers, preventing human rights abuses, along with implementing civic action projects, would convince the population to support the government. In theory, it was a formula for winning Salvadoran hearts and minds. Washington officially maintained that the Salvadoran military had improved its human rights record and followed US advice. US military strategists were concerned that continued human rights violations, combined with a lack of progress in outstanding legal cases such as the murder of the four US churchwomen, could potentially cause Congress to terminate funding. Nevertheless, the Reagan administration routinely downplayed such abuses and blamed them either specifically on the FMLN or on "unknown assailants."[50]

Throughout the war, the Salvadoran military proved hesitant to adopt the strategies promoted by its trainers.[51] As the CIA remarked in 1982, US military aid extended to this date had neither increased US influence over the Salvadoran Army nor made it substantially more effective. The limited deliveries with conditions attached and "on again off again time table" had left many Salvadoran officers believing US aid was illusory.[52] In spite of the massive amount of aid, the United States never had the requisite leverage to compel the Salvadoran military to fully comply with its wishes. The Salvadoran soldiers astutely realized that Washington was committed to their survival and feared "losing" another country to communism. In short, the Salvadoran military recognized that it had some flexibility and did not have to completely accept its US counterparts' advice—at least while the Reagan administration was in power.

That some Salvadoran officers resisted US advice should not have come as a surprise. Previous US experience in the region, including in its dealings with the military and oligarchy, should have been instructive. As a former US adviser who worked with senior Salvadoran officers noted, they were much "too nationalistic to allow the gringos to run them."[53] Although US advisers reserved the right to criticize senior Salvadoran officers, some of the fault also lay with the message and the messenger. The intervention did not fail because of incompetent locals who refused to heed US advice but because the principles themselves were inadequate. A similar parallel existed in the 1960s when US policy makers blamed the failure of modernization theory on supposedly incompetent natives. Even more importantly, the policies the United States devised did not address the root causes—socioeconomic inequality and lack of political space—of the insurgency.[54] Thus, even if the Salvadoran high command accepted US advice, it is unlikely the war would have ended differently.

Insurgent Strategy

Because the Salvadoran Army had numerous shortcomings, the FMLN strategy exploited and exposed its deficiencies. The FMLN represented the interests of five military and political factions with competing outlooks and strategies. Although it might have been united in its overall goal—to overthrow the Salvadoran government—its members often differed over the best means to achieve it, including the largest organizations, the FPL and ERP. The FPL, under the influence of its founder, Cayetano Carpio, the "Ho Chi Minh of Latin America," favored PPW, most famously executed by Vietnamese general Vö Nguyen Giáp.[55] Like North Vietnam's victorious campaign of reunification, the FPL hoped to drag the war out long enough to erode US resolve to the point where its support for the Salvadoran government would dry up. Conversely, the ERP pursued a more direct path of insurrection, hoping to provoke a massive uprising such as the 1981 Final Offensive. In spite of bitter internal conflicts, the FMLN general command managed to remain united during the war.

Throughout the civil war, the FMLN pursued a politico-military approach that aimed at defeating the Duarte regime militarily and undercutting its popularity across the country. Arguably, in the early 1980s, the Salvadoran insurgents emphasized the military aspect of the formula, hoping to inflict a series of military defeats against the regime that would lead to its collapse. After the failure of the Final Offensive, the FMLN established a force that imposed a series of military defeats on the regime. Until 1984, US officials privately worried about the possibility of a government collapse in El Salvador.

The FMLN used previous conflicts to design its strategy. At its core, it used an interrelated combination of military and political elements. The most commonly cited example was Vietnam, especially Giáp's theories about revolutionary war, which not only defeated the United States but exhausted its will to continue. FMLN rebels considered Giáp's strategy ideal and appropriate for El Salvador.[56] Prior to his death, Salvadoran poet Roque Dalton wrote an article that provided a synthesis of US strategy in Vietnam and the role of insurgents in a "guerrilla war." Among the most important tasks was destroying enemy forces through attrition. As the article noted, "Annihilating enemy forces will break the aggressive nature and strengthen the revolutionary forces."[57] The case study of Vietnam was also important for another reason: it provided the United States the COIN strategy it applied in El Salvador. Joaquín Villalobos considered his country a pilot project in irregular warfare. As he noted, "All that was applied in Vietnam, and subsequently improved and corrected, has been put into El Salvador without success."[58] Throughout the conflict, whenever the Salvadoran Army adjusted its strategy or tactics, the FMLN attempted to adapt and counter them.

Throughout the 1970s, the Salvadoran insurgents used urban insurgent tactics associated with the Tupamaros and the Brazilian radical Carlos Marighella to undermine the Salvadoran government. These urban insurgent tactics were especially useful when the Salvadoran left committed acts of urban terrorism, such as kidnapping wealthy businesspeople for ransom, along with organizing politically in the major cities. Meanwhile, the ERP and other insurgent groups drew inspiration from the Cuban and Nicaraguan revolutions (which some insurgents had experienced firsthand). Although Cuba and Nicaragua provided assistance to the Salvadoran radicals, their stories of triumph over US client regimes were not always considered relevant or applicable. Facundo Guardado, an FPL insurgent and future presidential candidate, believed that the Cuban rebels and the Sandinistas did not have the necessary experience to train the FMLN in the concepts of guerrilla warfare. The more practical and relevant example was the North Vietnamese. However, according to Guardado, the Sandinistas proved to him that overthrowing a corrupt regime was possible.[59]

As the conflict continued, the experiences of Giáp and Mao demonstrated their utility for several *comandantes*. Some rebels looked to other military writers for guidance. Comandante William Pascasio

(Comandante Memo) concentrated more on Carl Clausewitz's *On War.* Pascasio reasoned that the Salvadoran Army resembled a Prussian-style force, like that of the German-trained Chilean Army, and that the situation in El Salvador differed from the one in Vietnam.[60] The particular case models the insurgents studied were determined by the role they played in the insurgency. For those more involved in the politico-military aspect of the revolution, the Vietnamese model would have appeared more appropriate. For those strictly concerned with military matters, Clausewitz was more appealing because of the Salvadoran Army's conventional mind-set from the outset of the conflict.

The Prussian strategist has been indelibly associated with the conventional military approach to waging war. Recent military historians have been critical of Clausewitz, arguing that his approach to warfare is no longer applicable to today's conflicts. Historians such as Bart Schuurman and Christopher Daase believe that these critics are mistaken because of a fundamental misunderstanding of his writings on their part.[61] In particular, Daase argues that Clausewitz not only discussed guerrilla warfare but had a firm grasp of its essentials. Many of the strategies associated with this type of war, including small-scale attacks against enemy detachments or weak points, were highlighted during Clausewitz's various lectures on the subject. From Daase's standpoint, there is much to learn about guerrilla warfare from reading Clausewitz. Thus, although Clausewitz is generally associated with conventional war and the application of concentrated firepower, his writings also resonate with insurgents and are more proscriptive for them than generally imagined.

The FMLN divided its Revolutionary War of the People into three stages: growth and consolidation, strategic equilibrium, and the strategic counteroffensive.[62] The latter term was a staple of Mao and Giáp's approach to insurgency; it is also indicative of the influence they exerted over the FMLN's strategy. To implement PPW, the FMLN applied three different modes: guerrilla, maneuver, and attrition warfare.[63] Although revolutionary war was supposedly a linear process, it was flexible. FMLN members were not constrained ideologically to one particular strategy or approach, which enabled them to switch between them when it suited their needs.

After the failure of the Final Offensive, the FMLN regrouped and analyzed its failures. A subsequent investigation determined that its failure was tactical, not strategic.[64] Although the FMLN had a large force at its disposal, it lacked the necessary training and experience.[65] Assessing that the time was not yet ripe for a full insurrection, the FMLN turned its attention to successfully building and training a larger force.[66] Pablo Parada Andino (Comandante Goyo), military adviser to Salvador Sánchez Cerén (and current president of El Salvador), recounted the great difficulty of the years that followed. The lack of clothing, military experience, and resources made an already dangerous situation even more hazardous. One of the primary goals was simply to survive.[67]

Over the next several years, the FMLN fought the conflict using a combination of both conventional and unconventional strategies. Although occasionally fighting in large-scale formations, the insurgents continued using strategies associated with guerrilla or revolutionary warfare, including organizing politically, establishing "rearguards," and attacking when they had the advantage. Between 1981 and 1984, the FMLN inflicted a series of defeats on the Salvadoran government and destabilized the nation's economy. Nevertheless, in spite of these achievements, victory proved elusive.

One of the FMLN's central goals was to create additional "rearguards."[68] The rebels carried out important tasks such as recruiting, strengthening their popular organizations, and training military forces in these insurgent-controlled areas. They also established military schools to train elite commando units in the rearguards, including the ERP's La Brígada Rafael Arce Zablah (BRAZ) and the Fuerzas Especiales Selectas (FES).[69] The FMLN consolidated its rearguards in the northern and eastern regions of El Salvador. It established several others near Honduras, where insurgents could slip across the border, and close to the established refugee camps. Two of the more important rearguards were at Chalatenango and Morazán, dominated by the FPL and ERP, respectively. In contrast, the Salvadoran government focused on shoring up its bases of support in western El Salvador and the main cities, including San Salvador.

The three elements behind the FMLN's strategy were the destruction of national infrastructure, disruption of the constituent elections in 1982, and demoralization of the nation's armed forces. These would remain constant throughout the conflict.[70] Insurgent documents repeatedly mention the importance of wearing down the enemy forces. Referred to as *el desgaste*, or attrition, this tactic relied on surprise attacks, ambushing troops using small patrols, and later in the conflict using small, improvised mines. The Woerner report noted that 75 percent of all casualties were the "result of ambushes (primarily vehicular) and mines or booby traps."[71]

From 1981 onward, the FMLN campaign of economic sabotage and destruction of the country's infrastructure served several purposes. First and most obvious, it hampered the Salvadoran economy. Economic recovery was an essential aspect of both the US and Salvadoran COIN plans. Sabotage created uncertainty about the economy and triggered capital flight. It also dried up investment in the country, costing jobs and leading to further discontent.[72] Attacks on power stations, utility poles, hydroelectric dams, and coffee harvests were also designed to test the legitimacy of the government and its ability to provide essential services to the people and promote the socioeconomic development of the country.[73] In addition to disrupting the Salvadoran economy, targeting the nation's infrastructure also tied down army units to provide static defense at sensitive locations and limited their ability to carry out offensive operations against the FMLN.[74]

The FMLN policy wreaked havoc on the Salvadoran economy. The US State Department estimated that the FMLN caused $826 million in damage to the Salvadoran economy between 1979 and 1983.[75] According to a US government document, the FMLN caused approximately $263 million in damages in 1984 alone, roughly 6 percent of El Salvador's GDP. In 1985, total cumulative damages since 1979 were assessed at $1.2 billion.[76] These attacks severely taxed the Salvadoran government's resources and capabilities. Not only did the FMLN's strategy prevent economic growth but also kept its enemy dependent on US aid.

Yunque y Martillo

Early in the conflict, the Salvadoran Army responded to FMLN attacks and offensives by pursuing a policy of *tierra arrasada* (scorched earth). A sense of desperation and frustration motivated the military. For the first several years, civilians were forcibly relocated, and those suspected of supporting, or at least sympathizing with the insurgents, were killed.

Prior to 1983 the Salvadoran military did not take many prisoners. Soldiers refused to view captured guerrillas as prisoners of war. Rather they were classified as *delincuentes terroristas*, terrorist criminals, not owed any consideration. The same logic applied to civilians. They became *las masas*, or guerrilla supporters. Thus, entire areas in the Salvadoran *campo* were considered suspect and required purging. This was also euphemistically known as *la limpieza*, the cleanup. This strategy was aimed at removing the "fish from the water," or removing the population from the insurgents.[77] According to journalist Mark Danner, the areas "infected" by communism were "being ruthlessly scrubbed; the cancer would be cut out, even if healthy fish had to be lost too."[78]

As the army rampaged through the countryside, it often harassed or terrorized Salvadoran villagers and, in one instance, destroyed an entire village. The most brazen demonstration of this strategy occurred at El Mozote, where the Atlacatl Battalion—the most professional unit in the entire army—rounded up and deliberately murdered hundreds of civilians. On December 10, 1981, the force arrived in the village after a brief firefight with guerrillas. Upon arrival the soldiers did not find any guerrillas; instead they discovered women, children, and non-military-aged males along with refugees from the surrounding area. After rounding up the villagers the following day Salvadoran soldiers separated the males from the females and children and interrogated, tortured, and finally murdered them in an orgy of violence. The carnage El Mozote residents suffered is so striking because its inhabitants were not militants.[79]

Perhaps even more importantly, these systematic scorched-earth campaigns characterized the early Salvadoran way of war. A similar parallel existed in Vietnam.[80] As Binford has argued, the Salvadoran officers who directed the massacre viewed mass terror as a legitimate tactic of COIN; "in doing so they demonstrated that they had mastered, perhaps too well," the lessons imparted by their various US advisers, who not only trained the unit but also disseminated a paranoid anticommunist ideology—the National Security Doctrine—that reinforced preexisting fears and justified the use of any and all methods to defeat the enemy.[81]

The number of people killed at El Mozote is a subject of dispute. Reagan officials such as Enders and Elliot Abrams denied that a massacre ever occurred. A list compiled by Tutela Legal, the human rights office of the Archbishopric of San Salvador, claimed that 767 people died. Some authors, including Binford, among others, have argued that approximately 1,000 civilians were deliberately and systematically murdered. A forensic postexamination conducted after the war revealed the true horrors of the massacre: approximately 85 percent of the 117 victims discovered at what had been the sacristy of El Mozote's church were children under the age of twelve.[82] Today, the church's sacristy is a garden dedicated to the children murdered. It contains the names of approximately 400 victims. It was an excellent example of the now infamous statement attributed to a US officer in Vietnam: "It became necessary to destroy the town to save it."[83]

Ultimately, indiscriminate attacks against civilians were self-defeating. They incurred the ire of the US Congress and alienated rural Salvadorans. They also increased FMLN revolutionary activity and the insurgents' interaction with the people.[84] The failure of this approach strengthened the hand of the US trainers attempting to convince the Salvadoran Army to eschew killing insurgents in favor of civic action and development projects. In June 1983, these efforts paid off.

Building a Moderate and Centrist Political Force

Political reform in COIN is meant to create institutions that build foundations of support among the people. Its ultimate goal is to bestow national and international legitimacy upon the government. In El Salvador, the strategy involved holding elections and establishing a viable, moderate political center against the extreme left and right. The goal was to replace formal military rule with a "third-force" civilian government capable of capturing support at home and abroad.[85] The major component of this program was holding scheduled Constituent Assembly elections in 1982 and presidential elections in 1984.

Elections were seen as a critical element in the US COIN effort. They were considered a means of enhancing the regime's legitimacy and a nonviolent way of resolving the conflict between the Christian Democrats and the right. They were also used to establish a centrist party acceptable to the US public and Congress and maintain congressional funding. Washington's concept of democracy, though, was limited to holding elections and curbing human rights violations. The United States never allocated any significant funds to strengthening the country's democratic institutions.[86] Both of these elections, however, excluded the FMLN as well as the smaller leftist parties in the country.

US officials repeatedly claimed that the Salvadoran leftists had no intention of participating. Rather, they preferred to shoot their way into power. Arguably, there were several individuals and factions within the FMLN who had no interest in participating. However, even if they had wanted to, their security could not be guaranteed. Members of the center-left FDR remained unwilling to participate because of fear they would be murdered, as their leadership was in November 1980. More importantly, the Salvadoran military opposed the participation of the left in the elections.[87]

The 1982 Constituent Assembly elections occurred in the midst of the fighting. The FMLN attempted to disrupt the elections, especially in the eastern portion of the country. It also issued a series of warnings to civilians to stay at home and avoid travel and military garrisons. Some of the factions refused to participate. According to one comandante, the ERP and the FARN were the only groups that attempted to disrupt the elections. Other rebel groups, especially the FPL, considered their actions "petit-bourgeois" and irrelevant to their strategy of PPW. They believed that trying to disrupt the elections would not lead to the decisive battle that would open the solution for a military or negotiated end to the conflict. In other words, it was a waste of effort and resources.[88]

To disrupt the Constituent Assembly elections, the groups within the FMLN who supported this policy concentrated on probing attacks on urban centers, destroying the means of transportation and other infrastructure, and intimidating voters. The Salvadoran insurgents launched several small attacks against cities in the provinces of Usulután and Morazán. The US ambassador believed that the aim of these attacks was to demonstrate insurgent strength and achieve propaganda victories ahead of the elections. In spite of the FMLN actions, the US Country Team predicted that the elections would proceed as planned.[89] Its predictions turned out to be accurate.

Ultimately, the FMLN failed to significantly disrupt the scheduled constituent elections, except in areas it effectively controlled.[90]

Comandante Balta conceded that the elections were a triumph for the Duarte government, especially because it held them in the midst of the war and prevented the FMLN from derailing them.[91] An insurgent publication produced during the war agreed, noting that the military tactics it employed during the elections were inadequate.[92] On Election Day, a record number of Salvadorans cast their ballots. Some sources claim that approximately 85 percent of Salvadorans voted. As Alexander Haig proudly noted in a telegram to diplomatic posts, in past Salvadoran elections as many as 50 percent of voters in some departments had submitted blank or defaced ballots; in this election the number was approximately 12 percent.[93] The Reagan administration cast the election as a resounding success and vindication not only for US policy but also for the spread of democracy in the region.

The 1982 elections, according to Cynthia McClintock, were probably the least fair of all those held during this period. Voter turnout was inflated by double voting, ballot stuffing, and manipulation of tallies. The president of el Consejo Central de Eleciones (the Central Election Commission) asserted that more than 25 percent of the votes cast were fraudulent.[94] Voting, furthermore, was mandatory for civilians and enforced by security checks. To protest, voters often submitted defaced or blank ballots rather than not participating at all. In spite of this, two decades later, Dick Cheney used the 1982 election to support the George W. Bush administration's policy of holding constituent elections in Iraq.[95] Much as Vietnam had served as a precedent for El Salvador, the Salvadoran conflict provided a useful example for a future conflict: the second Iraq War.

Even before the election results were announced, US policy makers were concerned about the likelihood of ex-major Roberto D'Aubuisson's party winning the elections. The previous year, the former intelligence officer accused of orchestrating the assassination of Archbishop Óscar Arnulfo Romero had founded his own political party, the Alianza Republicana Nacionalista (ARENA), which had strong links with the extreme right in Guatemala City and Miami. Reportedly, the CIA spent $2 million to prevent the election of D'Aubuisson. The prospect of D'Aubuisson being elected was a nightmare; keeping Duarte in power was crucial for continuing congressional support. The CIA feared

D'Aubuisson's victory because it could lead to the political isolation of the regime and potentially boost the credibility of the FMLN.[96]

Agrarian Reform

Agrarian reform, a key element of COIN strategy in rural areas, continued under the Reagan administration. The program aimed at not only restructuring El Salvador's unequal land tenure system but also undercutting support for the FMLN. Under this initiative, privately held land was to be managed through collective ownership by government-run agricultural organizations. After land was identified and expropriated, these groups would help manage the properties and pay the government for their usage. Agrarian reform, however, was beset by challenges from both sides of El Salvador's political spectrum. Even some of Reagan's supporters questioned the reform.[97]

The American Institute for Free Labor Development (AIFLD), an agency based in Washington, administered and advised the land reform campaign. AIFLD also created peasant unions to support the agrarian reform program and, later, form worker and peasant coalitions to support Duarte and his political party.[98] Created in the 1960s as the international arm of the AFL-CIO, the AIFLD received the majority of its funding from USAID. Under Carter, the Salvadoran government closed the AIFLD offices. Nevertheless, prior to the overthrow of the Romero regime, the US organization was allowed to return, but the JRG coup prevented the necessary signature to reopen the office.[99]

Agrarian reform in El Salvador contained three distinct phases, meant to proceed in linear fashion. Phase 1 of the agrarian reform initiated the process of transferring land from the large landowners to the peasants. Properties in excess of 500 hectares were expropriated and their owners compensated by bonds determined on the declared value on their tax statements from 1976 to 1977.[100] As elsewhere, landowners undervalued their reported earnings or simply parceled their land into smaller sizes to avoid their inclusion in Phase 1. The implementation of Phase 1 aroused the ire of conservative Salvadoran landowners and the military, who demonstrated their hostility by assassinating three agrarian reform officials, two of them American, in January 1981.

Phase 2, announced in March 1980, concentrated on farms ranging between 100 and 500 hectares. The land reform targeted 23 percent of the nation's best farmland and nearly 75 percent of the nation's export crops.[101] Many of the farms affected grew coffee, one of the country's most important crops, and belonged to prominent Salvadoran families.[102] Even though it was considered the heart of the reform program, it was never formally implemented. In addition to wanting to avoid alienating key sectors of the Salvadoran right, the US government did not want to weaken the already shaky Salvadoran economy.[103] As a US Embassy briefing book noted, Phase 2 required administrative, financial, and personnel resources beyond those available to the Salvadoran government.[104]

Phase 3, promulgated in April 1980, was designed to transfer title of land ownership to Salvadoran *campesinos* (peasants) who had rented the land they plowed. Excluded from the decree were owner-operated farms of less than 100 hectares, which constituted about half of the country's farms and half of the land in farms.[105] Phase 3 drew criticism from both Salvadoran and US quarters. From the outset, it was not well adapted to Salvadoran conditions. Most renters worked plots of less than three acres of very poor land — not nearly enough to support the average family of six. The land's low quality required frequent rotation of crops to avoid soil exhaustion, so peasants rarely rented the same plot two seasons in a row.[106] Officials within the Salvadoran government, including within the Ministry of Agriculture and the Instituto Salvadoreño de Transformación Agraria (ISTA) opposed the decree. Although officials from ISTA generally supported Phases 1 and 2, they condemned the rigidity of the law and felt that it provided its beneficiaries with little more than "token benefits." As one document stated, Decree 207 would create "'*minifundistas*' of the most diminutive order, and their lives would be just as precarious as ever."[107]

The greatest political liability of Phase 3, according to an internal AID document, was that it was "designed virtually in its entirety by Americans and slipped into legislation without their [Salvadoran government] being consulted. The fact is known and resented."[108] This was a sticking issue in the program not only in the land reform but also, as will be discussed later, the military aspect. The author of this phase, Roy Prosterman, modeled the "land to the tiller" on an agrarian reform effort he launched in Vietnam.[109] Prosterman believed that these efforts would preempt support for revolution by restoring peasants' economic security and giving them a stake in the incumbent regime.[110]

Phase 3 had strong political undertones as well. According to US journalist Raymond Bonner, Prosterman's Land to the Tiller Program was meant to emulate Douglas MacArthur's land reform efforts in postwar Japan. In Prosterman's opinion, MacArthur's program effectively destroyed communists as a political force in Japan. He also told a hostile audience of Salvadoran businesspeople that the program would be successful, "breeding capitalists like rabbits."[111] Former ambassador Robert White also agreed, remarking that Prosterman thought "it was going to build a middle class, a group of people who had a stake in society."[112] In theory, Phase 3 would create a group of small land-holding Salvadoran farmers who would naturally be procapital. This new class of *campesinos* could also conceivably become the moderate and centrist force in El Salvador to counterbalance the extreme left and right.

As violence against *campesinos* and cooperative members continued, AIFLD officials were concerned that members of the Unión Comunal Salvadoreña (UCS), especially in western portions of the country, might renounce their membership. This organization was especially strong in the departments of Santa Ana, Ahuachapán, and Sonsonate, areas with high rates of violent incidents against agrarian reform officials and supporters of the program. A network of Salvadoran AIFLD members in the 1960s established the UCS to improve the plight of the Salvadoran peasantry through self-improvement projects. Its membership quickly expanded from 4,000 members at its inception to 70,000 six years later and 120,000 by 1980.[113] Because of its attempts to co-opt peasants and bring them under effective government control, the UCS was routinely accused by its critics of being an appendage of the US government. Although acknowledging the merit of these claims, Molly Todd believes they are also overblown. For Salvadoran peasants, their affiliation with the UCS proved beneficial not only in terms of material acquisition and skills but also because they gained economic and political awareness and experience with political organization. In Todd's opinion, the UCS actually paved the way for future *campesino* organizations.[114]

Violence against *campesinos* soared after the Constituent Assembly elections. By the middle of 1982 opponents of the reform effort won key positions within the Salvadoran government and began to strip important provisions from the legislation. After winning control of the Constituent Assembly, D'Aubuisson used his powers to end transfers of land under Phases 1 and 3 and delay the implementation of Phase 2. Moreover, he obtained key posts for his supporters within ISTA and the FINATA.[115] Nevertheless, the US government maintained that the agrarian reform program was working by arguing that land reform had passed its political crisis point and violent resistance had been defused.[116] In spite of these optimistic pronouncements, the following year, death squads resumed their practice of targeting agrarian reform activists and supporters in the Salvadoran government by sending them death threats. The intimidation worked, further truncating and blunting the reform's effectiveness.[117]

Beyond its intended role of defeating and discrediting Marxist insurgents, the agrarian reform program in El Salvador also had the rather straightforward goal of simply ending the country's pervasive wealth disparity. Unfortunately, eleven years after the program began, wealth had become even more concentrated, and the gap between rich and poor had grown.[118] Although the program arguably diminished the further radicalization of the peasantry, it never broke FMLN power over the countryside. The most important stage of agrarian reform — Phase 2 — was not only delayed but also it was opposed by key sectors in both the US and Salvadoran governments. The political right proved indefatigably hostile by first trying to prevent the program's implementation and eventually killing the program altogether.[119] This opposition was compounded by violence against agrarian reform officials by the FMLN and the coffee oligarchy and its various paramilitary networks. Ultimately, agrarian reform failed to achieve its lofty ambitions. El Salvador also attempted to address land reform after the conflict through the Land Transfer Program. Unfortunately, it resembled its predecessors in a disconcerting way: it did not seriously attempt to address the land issue or touch the nation's most valuable acreage. Instead, it was mainly used as a means to reintegrate the FMLN supporters into society.[120]

Regional Peace Initiatives

In January 1983, officials from Colombia, Mexico, Panama, and Venezuela gathered at Contadora, an island off the coast of Panama. Known as the Contadora Group, these countries tried to devise a plan to end the conflicts that ravaged Central America. In particular, the Contadora mediators believed that their collaboration could lead to a decrease in intrusive US intervention in the region and force the principle belligerents to negotiate.[121] In September 1983, the group produced a twenty-one-point agreement that called for an end to the militarization of the region and for further democratization. The following September, it issued an agreement that included advancing the promotion of democracy, ending the region's conflicts, and increasing economic cooperation. To enforce compliance, the Contadora Group created regional committees to evaluate and verify the implementation of its protocols.

The Contadora Group's preferred method of work consisted of dialogue among foreign ministers. They made no effort to include nongovernmental regional actors such as the FMLN. Central American guerrilla forces were excluded because they were considered illegal actors. Consequently, the FMLN viewed the group's initiatives cynically and actively opposed them.[122] This was a curious claim, because two years before, the FMLN had been recognized by France and Mexico as legitimate political actors.

The Mexican government's policy was completely at odds with its northern neighbor. Unlike the Reagan administration, the Mexican government believed that the various military governments in Central America would not be able to survive growing demands for political and social change. The Mexican government also recognized that bolstering repressive regimes prolonged instability and radicalized calls for change. As a Mexican diplomat informed Washington, "We recognize that the pressures for change can no longer be smothered. These countries have to find their own solutions, even if this means revolutions. Otherwise they will never be stable."[123]

The Contadora Group's proposals received a mixed response from the Reagan administration. Secretary of State George Shultz, a political moderate, preferred a diplomatic solution. On the other hand, hardliners within the administration, especially the NSC, denounced the pact because it legitimized the Sandinistas in Nicaragua.[124] As Walter LaFeber acknowledged, "The United States set out to destroy the Contadora agreement."[125] The hardliners within the Reagan administration ultimately won. After it was ratified by Nicaragua, the Reagan administration refused to sign the document, calling it a publicity stunt.[126] The United States then successfully pressured its closest allies in the region, including Honduras, Guatemala, and El Salvador, to reject signing the convention and participating in outside mediation.

Despite the lack of tangible progress, these initiatives began the process that produced the Esquipulas Accords. These proposals provided a nonviolent means of ending the region's conflicts that clashed with the Reagan administration's preference for securing military victory. Ultimately, Latin American initiatives, rather than anything that emanated from the White House, ended Central America's bloody conflicts. Whereas US diplomacy and military intervention have been decisive in terminating other conflicts, the same cannot be said for the Salvadoran Civil War. As I will discuss later, the termination of the war had little to do with US COIN strategy. In addition, this also contrasts with the "success" narrative promoted by COIN advocates and supporters of US policy during the conflict, who claim that the US COIN effort led to the end of the conflict and promoted democracy in El Salvador.

Pacification

According to General Wallace H. Nutting, commander in chief of SOUTHCOM (1979–1983), the situation at the end of 1982 and early 1983 was dire. After finishing his tenure, he told interviewers that "at the end of '82, early '83" the "whole thing was about to go down the tubes. The leftist guerrillas . . . were very strong. The armed forces did not yet have their act together."[127] The CIA also agreed, commenting that the stalemate that began in 1981 had continued.[128] Most contemporary accounts argued that although the political and security situation had improved, the Salvadoran rebels still remained a formidable force.

US government agencies registered their concern. The DIA acknowledged that although "the ESAF has improved its capabilities both qualitatively and quantitatively since 1980, the essential political ingredient still eludes the government. Until the GOES can bring the kind of secure environment and economic development to rally support among the general population," the Salvadoran Army COIN campaigns could only inflict brief setbacks on the insurgents.[129] One official portrayed the stakes in drastic fashion: "If pacification fails, we're sunk. We'll either have to give up the Salvadoran effort entirely . . . or we'll have to make a larger commitment—maybe even troops."[130]

In June 1983, the Salvadoran Army embarked on an ambitious civic action and pacification plan known as the NCP to regain momentum in the countryside. Calling the NCP a "turning point in the war," a US military official acknowledged, "We will win or lose on this operation."[131] The State Department agreed, viewing the campaign as a vital test of the commitment and capabilities of the Salvadoran military to counter the guerrilla advances of recent months.[132] The plan's blueprint was loosely based around CORDS, a program originating in Vietnam and remembered as a success story in what was otherwise a costly debacle.

The NCP attempted to win popular support and regain government control over contested zones, especially the San Vicente and Usulután Provinces, both economically and strategically important areas. According to Todd Greentree, the NCP embodied a US "can-do approach" founded on solid accumulation of lessons learned from other COIN experiences. The only problem was that it would have been a stretch for even the most developed country to carry out, let alone an underdeveloped country in the midst of a civil war and political transformation.[133] In other words, the US-designed policies were, at best, difficult for the Salvadoran government to implement, especially under wartime conditions.

The pacification effort included four phases: planning, offensive, development, and consolidation.[134] The first order of business required the Salvadoran Army to flush the insurgents out of the vicinity via military sweeps of the area, securing it and stationing troops to protect the population. The second phase initiated extensive civic action projects, including building hospitals, schools, and other institutions to transform the civilians' lives. In COIN theory the consolidation phase is the most important phase of the process. After removing the insurgents and beginning development projects, the Salvadoran Army handed over security to local security forces. According to a State Department fact sheet, this phase of the operation would address the causes of the insurgency through goodwill and building popular support.[135]

The National Commission for the Restoration of Areas (CONARA) oversaw the NCP. Its main goal focused on rebuilding communities devastated by subversive violence or natural disasters and improving their standard of living. One of their essential tasks was restoring public services to the affected communities. CONARA consisted of a series of short-, medium-, and long-term reconstruction projects. Reconstruction was envisioned as a three-step process: an immediate phase of providing and restoring aid, an escalation of the process, and then consolidation.[136]

Corruption was rampant in CONARA. US officials referred to the agency as a "notorious black hole," swallowing money without results, and as one US official quipped, "It was the worst agency you could ever set up."[137] One report detailed a former director who had misused and stolen funds provided for the agency. This scandal proved to be only the tip of the iceberg.[138] Like many other US COIN efforts, including in Vietnam and Afghanistan, US aid was siphoned off by corrupt officials, never reaching those it was intended to. Rampant misuse of funds not only drains a country's treasury but also, when it becomes accepted and institutionalized, threatens the viability of the state. As history and the collapse of dictators attest, people are less likely to place their lives on the line for corrupt and venal regimes unless their survival depends upon them.

One hundred days after the launch of the NCP, the Salvadoran Army had achieved or surpassed all of its objectives for the province of San Vicente. CONARA had also reopened schools and built health-care clinics and cooperative farms and, along with the US government, provided loans to small businesses such as banks and poultry farmers. As one embassy official noted, "While 1983 opened poorly for the El Salvadoran Armed Forces, new leadership, an increase in resources due to US assistance, and the impetus of the combined National Campaign Plan had given a new sense of purpose, with the army in the field and morale high." Nevertheless, embassy officials warned that it was too "soon to know if the trend can be sustained."[139]

In spite of the optimism, the Salvadoran government lacked the essential resources to pursue the combined civil-military operations actively outside the priority areas.[140] It was a classic case of "good intentions sabotaged by inadequate resources."[141] A lack of adequate resources confounded similar pacification efforts in the months ahead. CIA reporting made note of modest successes between June and August. It also noted that the NCP produced some positive results; however, the FMLN launched a series of counteroffensives that halted these gains. The insurgents capped off their advances the following year by overrunning a major army garrison and destroying a vital bridge.[142]

The NCP also featured the use of civil defense units (CDs). The development of CDs continues to be a mainstay in US COIN strategy, including in Iraq. These units provided static security after the military's departure. They also collected intelligence and regulated the movement of civilians to quarantine them from the guerrillas.[143] In addition to bolstering efforts by regular forces to control the countryside, CDs also provided a mechanism for inducing people to support the government.[144] Many of the people recruited for CDs, however, were very likely former members of ORDEN, linked to previous human rights abuses. Unpleasant memories of ORDEN and other death squads were partly responsible for this lack of enthusiasm.[145]

Poorly armed CDs were also ineffective against insurgent forces returning to San Vicente during the NCP. They were also insufficiently armed and consistently outgunned. Compounding this tactical weakness was the all-too-common practice among CD personnel of abandoning their weapons when fleeing from the enemy. As one Salvadoran colonel wryly observed, "Sending them out on patrol is a better supply for the rebels than the Nicaraguans."[146] This pattern of failure led to the creation of a national-level program for training and equipping CD forces.[147] This new training program was based on the US Marine Corps Combined Action Programs from Vietnam—combining Americans and Vietnamese civilians—aimed at correcting abuses and corruption and creating a defense structure that would complement the COIN effort of the ESAF.[148]

After the army moved into the area, the insurgents largely disappeared, allowing it to occupy the territory. The insurgents employed the classic guerrilla warfare strategy of avoiding superior forces. Theoretically, the military was supposed to remain until the insurgents were defeated. Salvadoran government forces, however, never had enough troops to permanently occupy the territory, even with subsequent increases in troops. Eventually, the battalions had to move elsewhere to provide security or be redeployed to carry out operations against the FMLN. Instead of attacking locations where the Salvadoran Army was strongest, the FMLN assaulted vulnerable locations, requiring the ESAF to move.

In response to the NCP, the guerrillas directed their actions away from San Vicente, the focal point of the program, toward areas where the army was weaker. Beginning in September 1983, the FMLN launched another offensive, seizing new areas across the eastern third of the country, including in the provinces of San Miguel, Usulután, and Morazán. It followed up these attacks with another set of devastating attacks against the army a few months later. In late 1983 and early 1984, the ESAF was routed in two separate areas—El Paraíso, an army barracks designed by US engineers and said to be impenetrable, and the Cuscatlán Bridge. According to the Salvadoran Army, El Paraíso was the battle with the government's single-highest casualty count in four years of war.[149] The destruction of the Cuscatlán Bridge severed the main route of traffic to the eastern third of the country.[150] These failures showed that, despite the ambitious campaign, the rebels were still able to determine the pace and initiative of battle.

After the Salvadoran military vacated a region, the FMLN returned and set up its own shadow governments, including local governing bodies, defense forces, hospitals, and a rudimentary legal system. The strategic goal was to establish these areas as strongholds or bases from which it could launch attacks. According to journalists who visited these areas, the disposition of the local population ranged from passivity to support. Reflecting the general mood, one local woman stated, "The only thing preventing massive incorporation is fear that the army will return."[151]

A *Newsweek* reporter who traveled to a rebel stronghold noted that the villagers were as intimidated by the rebels as by the army.[152] Even if the civilians were not uniformly supportive of the insurgents, they at least tolerated them. This made cooperation with the ESAF even more difficult.

Ultimately, US-backed pacification efforts failed for a variety of reasons. The COIN operations devised for the Salvadorans were contingent on the availability of considerable troops and resources.[153] Civic action offered protection and services to people who did not necessarily view the FMLN as the enemy. Although civilians accepted the program's benefits, it is also entirely conceivable that they did not simply forget that many of these same institutions providing aid to them had been hostile in the past. In addition to the corruption within the state apparatus, these efforts were also hampered by the conspicuous presence of US fingerprints that simply would not wash off. No matter how much aid the United States put into El Salvador, it could not have achieved US objectives, given the illegitimacy of the Salvadoran government.

There was also a question of will. As Greentree notes, it was never entirely clear just how determined the ESAF was to win, either on US terms or at all. The ESAF had been fighting communism in its own way since 1932 and had not hesitated to sever its formal ties with the US military in 1977 over what it considered the indignity of the Carter human rights policies.[154] According to the *Colonels' Report*, written and published during the conflict, the failure of the NCP convinced hardline Salvadoran commanders to forget about winning hearts and minds and focus on pursuing and killing the guerrillas.[155]

Conclusion

Near the end of 1983, it appeared as if Reagan's Salvadoran strategy was proceeding as planned. With help from the United States, Duarte's party had emerged victorious in the Constituent Assembly elections in 1982, the Salvadoran military had avoided defeat, and a number of reform efforts were under way. Large-scale pacification efforts such as the NCP, however, although achieving some short-term gains, failed to meet expectations. By 1984, it was hard to argue that the massive expenditures had brought the administration closer to achieving its foreign policy goals in El Salvador.

The insurgents were arguably at their strongest in 1983 and early 1984. Villalobos, in an interview conducted during the war, offered an earlier date of June 1982.[156] Estimates of how much territory the insurgents controlled varied from one-fifth to as much as one-third. Raúl Mijango promotes a higher figure, claiming that the FMLN controlled almost as much as 60 percent of Salvadoran territory.[157] In an internal FMLN report, in the year between June 1982 and July 1983, the FMLN obtained control of an additional one-fifth of El Salvador's territory. The same document claimed that the insurgents controlled more than 3,000 miles, seventy municipalities, and "80 percent of strategic military territory."[158] Whatever the exact figure, the FMLN's ability to control up to one-third of a country the size of El Salvador is a testament to the popular support the rebels received from the Salvadoran people. Even if not all of the civilians actively provided help to the guerrillas, their mere passivity is also indicative of FMLN influence and power.

Many of the COIN initiatives launched during this phase of the war continued until the end of the conflict. Agrarian reform began with noble intentions, but determined opposition from its opponents, lack of technical experience, bureaucracy, and the cancellation of its most important phase doomed the effort. Americans outside of the MILGP also initiated a resolute effort to create new and better-trained CDs to defend areas repopulated by peasants. Their efforts, however, were hampered by a lack of participation, distrust of the government, and fear of insurgent reprisals. Even though the Salvadoran military began to focus less on a scorched-earth policy and more on US-style pacification efforts, victory proved elusive. This switch also was not indicative that the Salvadoran high command had fully embraced US advice.

The embrace of the low-intensity conflict strategy recommended by the US military carried a hefty price tag that continually taxed the Salvadoran government's resources. As an internal memorandum warned, no country the size of El Salvador could maintain this brand of "costly assistance" without permanent outside funding.[159] The memo's author had good reason to be concerned. The Salvadoran state's continued reliance on US aid could potentially damage its political legitimacy, especially if it appeared that Washington pulled the strings. Although some US officials realized the misguided nature of Washington's security strategy in El Salvador, US operatives on the ground, with input from their Salvadoran counterparts, continued to design programs that stretched San Salvador's meager resources even further.

Washington's enemies had a firm grasp of the joint US-Salvadoran COIN strategy and how to counter it. Viewing these programs as replicas of those used in the Vietnam War, the Salvadoran rebels used that conflict and its leading strategies to devise a response. As with belligerents in other wars, the FMLN experienced successes and defeats during the first years of the conflict. Until early 1984, the insurgents often held the momentum and, in spite of the massive US aid, still remained a formidable foe. However, that same year, the nature of the conflict changed. Although they might have correctly perceived US strategy, they did not have the resources—or the international support—necessary to reverse the outcome of the war. Their inability to avoid defeat in spite of the massive intervention should not be dismissed.

Starting in middle to late 1984, the insurgents switched tactics, seeking to wear down the Salvadoran government and dry up US support by prolonging the war. Duarte's government also changed its strategy by embarking on a more aggressive and sustained air war against the FMLN. The infusion of US helicopters and aircraft devastated and depopulated portions of the country, displacing Salvadorans, who either fled to Honduras, joined the rebels, or emigrated to the United States. Although the Reagan administration turned its attention elsewhere in the region, the war continued and exacted a heavy toll on El Salvador and its economy.

Chasing Victory, 1984–1988

In El Salvador, 1984 literally began with a bang. On New Year's Day, the FMLN launched two large-scale and high-profile attacks. The Salvadoran insurgents assaulted El Paraíso, a modern US-designed military barrack, and briefly captured it; during another operation, they destroyed the Cuscatlán Bridge, severing the main link between eastern and western El Salvador. In addition to demonstrating the FMLN's continued ability to carry out spectacular operations, these attacks damaged the morale and psyche of the Salvadoran Army. Following the attacks, a high-ranking Salvadoran official lamented, "We are losing the war . . . and the only way to salvage the situation is to give the troops something to fight for. Until that time, we cannot be saved, no matter how much military equipment arrives from the United States."[1]

The attacks represented another setback for the White House's Central American ally. Secretary of State George Shultz admitted that these had been "tough blows for the army and government." Discussing the destruction of the bridge, Shultz noted that the guerrillas made excellent use of "diversion, lax security, and first-rate intelligence."[2] Although these attacks demonstrated the ability of the FMLN to continue inflicting military defeats upon the government, by the end of the year, the strategic outlook had been reversed. US aid not only stabilized José Napoleón Duarte's regime but also changed the Salvadoran government's fortunes. Over the course of the next several years, the counterinsurgents made some notable gains against their adversary; nevertheless, the FMLN remained an unvanquished force.

Although the beginning of 1984 might have unsettled US policy makers, they felt more confident as the year progressed. For many, Duarte's election as president in 1984 marked a decisive turning point in the war in favor of the Salvadoran government. US aid also constructed a larger Salvadoran Army and, with the help of US advisers, improved its overall performance. From 1984 until 1988, this trend generally continued.

Even though the military outlook had stabilized, several negative trends continued. In particular, the number of displaced civilians grew steadily. Aerial bombardment and large military sweeps caused massive dislocation in the countryside. The number of impoverished Salvadorans also rose amid deteriorating economic conditions. According to the executive director of the Central American Refugee Center, Sylvia Rosales-Fike, approximately 10 percent of the nation's population lived in squalid squatter camps by 1989.[3] To escape economic turmoil, war, and violence, thousands streamed across the border into neighboring Honduras. Salvadorans also immigrated to the United States, where more than 400,000 illegally crossed the nation's borders during that period.

The Salvadoran economy also continued to flounder. Key statistical indicators in every important category had dropped precipitously since 1980, including unemployment, capital flight, investments, and declining GDP. As the war dragged on, Duarte's US advisers pressured him to adopt austerity measures, which ultimately damaged him politically.

Similarly, the various reform measures implemented before 1984 (including agrarian and banking) continued. These efforts were designed to stabilize El Salvador's economic and political system and address the root causes of the conflict. Despite benevolent intentions, these reforms failed in part because of the elites' intransigence and the continuing deterioration of the economy. Nonetheless, Washington continued to maintain that these efforts were promoting progress and reform for the vast majority of Salvadorans.

This chapter will continue to elaborate upon the various COIN tactics the United States and its ally used to defeat the FMLN between 1984 and 1988. Many of the programs already established prior to 1984, such as civic action, persisted. US tacticians and their Salvadoran counterparts also experimented with what was, in many ways, a national-level version of the NCP and reaped similar results. When not trying to win hearts and minds, the Salvadoran military spent its time augmenting its forces and incorporating new US military hardware into its arsenal.

For the next several years, conventional logic in Washington assumed that generous US aid had enabled El Salvador to make progress in improving its human rights record, promoting democracy, and defeating the FMLN. On the positive side of the ledger, CIs eventually reduced the ranks of their nemesis, and their tactics also forced the insurgents to reappraise their strategy. The guerrillas also contributed to their reversal of fortune by relying on forced recruitment to increase their ranks and perpetrating indiscriminate use of mines. The Salvadoran guerrillas also refocused their attention toward political organizing and preserving their forces beginning in late 1984. Despite the FMLN's declining military prospects, it avoided decimation in a large and decisive battle. The Salvadoran rebels spent the next several years preparing to launch one last, large-scale offensive to take power or improve their bargaining stance at the negotiating table. It proved to be an apt decision. More importantly, even though both sides were not strong enough to defeat their adversary, the Salvadoran people had tired of years of constant war, deprivation, displacement, and violence.

Death from Above: The Expansion of the Air War

After attempting to win the war through the hearts-and-minds approach in 1983, the Salvadoran Army high command embraced US firepower and its technological advantage over the FMLN. The various bombing campaigns directed by the Salvadoran Air Force aimed at disrupting the guerrillas' activity, destroying their forces, and making life unbearable for their supporters and civilians. For the next several years, air power increasingly assumed a prominent role in the US-supported war effort. Ever since the surprise attack at the Ilopango Airbase in 1982 in which the FMLN destroyed most of the Salvadoran Air Force, the US government had gradually restocked their ally's inventory of helicopters and fixed-wing aircraft. Helicopters assumed a crucial role. They served a variety of purposes, including transporting troops quickly across the nation's territory, negating the enemy's speed, and establishing the element of surprise. Their primary functions, however, were transporting infantry forces for offensive operations and providing firepower.[4]

After the US Congress approved virtually all of the Reagan administration's funding requests in 1984, the Pentagon doubled the size of the Salvadoran Air Force almost overnight. At the beginning of the year El Salvador possessed nineteen aircraft. By year's end, it had forty-six at its disposal.[5] The Salvadoran Air Force inventory eventually included Huey (UH-1) helicopters, A-37 jets, and the AC-47 "Spooky" gunship. The latter plane, affectionately dubbed "Puff the Magic Dragon," contained powerful guns that could fire thousands of rounds per minute. These planes provided close air support to US combat troops during the Vietnam War and pulverized the Vietnamese countryside. Nevertheless, those destined for El Salvador were not outfitted with the regular weapons out of fear that their indiscriminate use could produce heavy civilian casualties.[6]

Beginning in 1984, the Salvadoran Air Force repeatedly attacked contested areas, included Chalatenango, Morazán, and the Guazapa Volcano. In the words of political scientist Jenny Pearce, between 1984 and 1985 the bombing practices of the Salvadoran military established a "free-fire" zone in Chalatenango. In such areas, military forces are permitted to use indiscriminate fire without receiving prior authorization. Individuals residing in these areas were considered either guerrillas or their supporters and were thus viewed as legitimate targets. One Salvadoran officer offered the following explanation behind this strategy, claiming, "There are no civilians. There are only concentrations of guerrillas, so we keep these areas under heavy fire."[7] According to a Salvadoran military spokesperson, "The people who move in zones of persistence are identified as guerrillas.... Good people—the people who are not with the guerrillas—are not there."[8]

Residents of these areas were subjected to artillery barrages and blistering aerial assaults. These were followed by large sweeps of the suspect villages by Salvadoran troops. The Salvadoran Air Force also reportedly used napalm and white phosphorous munitions against civilians.[9] These military maneuvers were intended to "drain the sea" by forcing the area's inhabitants to flee (or killing them), thus depriving the FMLN of access to food, intelligence, or shelter. Colonel Sigifredo Ochoa, a favorite of US officials, summed up the strategy aptly. "Our first goal is to clean up the province militarily. . . . This means we cannot permit civilian contact with the rebel army. We must separate the people from the guerrillas and then crush the guerrillas. . . . Without a civilian base of support, the guerrillas are nothing but outlaws."[10] As Americas Watch argued, the frequency with which air attacks were followed by ground sweeps left little room for doubt that the Salvadoran military considered noncombatants legitimate targets.[11] Viewing civilians in insurgent strongholds as "legitimate targets for attack," the Salvadoran Armed Forces destroyed numerous communities in an effort to deprive the guerrillas of their support.[12]

These practices increased civilian displacement. After 1985, the number of individuals uprooted by the war spiked dramatically, creating an exodus "unprecedented in the hemisphere."[13] By 1987 approximately 500,000 Salvadorans had been displaced—10 percent of the population.[14] Two years later, that figured had increased to 600,000, and another 1.5 million had fled beyond the nation's borders.[15] Instead of fleeing across the border to Honduras, hundreds of thousands of Salvadorans illegally immigrated to the United States. The Salvadoran population in the United States increased from approximately 100,000 to half a million in 1990.[16] The US government refused to admit Salvadorans as refugees displaced by war despite the fact that many fled for that very reason. Accepting that San Salvador had persecuted its own people—with substantial US support—would have contradicted US government policy toward the country.[17]

Even as the numbers of dislocated civilians increased, Salvadorans attempted to return home and resume their lives. In July 1985, the archdiocese of San Salvador, with the tacit acceptance of the Salvadoran military and FMLN, established a repopulation community in Tenancingo to settle displaced civilians.[18] Years later, refugees in Honduras also began the grueling process of returning to El Salvador. The Salvadoran government initially resisted their efforts. Nonetheless, Duarte and his successors eventually acquiesced not only because of the determination of the displaced but also because their efforts received considerable media attention. The process of their fleeing (*la guinda*), resettling in Honduras, and returning home carried political ramifications for the Salvadoran government. Through their actions, the *campesinos* forced the state to recognize them as "agents, citizens, and members of the national body. By going home they reclaimed fundamental civil rights."[19]

Even though the aerial bombing raids caused civilian casualties and displacement, they, and the increased use of helicopters, also caused considerable damage to the FMLN. As several *comandantes* recounted, helicopters and airpower, not US COIN doctrine or the various strategies and tactics associated with it, caused the FMLN significant consternation. The increased reliance upon and use of air power was an important factor that led the insurgents to decentralize their forces.[20] In an already beleaguered and taxed rebel army, some units were forced to assume another burden of war: responsibility for the people's care and well-being.[21] Over the next several years, the FMLN attempted to counter the helicopters and fighter jets, but it was not until 1989 that it acquired the means—antiaircraft weapons—to challenge its enemy's dominance of the skies. Despite never adopting a successful antihelicopter strategy, the Salvadoran insurgents avoided encirclement and wide-scale annihilation of their forces through luck and intimate knowledge of the terrain.[22]

Removing a Thorn in the President's Side

Throughout Ronald Reagan's first term, his Salvadoran policy faced resistance from the legislative branch. From 1981 to 1984, Congress attempted to shape the administration's Salvadoran policy by attaching conditions to aid. These measures included reining in security force abuses, making a concerted effort to comply with internationally recognized human rights standards, honoring a commitment to holding free elections, and making continuing progress in land reform. Although Congress criticized the president, it failed to halt US aid to El Salvador in spite of continuing abuses and corruption. As Assistant Secretary of State for Human Rights and Humanitarian Affairs Elliot Abrams noted, Congress "didn't cut off aid because it didn't want to risk being blamed if the guerrillas won as a result for 'losing' El Salvador. Instead, they required certification—which is to say, they agreed to fund the war while reserving the right to call us Fascists."[23]

To create a bipartisan consensus on US policy toward El Salvador, President Reagan nominated former secretary of state Henry Kissinger in July 1983 to chair a commission to support the administration's policies. Rather than presenting new ideas, the Kissinger Commission simply validated Reagan's anticommunist policies.[24] The commission's findings, presented in January 1984, provided another foundation upon which US strategy toward El Salvador rested.[25]

The Kissinger report viewed regional instability as caused by external actors who exploited socioeconomic conditions, an argument most Latin American specialists and critics of the Reagan administration hotly disputed. Although the commission placed the burden of responsibility on external actors, it spent little time addressing the internal conditions that triggered the outbreak of the civil war in the first place. The commission's report advocated a thorough application of US COIN by promoting a strategy of political, social, and economic development as the key to defeating insurgency.[26] Nevertheless, the Kissinger Commission's focus on the struggle for political legitimacy conspicuously excluded an important actor—the FMLN. The Reagan administration denied the legitimacy of any presence of the FMLN in the political process. The US government had, and still has, a long history of denying the legitimacy of popular movements that have opposed right-wing US allies, including in El Salvador and Vietnam.

After the commission presented its report, the battle went back to Congress, where considerable opposition to Reagan's policies persisted. Various government officials tried to win support on Capitol Hill by promising military victory in El Salvador. At a congressional hearing discussing SOUTHCOM's role in Central America, General Paul Gorman, its commander in chief, predicted that the Salvadoran Armed Forces could have 80–90 percent of the country under "effective" control within two years if Congress implemented the findings of the National Bipartisan (Kissinger) Commission.[27] National Security Adviser Robert McFarlane was even more optimistic, declaring that the war would be over within a year.[28] Despite the rosy predictions, the conflict outlasted the Reagan administration.

Two years after the Constituent Assembly elections, Salvadorans returned to the polls to elect a president in March 1984. Policy makers in Washington were not overly enthusiastic about either of the front-runners. In spite of the generous aid provided by the United States to Duarte's government since 1982, he was not the Reagan administration's favored candidate. The White House's first two choices failed to capture either their party's or the voter's support. Ultimately, the race came down to Duarte and Roberto D'Aubuisson. Because the latter had been labeled as a "psychopath" and "mentally unstable" by the CIA, it was an easy choice to back Duarte. The United States provided Duarte $10 million to pay for expenses and another $1.4 million directly for his campaign.[29]

After Duarte's election, many moderates in Congress became reluctant to oppose aid despite evidence that the military, not Duarte, was still in control and that the military corruption and repression were continuing.[30] Moreover, with Duarte and his Christian Democrats in office, the Reagan administration could convince Congress—previously reluctant to back an obvious rightist and authoritarian regime—to increase economic and military aid.[31] If Duarte had not won the 1984 presidential election, it would have spelled the end of Reagan's policy in El Salvador.[32] Duarte's election allowed the White House to focus its attention elsewhere in the region. For the next several years, Reagan's Salvadoran policy took a backseat as the administration focused on Nicaragua.

Duarte's election in 1984 accomplished what the Kissinger Commission could not—a solid majority coalition in Congress behind virtually unlimited military aid.[33] Until 1989, Congress approved US aid to El Salvador largely without any reservations. Several months after Duarte's election, Reagan won reelection in a landslide. After winning a second term, the administration focused less on El Salvador and turned its attention toward destabilizing Nicaragua by using a covert army, the Contras. Although the White House might have placed more emphasis on Nicaragua, it did little to diminish the fighting in El Salvador.

The FMLN's Strategic Reappraisal

By the middle of 1984, US military aid had altered the nature of the conflict. As the Salvadoran military expanded and received more weapons, its new firepower greatly increased insurgent casualties. FMLN insurgents also noticed a difference in their adversary's behavior, especially in terms of tactics. Most noteworthy, the Salvadoran military created additional units, in addition to the rapid-reaction battalions, that could carry out the long-range, small-unit tactics cherished by the US advisers.

US Special Forces troops also continued their mission of attempting to professionalize the Salvadoran military and persuading its leaders to adopt tactics derived from US COIN doctrine. In particular, US advisers repeatedly emphasized the need for nighttime patrolling, small-unit action, and long-distance reconnaissance missions. US operatives had identified their lack of use by their allies as tactical deficiencies. For some US advisers, including Colonel John Waghelstein and General Fred Woerner, these measures had been successfully used against their adversaries in Vietnam. Eventually, their patience was rewarded.

The creation of Las Patrullas de Reconocimiento de Alcance Largo (PRAL), mobile forces that operated using "irregular tactics" in the FMLN rearguard, was of particular concern to the Salvadoran rebels.[34] They conducted lengthy reconnaissance and small-unit actions against the guerrillas. These units disrupted many FMLN offensive operations.[35] They also inspired *la pralitis* (fear) among the insurgents, especially those stationed around the Guazapa Volcano. According to one account, no one wanted to move, pick up food, or go on patrol out of fear of being ambushed by a PRAL unit.[36]

PRAL units were trained by the 7th Special Forces detachment, along with CIA advisers, and modeled on previous US COIN experiences. Prior incarnations included the "hunter-killer" teams used in the Philippines to search for and destroy the Filipino insurgents. Acting on specific military intelligence, the primary functions of these aggressive, small-unit formations were to track and locate guerrillas, disrupt their operations, and either capture or kill them.[37] These units were intended to remain in the field for several weeks, apply persistent pressure on the rebel army, and never give it any respite. PRAL was eventually renamed El Grupo de Operaciones Especiales and maintained close command-and-control ties with the CIA.[38]

A study written by a former US adviser agreed with a former insurgent, noting that this kind of unit has "accounted for hundreds of guerrilla casualties and has been instrumental in disrupting guerrilla combat operations, logistical nets, and base camps. The unit has proven that El Salvadoran troops, with the proper training and leadership, can operate effectively in small groups, and they have set a standard for valor for the rest of the ESAF."[39] To combat these units, the FMLN increasingly relied on its local militias and the masses. The former were used to impede the PRAL movements, and the latter were used to alert FMLN combatants if these units penetrated camps.[40] Their countermeasures failed to halt these units' ability to infiltrate and attack their rearguards.

Over the next few years, the repeated bombings, growth of the Salvadoran military, and its ability to operate for longer periods reduced FMLN effectiveness as well as its number of insurgents. Although estimating the exact number of insurgents was notoriously difficult, one estimate offered between 6,000 and 7,000 troops. That number was a sharp decline from the height of FMLN power in 1983.[41]

In contrast, as the rebel forces diminished, the Salvadoran military grew exponentially. US aid and training expanded Salvadoran forces by between 40,000 and 50,000 by the end of 1988. In 1989, government forces totaled 55,000. As one analyst noted, this represented a 300 percent increase in the size of the army.[42] Colonel Waghelstein cited a ratio of 4:1 in favor of the Salvadoran government.[43]

The ERP leading strategist exposed a flaw behind the theory that creating more troops would lead to victory:

> It revolves around the assertion that the army has more battalions, more helicopters, more artillery. . . . It excludes the political and social factors and tries to establish and justify the following thesis: "We have an army that is so big, and the North Americans help us so much that we cannot possibly lose the war." . . . But history provides us with lessons. We must remember that Somoza began his war with 7,000 troops . . . and lost when he had 15,000! . . . The North Americans began their intervention with 3,000 advisers helping an army of 125,000 South Vietnamese. . . . They lost when they had 500,000 troops supporting 1.2 million Vietnamese.
>
> In no case was the war won by the revolutionaries through the achievement of military superiority. These wars were won because

the revolutionaries knew how to carefully use available military resources as part of the ongoing political struggle while bringing all of the people into the war. . . . Our goal is to . . . wear the enemy down.[44]

As Joaquín Villalobos adroitly realized, US taxpayer money built the region's second-largest military force behind that of Nicaragua, and as with its neighbor, victory in El Salvador proved elusive. For William Meara, a former Special Forces officer who advised the Salvadoran military in PSYOPS, the US military's infatuation with building a large army reflected the institution's conventional background. In his opinion, the US Army's intellectual and organizational culture was a major impediment to a decisive victory for the Salvadoran government.[45] In the end, the prodigious size of the Salvadoran military built by US policy could not overcome the Duarte government's inability to end the war or improve the people's well-being through his economic measures or development programs.

Prolonged People's War

From 1984 onward, the FMLN increasingly emphasized the political nature of the conflict. Before then, arguably, the political aspect of the Salvadoran guerrillas' strategy had been subordinate to the military component. For the next several years, the insurgents adopted PPW, closely related to the Vietnamese strategy authored by Vö Nguyen Giáp and used to devastating effect against France and the United States. Increasingly, the FMLN relied on political organizing and establishing (and in some cases reestablishing) greater links with the civilian population. Of all the organizations within the FMLN, this strategy was most associated with the FPL.

As the name implies, the ultimate goal under PPW is to carry out a lengthy and protracted struggle that eventually topples the government. Rather than trying to annihilate the enemy in one decisive battle, PPW relies upon political organizing and eroding the enemy's will to fight by causing enemy casualties and desertions. This strategy is predicated on creating the conditions necessary for a massive uprising that leads to the overthrow of the government. From the US Embassy's viewpoint, this FMLN approach was explicitly based on the expectation that one day US assistance to El Salvador would be terminated. By creating a prolonged political and economic crisis, chaos and instability would create the conditions for Duarte's removal.[46]

Strategies such as PPW enabled suppressed colonial and subaltern peoples with the means to challenge much larger, more economically developed powers, or technologically sophisticated governments, and win. It also provided the FMLN a purpose and the will to succeed. By prolonging the conflict and negating their enemies' strengths, especially their reliance on technology, the Salvadoran insurgents battled a vastly superior army to a stalemate. As in Vietnam, Washington failed to convince most of the Salvadoran people to abandon their support for the FMLN or view US enemies as their own. The fact that a group of revolutionaries derived from and supported by the people (or a significant portion of them) could challenge a US-designed and heavily supplied and funded regime in the US sphere of influence and fight it to a stalemate is truly remarkable.

Increasingly, the Salvadoran insurgents focused their efforts on establishing the conditions necessary to launch one last, large-scale offensive, known as the strategic counteroffensive. Modeled along the lines of the 1981 Final Offensive, this plan required the establishment of a military and political vacuum for the FMLN to exploit. To create the necessary climate, the rebels focused on five essential tasks: attrite enemy forces, organize the masses, break down the enemy ranks, destabilize and sabotage the economy, and increase their forces. These tactics remained significant features of the FMLN strategy for the next several years.[47]

Starting in the summer of 1985, the FMLN decided to rely on an economy of force and preserve its own units. Thus, its leaders dispersed their forces and reduced their size from operating in company formations to platoons. This strategy was more adept at carrying out a conventional guerrilla war. As it unveiled its new strategy, its slogan became *"Convertir El Salvador en un mar de guerrillas y pueblo organizado!* [Convert El Salvador into a sea of guerrillas and organized villages!]"[48] The decision has often been attributed to the increased use of airpower and the growing effectiveness of the Salvadoran military. During the middle of the war, the FMLN disputed such efforts, claiming that its strategic reappraisal was an initiative launched from within, not forced upon it by the Salvadoran military.[49] Even though it broke its forces down into smaller units, it still occasionally massed its troops to launch spectacular attacks. The guerrilla leaders also extolled the virtues of the switch. As they noted in one of their documents, although the enemy would continue to try to destroy as many insurgent forces as possible, the Salvadoran military would still never be able to create a force large enough to destroy them or to sustain continued action against the FMLN.[50]

Economic Sabotage

Insurgent attacks against the Salvadoran economy skyrocketed. Statistics indicated that during the first six months of 1985, economic sabotage increased more than 550 percent over that of the same period of the previous year. Electrical facilities were a favored target. In 1986 insurgents destroyed nearly forty electrical pylons, causing lengthy blackouts in San Salvador and eastern portions of the country.[51] Their objectives included not only capital-intensive sites, such as power plants and dams, but also key agricultural products, in particular coffee and sugar. This strategy forced the Salvadoran military to redirect soldiers to protect the harvests. Otherwise, farmers simply left their fields fallow. As the conflict continued, these attacks exacted a heavy toll on the country's economy.

Economic sabotage caused considerable damage to El Salvador's financial system and hobbled its recovery. Total cumulative damages caused either by FMLN attacks or by other factors between 1979 and 1985 potentially exceeded $1.2 billion.[52] Several years later, a US AID study in 1987 approximated that the costs to repair and replace infrastructure damaged by FMLN attacks was $600 million, and lost production hovered at $1.5 billion.[53] By attacking the nation's infrastructure, the insurgents forced the United States to divert money from weapons to repairs.[54] Not only did these attacks hinder economic recovery but also they undercut President Duarte's popularity.

Insurgent attacks forced Washington to address the regime's most serious liability, the economy. The country's economic tailspin had been dramatic. Leading economic indicators were staggering. By 1985, the unemployment rate was 30 percent, with another 30 percent underemployed. Inflation continued as well; that same year US officials estimated it at 22 percent.[55]

AID helped keep Duarte in power. By 1987 it had contributed more than $1.5 billion in economic assistance. The Economic Support Fund (ESF) program in particular constituted almost half of the country's import bill and provided almost one-third of the government's total operating expenditures. ESF also contributed to development projects, especially restoring war-damaged infrastructure, and to earthquake recovery efforts.[56] Although the funds might have prevented Duarte's collapse, very little, if any, of the money used by AID was devoted to economic programs aimed at improving the basic living conditions of the poor and the landless.[57] Between 1985 and 1989 less than 10 percent contributed to agrarian reform, education, or democratization.[58]

To engineer the Salvadoran economy's revitalization, US policy makers argued for the implementation of classic, neoliberal, economic principles. The ideas touted included financial restraint, promotion of private enterprise, and termination of social subsidies.[59] With no end in sight, Duarte increasingly became more dependent on US aid. As his government's reliance grew, Washington pressured the Salvadoran president to adopt its solutions to halt the economy's further deterioration.

Originally, Duarte promised an economic recovery project that emphasized public-sector jobs and ongoing government subsidies. He hoped to address the nation's unemployment crisis and alleviate the burdens faced by his poorest urban constituents. Duarte's policies did not please the DIA, which complained that his "hesitation to take needed austerity measures, show clear resolve in enforcing public sector labor codes, and to work sincerely with the private sector to reactivate the economy" were halting economic progress.[60] US officials demanded that the Salvadoran president tighten his financial belt and slash social spending.

Under pressure from the United States, Duarte unveiled an economic package that alienated both sides of the political spectrum, including his most supportive constituents. Known as the Economic Stabilization and Reactivation Plan (1986), its measures included reducing spending on subsidies, adopting a policy of monetary restraint, and devaluing the *colón*. Consequently, opposition to the president increased, and San Salvador experienced a series of strikes, including the largest since 1980 led by the National Union of Salvadoran Workers (UNTS). In the end, Duarte's inability to end the war and improve the economy caused considerable political damage to his party.

Organizing Las Masas

Although the FMLN might have scaled back its offensive operations, its work with the masses continued. To further strengthen its links with civilians, the FMLN unveiled a new strategy: *Poder Popular Doble Cara* (Double-Face Popular Power). The insurgents aspired to extend their rearguards in *el campo* to the nation's main population centers. In many ways, Poder Popular mirrored Mao's strategy of moving the struggle from the periphery to the center. Its ultimate intention was to create the conditions necessary in the country's primary population centers for a massive uprising. During the 1970s, the Salvadoran left had established an impressive array of urban networks and activists who brought the Romero regime to its knees. Reactivating the revolutionary struggle in the cities was necessary because years of repression by the Salvadoran security forces and death squads, combined with the failure of the Final Offensive in 1981, had decimated its urban networks. By 1981, the main bulk of the FMLN urban cadre either had been killed, fled to *el campo*, or become dormant.

Under Poder Popular the FMLN created legal and transparent organizations to establish links with civilians, organize them, and elevate their political consciousness. The double-sided feature of this plan envisioned creating shadow networks within these groups that would expand the FMLN's influence and enact its strategy. In particular, two groups targeted by the insurgents included labor unions and student organizations. Crucially, these groups would establish the groundwork, and after the decisive battle began, help lead the progressive forces to victory. The FMLN also attempted to infiltrate its cadre into the PDC.[61] After the creation of new organizations or the infiltration of existing ones, insurgents and their sympathizers carried out open and transparent organizing and developed labor and logistical networks among the people.

The rebel leadership hoped the agitation and radicalization of the popular forces would provoke a confrontation with the Salvadoran government and its security forces. According to CIA analysts, repression could potentially alienate the Salvadoran working and middle classes, two of the president's key constituencies. A violent response by the Salvadoran government could also be used as a propaganda tool for the FMLN to potentially weaken US public and congressional support for continued funding.[62]

An assessment conducted by the CIA stated that the insurgents' decision to resurrect their urban strategy reflected their sagging military fortunes in the field.[63] From this perspective, the FMLN decision was born out of weakness. Yet, political organizing and establishing networks with sympathetic individuals had been a hallmark of FMLN strategy even predating its formation in 1980. Although it could be argued that its military decline had forced certain elements within the insurgent high command to abandon pursuing the decisive battle, Poder Popular was not indicative of the guerrillas' weakness. Rather, as the CIA would belatedly realize years later, this strategy altered the outcome of the conflict.

Expansion of Guerrilla Networks

Throughout the conflict, insurgent rearguards played a prominent role in the FMLN strategy. As the term is often described, a rearguard is part of a military formation that protects the rear and flank of the main force either before the assault or during withdrawal. The FMLN offered a different conception of this strategy. From the beginning of the conflict, the Salvadoran guerrillas established rearguards in areas where they were dominant. Each organization within the FMLN had its own rearguard. They served a variety of purposes, but according to a US government appraisal, their primary functions included staging and supporting military operations.[64] Nevertheless, they often played other roles as well, including political efforts to spread FMLN influence and undermine the government's legitimacy. As the conflict progressed, the guerrillas increasingly expanded their network of rearguards and tried to prevent their enemy from extending its reach into these zones.

The FMLN established three types of rearguards, each of which served a different purpose. Strategic rearguards, often located in northern El Salvador, offered support and protection for the FMLN senior leadership and major concentrations of its forces. They also served as its political base, primary source of recruits, and material support. Operational rearguards, including the one at the Guazapa Volcano, served as forward operating bases—small military bases used to support tactical operations—and linked the other two rearguards. The third and final type of rearguard, tactical, offered support during offensive operations and provided rest for the troops, medical attention, food, and other basic necessities.[65]

Rearguards also served an important role in the informational and psychological struggle between the two belligerents. Radio Venceremos, a rebel-run radio station, broadcast from one of the ERP's strategic rearguards. This radio station served as a propaganda outlet for the FMLN for domestic and international audiences. It also provided stirring accounts of the insurgents' recent exploits and in some cases comedic relief. For many Salvadorans it was their key source of information. In spite of considerable obstacles and numerous attempts to knock the station off the airwaves, Radio Venceremos continued operating almost uninterrupted. Destroying the radio station was an obsession of Lieutenant Colonel Domingo Monterossa, who lost his life trying to seize one the radio's transistors.

Beginning in 1985, the FMLN initiated a strategy of repopulating its rearguards with displaced persons. In particular, they targeted the Salvadoran refugee camps in neighboring Honduras. These exiles often had subtle or explicit connections with the rebels. Molly Todd's research has demonstrated that the relationship between these actors varied between individual refugees and their camps. In Todd's words, "it is safe to say" that "the majority of the refugees (with the exception of those at Buenos Aires) identified with the basic principles of the FMLN's struggle and therefore were at least partially sympathetic if not active contributors."[66] According to one US estimate, between 1988 and 1991 the insurgents repopulated approximately 16,000 refugees into settlement areas near their bases.[67] These resettlement communities played a key role in FMLN strategy by expanding its rearguards and influence throughout the Salvadoran countryside. The FMLN's repopulation of rearguards with displaced persons forced the Salvadoran military to modify its strategy. In particular, the Salvadoran military was forbidden to enter these repopulation communities and could not conduct military operations within 1 mile of these communities, a concession that most likely caused unending frustration to FMLN enemies, including US tacticians.[68]

Attrition

Before the insurgents could launch the strategic counteroffensive, they needed to lay the groundwork militarily as well. Although political organizing was extremely important for their overall goal, the high command continued to envision that they would achieve power through a coordinated military offensive. Unlike the previous stage of the conflict, when the FMLN leaders concentrated on inflicting a decisive military defeat upon the Duarte regime, the means changed. Arguably, their most pressing goal was weakening the morale of the Salvadoran Army. To accomplish such a task, the insurgents relied on the policies of *el desgaste*, infiltration of the Salvadoran military, and incorporating classic aspects of guerrilla war doctrine. These tactics included perpetrating sneak ambushes, shadowing enemy units, launching pinprick attacks, and occasionally conducting massive assaults on a fixed position.

To demoralize Salvadoran troops, the FMLN focused on expanding the war into areas where it had previously been inactive. Doing so would disperse the enemy's units and not allow it to concentrate its forces. The guerrillas attempted to extend the conflict to the western departments, far from their strongholds. Unlike in the 1930s, when western El Salvador was a hotbed of agitation and unrest, this region of El Salvador remained quiescent for most of the conflict. The FMLN attacked Sonsonate, where it destroyed machinery at a local coffee processing plant, damaged buildings, and sacked a bank. All of this occurred within a fifteen-minute drive from a major army base.[69]

Antipersonnel land mines played an important role in the FMLN strategy. Even though the insurgents had relied on these weapons since 1980, their use skyrocketed beginning in 1985.[70] Mines performed a variety of functions, including injuring or killing enemy soldiers and weakening their morale. In particular, land mines were used to slow down the large military sweeps that followed aerial bombardment. By thinning the Salvadoran military's ranks, this would limit its ability to carry out operations and possibly prevent it from conducting more aggressive maneuvers, especially in the FMLN rearguard. Most of the mines used by the FMLN were homemade varieties employed to attack columns of troops or military vehicles such as jeeps.

These weapons increasingly caused the majority of the Salvadoran Army's casualties. In 1985 mines caused approximately one-third of all combat-related deaths.[71] The following year, they accounted for nearly two-thirds of all military fatalities. Medical care required for individuals injured by mines also placed further strain on the fragile Salvadoran economy, draining the government's dwindling resources.[72] After the end of the war, the high numbers of veteran amputees compelled the Salvadoran government to provide disability pensions and transitional job training.[73]

Civilians also paid a heavy price. The indiscriminate use of mines in the Salvadoran *campo* caused a sharp rise in amputees, especially among children and farmers. As members of the FMLN admitted to the UN Truth Commission, they often laid mines with little to no supervision. According to various accounts, in 1985, between 31 and 46 people were killed by the FMLN mines.[74] The following year, at least another 46 people were killed by mines as well as an additional 162 wounded.[75] Establishing a comprehensive estimate of the number of civilian casualties caused by land mines has proven elusive. Washington and San Salvador exploited the FMLN use of mines by placing posters emblazoned with people maimed by these weapons in prominent places, including at El Salvador's international airport.[76] Yet, although the use of land mines should be condemned, the overwhelming majority of war crimes were committed by the Salvadoran state and its security forces, not the Salvadoran rebels.

High-Profile Attacks

Despite the turn toward PPW, the FMLN still maintained its capability to launch several high-profile attacks, including in El Salvador's main cities. Rebels hoped to precipitate a military and political crisis in El

Salvador's cities by sowing chaos and disorder. The insurgents' continued ability to launch attacks was also meant to demonstrate the government's inability to prevent them. Assassinations of government officials
and former military officers associated with repression delivered a powerful message to the nation's elite: the FMLN could still reach into the
heart of San Salvador. For example, the rebels assassinated military officers such as José Alberto "Chele" Medrano, founder of ORDEN, as
well as government officials, to commemorate Archbishop Romero's
murder. Insurgent attacks in the nation's capital increased by nearly 50
percent, from thirty-six in 1985 to fifty-four in 1986, and acts of sabotage
also rose 35 percent, from fifty-four to seventy-three.[77] These forays also
included artillery barrages against government targets with homemade
munitions. Wildly inaccurate, these attacks caused civilian casualties,
increasing anger at the FMLN.[78] These activities laid the groundwork
for the strategic counteroffensive. Nevertheless, although these attacks
might have caused disorder within the nation's main cities, they never
posed a major threat to the existence or functioning of the government.

Concentrated attacks against various government installations also
continued to be a mainstay of the FMLN military repertoire. Some of
the more infamous examples included the attack on the Cerron Grande
Dam, the 3rd Brigade Headquarters at San Miguel, and El Paraíso, the
same base the FMLN overran in 1983. The following year the FMLN
struck again at San Miguel in a well-coordinated assault. Although the
insurgents left without taking control of the installation, the Salvadoran
military turned the assault into a public relations disaster by lying about
the numbers injured and killed and then being caught by the media.
After the attack, when asked by a US soldier about the incident, a US
adviser confidently claimed that it was "completely insignificant militarily" and believed that it did not represent a shift in the "military
balance." Instead, the FMLN had merely "concentrated its forces" and
staged a "spectacle" that "didn't mean anything."[79]

The continuation of these attacks served as a troubling reminder that
the FMLN could continually strike at a time of its choosing and create unease within important sectors of the government. From a conventional view, these spectacular attacks might not have been a rousing

military success. Perceptions, however, are just as critical as battlefield success in an insurgency. Thus, even if a particular event does not alter the strategic balance in the war, its wider impact can be felt by affecting civilian perceptions. Paradoxically, counterinsurgent forces can defeat insurgent forces militarily but lose the political battle at the same time. The Lyndon Baines Johnson administration experienced this firsthand in the aftermath of the 1968 Tet Offensive. The Salvadoran government and military also learned this lesson the hard way in 1989.

Diminishing Popular Support

In order to compensate for their diminished ranks, the insurgents began relying on forced recruitment. Several former insurgents believed this policy greatly harmed their reputation in the countryside.[80] When the Salvadoran guerrillas entered a village, they offered the residents a stark choice: either serve with the FMLN or fight for the enemy.[81] In many instances, military-age males selected an option not included — they fled. For suffering civilians, forced recruitment represented another taxing burden. Along with military sweeps and bombing attacks, this practice created a substantial amount of displacement in the *campo.* As Americas Watch noted about the practice, "It is clear that the Salvadorans regarded forced recruitment as sufficiently onerous that they fled their homes, preferring misery to coerced military service with the guerrillas."[82]

Even FMLN supporters recognized that its reliance on urban terrorism, assassinations, and forced recruitment had cost popular support. Father Ignacio Ellacuría criticized the insurgents for their forced recruitment and attacks against civilians and called for an end to economic sabotage, including "respect for agricultural crops and the economic livelihood of the civilian populace." To regain lost momentum, in his opinion, the FMLN needed to humanize its conduct (as well as the government) and negotiate in good faith. According to US ambassador Thomas Pickering, several years before his death, Ellacuría realized that the FMLN would never win the war even though it had switched tactics.[83] Ambassador Edwin Corr agreed with Pickering's assessment, noting that the Jesuit priest believed the FMLN was losing and called for dialogue.[84] As the conflict progressed, Ellacuría used his contacts and influence with the FMLN senior leaders to try to persuade them to negotiate an end to the struggle and moderate their demands.

After the Salvadoran government regained the initiative in 1984, the FMLN had largely been forced onto the defensive. For the next several years, the insurgents adapted their strategy to meet the existing situation on the political and military fronts. Slowly but surely, the guerrillas pursued their newly revised strategy. US and Salvadoran analysts mistakenly viewed the new FMLN tactics as a sign of weakness, whereas in reality they were methodically expanding the scope of the war. In 1987, the FMLN high command sensed an opening. The cumulative effects of the earthquake that leveled parts of San Salvador, the incompetence of the Duarte regime, and economic malaise had produced discontent. Sensing the country was on the verge of insurrection, the FMLN unveiled a new strategy, Plan Fuego (Plan Fire).[85] Plan Fuego attempted to accelerate the revolutionary process by precipitating a military and political crisis using many of the strategies employed throughout the conflict. More importantly, it initiated the process that led to the strategic counteroffensive, which rocked San Salvador in 1989.

Destroying Local Power

By the end of 1982, the FMLN considered local power a central part of the US COIN strategy. Mayors increasingly assumed a crucial role in anchoring the various COIN initiatives used in rural El Salvador. Originally, the insurgents intended to combat *el poder local* (local power) through political means.[86] Nevertheless, their original strategy failed; in response, they resorted to violence to destroy the representatives of the central government in the countryside.

Beginning in 1985, the FMLN, especially the ERP, increasingly targeted mayors throughout the country. These officials often received death threats, endured harassment, or in some cases were either kidnapped or murdered. The guerrilla leadership viewed mayors as legitimate targets by describing them as the "repressive apparatus of local control designed to prevent the masses from organizing themselves."[87] These officials represented the central government's presence in the countryside and were often responsible for implementing San Salvador's policies. Thus, mayors were viewed as collaborators who organized counterinsurgency efforts, created paramilitary groups, and administered civic action programs.

By assassinating mayors, the FMLN strove to dismantle local governance and sever the link between the nation's capital and the rest of the country. Destroying the central government's political and military rural apparatus would prevent the Duarte government from enacting its various policies aimed at combating the FMLN. Furthermore, it served to reduce the reach and visibility of the government. The FMLN strategy forced the US Embassy to admit the tactic "successfully hindered, if not altogether eliminated in some towns, local government."[88] Yet, the policy also cost the FMLN some degree of popular support because the targets had been trying to implement much-needed development programs.

The FMLN efforts caused considerable damage to civic action efforts in the *campo*. The often abrupt departure of mayors as well as dissolution and disruption of the council meetings, in the words of a CIA analysis, "interrupted the flow of millions of dollars in economic assistance and government service. While the military can eventually assume the functions of the civil authorities in most cases, the ability of the government to deliver much-needed services, such as potable water, electric power, schools, medical facilities, and transportation has been seriously eroded in many areas."[89]

Killing civilians also served as a means of intimidation. The insurgents did not have to assassinate the mayors to make a point. Harassment or death threats could achieve the desired results. Executing mayors demonstrated a stark contrast between the central government's inability to protect its allies and the FMLN's ability to act with impunity. Instead of relying upon indiscriminate violence, the FMLN chose specific individuals for assassination. The Salvadoran rebels were not simply draining the swamp.

Unfortunately for the FMLN, not all of the mayors marked for execution were despised by their constituents or corrupt. Nor was attacking local mayors viewed as a legitimate or viable strategy by all FMLN *comandantes*. Father Ellacuría and some *comandantes* realized that, although this policy successfully eliminated local representatives, it also damaged FMLN standing. According to a former FPL insurgent, the benefits of killing mayors were outweighed by the tangible benefits that sometimes resulted from working with them, such as information about the Salvadoran military and its movements.[90] Not all mayors suffered the reputation of being corrupt party hacks, "enemies of the people," or beyond reproach.

After the war, the UN Truth Commission investigated the FMLN campaign of assassination against the mayors. The commission focused specifically on the ERP activities, including eleven executions carried out by this faction. Indeed, one of the more striking aspects of the Truth Commission report is an almost complete absence of discussion of war crimes committed by the other factions of the FMLN. Nevertheless, as the report observed, this practice violated international humanitarian and human rights law.[91] Even more important, killing mayors cost the insurgents broader popular support.

Dialogue

Over the following years, the two antagonists met six times, including at La Palma in 1984; Ayagualo in November 1985; Sesori in October 1987; and Mexico City and San José, Costa Rica, in September and October 1989. Even though the belligerents held periodic talks, they produced very little in terms of substance.[92] For both sides, dialogue played a subordinate role to pursuing victory on the battlefield. The much-needed breakthrough did not occur for several more years, well after both sides had given up on achieving a decisive military victory.

In October 1984, President Duarte made a bold step: he decided to hold peace talks with the FMLN. His gambit represented the first time that the Salvadoran government had seriously proposed to engage in dialogue with the rebels. Archbishop Romero's successor, Arturo Rivera y Damas, offered to arrange a meeting between the Salvadoran government and the guerrillas. Both sides agreed to meet on October 16, 1984, at the village of La Palma.

The negotiations at La Palma were enormously popular in a country that had endured six years of war and economic privation.[93] After the talks concluded, both sides expressed optimism. Duarte considered the meeting to have "been the most transcendental hours in Salvadoran history."[94] The Reagan administration also reacted positively, claiming that the meeting offered a "vindication" of the president's strategy. According to the White House's logic, the administration's policy made the talks possible because US strategy had reduced violence in El Salvador, curbed human rights abuses, and "restored" democracy with Duarte's election.[95] Yet, hardliners remained on both sides who viewed dialogue with utter contempt. Included in this category was D'Aubuisson, Duarte's *bête noire*, who characterized the meeting as "a monologue between old friends who support the same cause: socialism. It was not real; they did nothing concrete."[96] Even though the dialogue at La Palma resulted in a lack of tangible achievements, both sides agreed to meet one month later.

Following on the heels of La Palma, the Salvadoran Army launched a major offensive against the FMLN. During this operation, Lieutenant Colonel Monterossa, the ideal prototype of US military strategists—even though he was involved in the massacre at El Mozote—was killed by a bomb planted in a radio transistor. These operations had been planned in advance. Senior US officials, including Fred Iklé, and the head of SOUTHCOM, Paul Gorman, believed the FMLN was on the verge of defeat. One week before La Palma, the undersecretary of defense announced that the Salvadoran military had broken the stalemate and could successfully neutralize the insurgents within two years. A senior Pentagon official interviewed by the *New York Times* also sounded an optimistic note, declaring that the "Salvadoran army has turned the corner."[97]

In November 1984, representatives from the FMLN and Salvadoran government met at Ayagualo. Unlike that of the first meeting, this round of dialogue produced nothing but frustration. At La Palma, Duarte had promised to discuss measures to "humanize the armed conflict," but under pressure from the Salvadoran military and Reagan administration, the Salvadoran president dropped the issue. Duarte demanded that the FMLN lay down its weapons, accept a general amnesty, and participate in elections. The guerrillas rejected his overtures by proposing a power-sharing arrangement—a gradual de-escalation of fighting followed by a cease-fire, then the formation of a new government, a new constitution, and reorganization of the armed forces before elections were held.[98] After the talks failed, the Salvadoran protagonists resumed the war. Peace would not come for several years.

The US Embassy under Ambassador Corr firmly supported Duarte's various talks with the rebels, a move supported by the Reagan administration. Before Corr's arrival in El Salvador, President Reagan had instructed his ambassador to win the war. The White House, however, supported a negotiated settlement as long as it was "acceptable."[99] Although the US ambassador may have supported dialogue, he was not impressed with the FMLN proposals. A November 1985 telegram characterized one insurgent peace proposal as "old wine placed in new bottles." The ambassador also believed the FMLN had hardened its position since the previous year. In addition, he perceived a rupture between the FDR, the diplomatic arm and international representative of the Salvadoran insurgents, and the FMLN. If true, he argued, it might be worth trying to exploit. As the telegram rhetorically asked, "Is the FDR attempting to distance itself from the baggage of preconditions and set the stage for its own talks with the GOES?"[100]

The various peace deliberations held before 1989 failed to produce any positive results in part because the belligerents believed that military victory was within their reach. Negotiations were subordinate to a military victory. In Hugh Byrnes's opinion, these periodic meetings were public-relations exercises because neither side wished to be portrayed as intransigent. They also failed because neither side reached a consensus on several issues. Their respective positions were far apart. Duarte demanded that the FMLN lay down its arms and participate in elections, whereas the FMLN claimed his government was illegitimate because it had conducted elections in the midst of a war and repression, and the insurgents must be included in a coalition government to guarantee a lasting peace.[101] Ultimately, several years elapsed before both sides realized that it would require a negotiated settlement to end the conflict.

Human Rights

Prior to Duarte's election as president in 1984, the Reagan administration routinely maintained that its ally had made dramatic strides in improving its human rights record. The White House's supporters offered several different justifications to support their claims, including a drop in death-squad violence, Constituent Assembly and presidential elections, and ongoing "progress" in criminal cases in which violence had been committed against US citizens. According to Ambassador Corr, Reagan instructed him to continue improving human rights in El Salvador.[102] Although Reagan publicly endorsed these endeavors, the White House also habitually denied or ignored the abuses committed by the Salvadoran security forces and military, attributing them either to unknown assailants or to the FMLN. Human rights organizations, church groups, and the United Nations have demonstrated that Reagan was not only mistaken but also blatantly and knowingly distorted the truth.

Supporters of US policy believed that the Salvadoran government turned the corner in 1984. Central to these alleged improvements was the pressure from the US government to reform or face a cutoff of aid and US military assistance. Periodically, US administrations had to threaten their allies by linking continuing funding to reform. Former MILGP commander Waghelstein tried to impart this connection to one of his Salvadoran counterparts. When his ally argued that El Salvador's "fight was the United States' fight," Waghelstein reminded him that "unlike Vietnam, where we'd committed 450,000 troops, it would not take me long to put the 55 trainers on an airplane." According to Waghelstein, his Salvadoran colleague understood his point.[103]

Whereas death-squad murders and large-scale massacres committed by the Salvadoran Army and security forces characterized the first several years of the conflict, these practices became less pronounced. By 1984 the number of victims killed by these entities dropped considerably. In 1982, 5,962 people were alleged to have been killed.[104] In 1985, the number of people killed by government forces dropped to 1,655. These trends continued until 1991, when the US Embassy discontinued tracking murders. Political killing, however, never stopped. If anything it became more selective. Death squads continued to operate, threatening labor activists and journalists, until the termination of the conflict. The common refrain offered by Washington, and repeated today by supporters of the US intervention, was that US aid and threats to cut off aid were responsible for the vast improvement in the human rights record and the drop in political murders.

The turning point occurred after Vice President George H. W. Bush's visit to El Salvador in February 1984. While toasting the Salvadoran president, the vice president reminded his listeners about the central tenets underlying US COIN strategy and criticized certain sectors within El Salvador.

> A guerrilla war is a long, arduous effort fought on many fronts: military, economic, social, and political. But the crucial battle is not for territory; it is for men's minds. The guerrillas never lose sight of that objective. They know the government is responsible for protecting the people. So their goal is to cripple the government, distort its priorities, and sow doubt about its legitimacy. For a government to survive a guerrilla challenge, it must continue to protect it even as it fights to defend itself from those who play by other rules—or no rules at all. As it does, it must continue to respect the rule of law and the rights of the individual. And it must honor basic human decencies. If it does not, it will lose that crucial battle for the support and approval of the people.[105]

In theory, the vice president's speech demonstrated the Reagan administration's newfound commitment to human rights to the Salvadoran rightists. Bush's remarks came after Ambassador Pickering voiced similar remarks to the Salvadoran Chamber of Commerce.

Pickering's predecessor, Deane Hinton, had made similar remarks before the chamber two years earlier. Unlike his successor and the vice president, Hinton's speech was interpreted hostilely by the Reagan administration, which ruffled the feathers of Reagan's more intransigent administration officials, including National Security Adviser William Clark. It cost Ambassador Hinton his position. Fortunately for Pickering, the hardliners within the president's cabinet had been sidelined temporarily, although they continued to shape the administration's Central American policy for the remainder of Reagan's tenure.

The intent was to threaten the withdrawal of US aid if the Salvadorans failed to reform. Nevertheless, doubts exist about whether the Salvadoran military and government ever took Washington's threats seriously. As political scientist William Deane Stanley observed, human rights reform only happened when serious money was involved, in a context of growing military danger, and then only to the degree absolutely required.[106] Salvadorans recognized, more so than most Americans, that the position of the Republican president and his Democratic opponents was identical on the important issues concerning El Salvador: both were adamant, for domestic political and geostrategic reasons, that El Salvador not fall to the FMLN. How, then, could the Salvadoran Armed Forces and far right be pressured to reform via threats if Washington had affirmed its determination to draw the line in that country?[107]

Critics, including independent human rights agencies, vehemently denied Reagan's assertions. The Lawyers Committee for Human Rights believed that US training played a minor role in the declining human rights abuses. Rather, the Salvadoran military and security forces reached the conclusion that the previous harsh measures used at the beginning of the war were no longer required.[108] Even though these activities declined, they did not stop. Rather, they occurred in smaller numbers, and no further massacres matched the size and severity of El Mozote. The failure of the Final Offensive in 1981 and continuing repression had either decimated the FMLN urban networks or had forced them to flee for the mountains and jungles. Abuses continued, but not on such a large scale. Nevertheless, the Salvadoran high command reverted to type after the insurgents brought the war to the nation's capital in 1989.

Nationwide Civic Action

Ever since General Woerner had completed his survey of the Salvadoran military in 1981, US tacticians had envisioned creating a national plan to conduct a nationwide, aggressive civic action and military operation that would gain the civilians' allegiance and turn the tide against the FMLN. Implementing such a program required close civil-military cooperation. Several years later, the Salvadoran government came the closest it ever did to launching a truly nationwide civic action effort to promote economic development and strengthen the central government's relationship with its citizens.

In 1986, the Salvadoran counterinsurgents unveiled a new COIN initiative modeled on the NCP. Unlike the previous incarnation, Unidos Para Reconstruir (UPR) expanded its area of operations to all of El Salvador's departments. UPR contained many of the same strategies used in the NCP, including a "clear, hold, and build" phase of operations. To remove insurgents, the Salvadoran military bombed these areas first, then initiated large-scale sweeps to force them out of the contested regions. After the areas were secure, or the guerrillas had fled, the civic action programs began. These programs were considered necessary to kick-start rural development and bind the civilians closer to the central government. Unfortunately, much like its predecessor, similar issues confounded the UPR.

Friction between military and civilian agencies continued. In spite of the US Embassy and MILGP's efforts, getting these two actors to fully commit and embrace the various operations proposed by the Salvadoran and US counterinsurgents proved a daunting task. As the CIA recognized, a "less-than-total commitment on the part of some civilian and military authorities" plagued civic action efforts in El Salvador.[109] Distrust between the two continued to be another reoccurring theme. For example, unlike those of the NCP, the UPR reconstruction efforts were handled by the military, not CONARA. The latter organization was widely recognized for its corruption and pilfering of funds earmarked for development. Even though civic action programs are supposed to include interaction between civilians and the military, it continued to be nonexistent under the NCP successor. Duarte's party was especially resentful of the military's role because party members viewed it as a thinly veiled attempt to eclipse civilian control, especially over the rural areas, where security was tenuous.[110] Declining budget allocation for civic action services represented an indicator of the government's lack of support for the program. Over a period of five years, funds for public works programs and services declined by about one-third.[111]

Lack of resources hindered the implementation of the UPR. Once again, a government struggling through a serious economic crisis was tasked—with generous US aid—to implement a resource-intensive and expensive COIN program. Perhaps even more importantly, Duarte's government lacked the proper bureaucracy to execute such a blueprint. The Salvadoran government's bureaucracies' inability and unwillingness to successfully implement the NCP should have given COIN tacticians cause for concern. Expecting that a government whose scant resources had been taxed by an operation that focused exclusively on two departments could successfully execute it nationwide represented a dubious proposition. Extending civic action efforts nationwide stretched its already meager resources thin. In the words of a critic of the Salvadoran military, by expanding the effort throughout the entire nation, "each of the regional commanders would get a piece of the pie. The problem was that by spreading its development effort around to keep the officer corps happy, the government insured that nowhere would its effort be decisive."[112] In October 1986, San Salvador was rocked by an earthquake that caused considerable damage. The already scant funds destined for the UPR were redirected toward the nation's capital to assist in relief and rebuilding.

The FMLN correctly understood the central premises behind the UPR.[113] The insurgent leadership viewed the program as a clear indication that the FMLN held the advantage in organizing the masses in its rearguard and that the military had failed to prevent the regrouping of its forces.[114] An insurgent publication issued during the war noted that there were three parts to the UPR: retake insurgent zones, contest insurgent expansion with *las masas*, and protect the government rearguard. Put another way, it was an attempt by the Salvadoran government to rebuild local government in the insurgents' rearguard.[115] The FMLN devised its own slogan for UPR: "'*quitarle el agua al pez*,' *ha pasado por ensuciar el agua y, en definitiva, acabar con el agua* [removing the water from the fish starts with contaminating the water and then completely draining the water]."[116] Other FMLN documents characterized the UPR as propaganda, psychological warfare, or a game of appearances that did not contain strategic concessions to the masses.[117]

Continuing on with this theme, the FMLN also adroitly realized another glaring issue with the UPR and most of US COIN doctrine. Essentially, this program was trying to salvage the economic system in El Salvador, not fundamentally reconfigure it. This worked in the FMLN's favor because in its view the people wanted reform, not a continuation of the same system.[118] Enacting far-reaching economic reforms through COIN has always presented a problematic and vexing conundrum for its practitioners. Historically, CIs—especially US allies in the third world—have fought to protect their interests, not reform them. The elite in El Salvador had no real interest in carrying out economic reforms, and the US government did not have the appetite for or the interest in pressuring them to make the necessary changes. If governments such as Duarte's had carried out the reforms, they would have validated the insurgents' grievances, providing them a form of legitimacy, something US policy makers attempted to avoid at all costs. In Michael McClintock's words, "Similarly, how could national elites . . . accept a real democratic process when they were convinced that it would bring precisely the changes demanded by the insurgents?"[119]

Grassroots Initiatives

After the UPR stalled out, US officials and Duarte reassessed their options. They decided not to completely abandon civic action but to reconfigure and improve its overall implementation. The result was a new initiative known as Municipios en Acción (Municipalities in Action, or MEA), an effort that began in earnest in 1988. Previous incarnations of civic action in El Salvador had been coordinated and carried out principally by the Salvadoran military, with MILGP and USAID backing but with limited and inadequate participation from the civilian side of the Salvadoran government.[120] Unlike with its predecessors, civilian involvement became more pronounced under MEA. Consequently, civilians worked with the US Embassy, Salvadoran government and military, and MILGP to promote development. After several failures, the CIs had finally established interagency coordination. A sympathetic appraisal of the program characterized the interaction as harmonious, noting, "The military provided the helicopters and trucks. USAID provided the edibles and healthcare. Humanitarian organizations contributed donated materials from the international community."[121] Although civilians were supposed to control the allocation of resources, critical US personnel noted that whereas this was "great in theory—wait until you get out in the Salvadoran ambience."[122]

Under MEA, Salvadoran mayors received US funding to carry out development projects. The plan aimed to eradicate corruption and ensure that its intended beneficiaries received the bulk of the funding. To avoid the notorious black hole, CONARA was mostly cut out of the loop. It continued, however, to disperse checks to local mayors.[123] Nevertheless, its role became increasingly marginalized as the conflict continued.

This new incarnation of civic action envisioned allowing Salvadoran *campesinos* to decide how to use the funds provided by US AID. Officials from this organization still felt the need to intervene in the decision-making process to ensure that their audience made the correct decisions. In the beginning, administrators made a deliberate effort to "guide" each village to request "five components": a school, a government building, electricity, telephones, and improved roads. These elements were viewed by the program's practitioners as necessary requirements to build and sustain local governance.[124]

MEA held *cabildos abiertos* (open town hall meetings) where civilians participated in discussing how development funds would be spent. Local mayors presided over these meetings and, after a consensus was reached on a particular project, contracted the required services.[125] A Salvadoran government brochure depicted these meetings as examples of "democracy in action" that provided a way to exercise "freedom within a participative context."[126] The program was intended to emphasize and generate "grassroots involvement."[127]

In contrast with other civic action initiatives, MEA has been considered a success. Unlike its predecessors, MEA continued for the remainder of the Salvadoran Civil War. A key indicator used by advocates to demonstrate the program's effectiveness was the number of municipalities that participated. By the time the ink dried on the peace accords in 1992, all but 19 of El Salvador's 262 municipalities had participated.[128] According to one source, there was minimal fraud involved. Even more importantly, MEA increased "government support and presence in the countryside."[129] Although local involvement was viewed as key to the program, Byrnes has accurately noted, it "did not necessarily equate to a winning of hearts and minds and was compatible even with allegiance to the insurgents."[130]

Regional Peace Efforts

As the US government continued to seek a military or political victory in El Salvador, regional actors moved toward an end to the region's conflicts, not their prolongation. Fearing that the existing wars could potentially convulse the isthmus in a larger clash, leaders from Central and South America had previously searched for a diplomatic solution. Their efforts had produced the Contadora Accords, derailed by the White House because of its lack of interest in peaceful coexistence with the Sandinistas.[131] In spite of the Reagan administration's best efforts to undermine the peace process permanently, it resumed in July 1985.

The Costa Rican president, Oscar Arias, effectively launched the second peace process in 1987. Known as the Arias Peace Plan, it promoted the democratization of the region through the electoral process. Another element envisioned by Arias was the cessation of external support for the various wars that plagued the region. In February 1987, Arias presented his proposal to other Central American leaders during a summit in San José, Costa Rica. These negotiations outlined a series of steps that could lead to regional cease-fires and demobilization.[132] Journalist Stephen Kinzer, who covered the Contra war extensively, noted that the "formula seemed utopian in its simplicity." Each Central American government would negotiate a cease-fire, declare a general amnesty, and hold free elections. Nonregional powers would be asked to terminate their support for the guerrillas.[133] In August, using a strategy he learned from reading Franklin Delano Roosevelt's biography, Arias arranged for the Central American leaders to meet without their aides present. In order to hammer out a consensus, everyone was locked into the room until an agreement had been reached.[134]

As with the previous Contadora Accords, the Reagan administration tried to destroy the Esquipulas peace process. To undermine Arias, the Reagan administration funneled $433,000 to his political opponents through the National Endowment for Democracy and the Republican Institute for International Affairs.[135] In September, barely a month after the Esquipulas Accords were signed, the Reagan administration announced that it was seeking $270 million in aid for the Contras, the CIA-trained paramilitary army trying to destabilize the Sandinista government.[136]

Certain members of the Reagan administration, especially Elliot Abrams, believed the White House would convince Congress to continue funding the president's paramilitary allies. As Abrams confidently declared, if nothing else, "the president is absolutely determined not to leave the Soviet Union dominant in Central America; we will never allow that."[137] Unlike in the previous regional peace efforts, US attempts to derail the agreements were resisted by congressional representatives opposed to a continuation of Reagan's proxy war in Nicaragua. The White House also met its match in Arias, who refused to be cowed by the administration's threats and who continued to argue for dialogue and the continuation of the peace process.

In El Salvador, support for the Esquipulas talks was muted. Duarte was concerned that the Central American democracies could be "picked off one by one in bilateral negotiations with the Sandinistas."[138] The FMLN realized that peace would mean giving up on revolution, and the Salvadoran military disliked the idea of negotiating with an actor they claimed to have defeated.[139] In spite of his distrust, Duarte eventually signed the accords. Three factors motivated the president. First, he sincerely wanted to end the conflict, even if it had put him at odds with his main ally, the United States. The agreement also unequivocally recognized the legitimacy of sovereign nations, reinforced elections, and granted no formal status to insurgent organizations. Finally, his Nicaraguan counterpart, Daniel Ortega, informed Duarte that he would comply with the terms of the agreement.[140]

Although the Esquipulas Accords made extensive efforts to end the Contra war in Nicaragua, they also placed the quest for peace in El Salvador on the regional agenda.[141] Their stipulations also allowed the FDR to return from exile and operate as a political party. Eventually, the FDR participated as a coalition in the 1989 presidential elections.[142] Especially crucial was the stipulation calling on outside powers to cease support for their respective clients. Using these agreements as a basis, the principle actors appealed in the following years to the United Nations for assistance in negotiating an end to the conflict. The international context also provided the necessary environment to establish peace.

Encouraging Signs?

Even though the White House, US military, and State Department collectively expressed optimism about the conflict, persistent doubts about the war continued. Critics within Congress, especially Democrats, steadfastly challenged the administration's interpretation of the war effort. In November 1987, the US Senate Arms Control and Foreign Policy Caucus produced a highly critical study of the US war effort, *Bankrolling Failure: United States Policy in El Salvador and the Urgent Need to Reform.*

The study's conclusion was blunt and damning. According to *Bankrolling Failure*, US policy was perpetuating, not terminating, the conflict. Rather than leading to a military victory, US initiatives were producing a stalemate. As the report caustically noted, the US government spent more than $3 billion dollars "bankrolling a failed policy."[143] Moreover, the committee's findings also faulted the US government for ignoring the very conditions that had provoked the outbreak of the civil war in the first place, especially a lack of arable land and continuing inequality and poverty.

Four US Army colonels also offered another critique of the war effort, the *Colonels' Report.* It offered a convincing argument that attempts to reform the Salvadoran military had produced mixed results. Despite hundreds of millions in aid, the Salvadoran high command still continued to fight the war according to its own prescriptions. Former US advisers admitted that it was very difficult to change the upper officers' opinions of how to wage the war. One former US operative characterized the senior officers as "real Neanderthals."[144] They noted, however, that training at the lower levels, especially among the noncommissioned officers, was much more effective.[145]

Some of the *Colonels' Report*'s criticism bordered on the comical. For instance, the report castigated the use of PSYOPS. From the authors' viewpoint, the use of PSYOPS in El Salvador had been a dismal failure. To illustrate its ineffectiveness, the study noted that in 1984 the army assigned an adviser who lacked fluency in Spanish to conduct PSYOPS — a critical deficiency, especially because the soldier could not effectively engage in conversation with his target audience.

The authors also found other key aspects of the US strategy in El Salvador wanting. Small-unit action languished. In the words of one US trainer, the Salvadoran military preferred to conduct "search and avoid patrols."[146] The four colonels also faulted the civil defense program for employing former paramilitary soldiers along with the "aged, lame, and the otherwise unfit" for military duty.[147] Even the civic action programs had failed to achieve their objectives, including the NCP and UPR, because of the Salvadoran bureaucracy's inability to implement these programs. Arguably, none of these factors was ever satisfactorily resolved at any point during the war.

Suffice it to say, US government officials did not appreciate the criticism. As one of the authors recounted, a senior official from the Department of Defense bluntly told him that the report was not welcome by the Reagan administration and "not needed at this time."[148] As one US Embassy official groused, the report was published in the "People's Democratic Republic of Massachusetts, where it's read five times a day, like the Koran. It's bullshit."[149]

Interestingly, neither study questioned the US intervention or the rationale behind it. The four colonels, like US policy makers before them, assumed that the United States would continue intervening in Latin America with positive results. Perhaps more importantly, as Tommie Sue Montgomery has noted, they perpetuated the belief in a need for US intervention to protect its threatened interests.[150] Instead, both studies focused their efforts on the implementation of US aid, which both agreed had been flawed.

In spite of the criticism, Reagan proceeded unperturbed. At a welcoming ceremony for Duarte at the White House in 1987, the "Great Communicator" fired a broadside at his critics and extolled his administration's accomplishments in El Salvador:

> It was not long ago that El Salvador was all but written off by many in this city's circles of power. The Communist guerrillas, it was said, were an irresistible force, and the cruel tactics of the right could not be thwarted. The cause of democracy was doomed, so they said. . . . Those of us who have stood in support of the democratic peoples of El Salvador are especially proud of what has been achieved in recent years. . . . In a relatively short time, you've [Duarte] brought the military under civilian control and helped turn it into a professional and respected part of Salvadoran society, a responsible force for both national security and democratic

government. You've reformed the police and set about to improve
the system of justice. You have created a climate of respect for human rights and the rule of law.[151]

In this particular speech, Reagan lauded the positive aspects of US aid.
According to the president, the United States had consolidated democracy under Duarte, improved the professionalization of the military,
and reformed the judicial system. Victims of abuses committed by death
squads and security forces, including US citizens, would have disagreed
with his sunny appraisal. The president's upbeat message regarding El
Salvador reflected Washington's conventional wisdom. Although there
had been setbacks, continued progress was certain. More importantly,
the war would end with a government victory.

From a conventional military and political view, between 1984 and
1988, the US ally had made notable progress. Politically, US policy makers believed democracy had been successfully entrenched in El Salvador
after ensuring Duarte's election as president. Generous US military aid
created the second-largest military in Central America and increased
the Salvadoran military's capability to carry out aggressive operations.
The region's largest army belonged to Nicaragua, busy fighting the US-
backed Contra forces, which terrorized the countryside. As with its
neighbor, constructing a large army also did not result in victory. It did
succeed in reducing the size and strength of the FMLN. The insurgents
also hurt their own cause with the practices of forced recruitment and
attacks on elected officials. Nevertheless, the FMLN adapted by switch-
ing its strategy to prolong the war and outlast the United States. For the
next several years, in spite of a reduction in its forces and undertaking
measures that cost broad support, the FMLN lived to fight another day.
Despite preventing an insurgent victory in the short term, the Salvadoran military was still unable to achieve a decisive victory over the
guerrillas.

Despite these positive factors, several notable issues continued to fes-
ter. Among the most important, the Salvadoran economy was still in dire
straits. Not only did insurgent sabotage against the economy delay economic recovery but also it damaged Duarte politically. His inability to
address the fundamental economic grievances that fueled the insurgency

also cost his government considerable legitimacy. Under pressure from Washington, the Salvadoran president adopted the rigid austerity measures prescribed by his allies, further costing him vital popular support from one of his largest constituencies. Consequently, money that could have been used elsewhere had to be used to pay for war-related damages.

The FMLN politico-military strategy continued to tie down a significant portion of the Salvadoran military in static defense, ensuring that the counterinsurgents did not have the resources to completely eradicate the insurgents as a military threat. The rebels' actions also prevented their adversary from stationing sufficient troops to provide security for the villages. Instead, civil defense forces—often poorly armed, funded, and trained—assumed this burden. Even if the Salvadoran military had been able to create a force of more than 80,000 troops, defeating a force that retained popular support still would have proven daunting.

In spite of a quantitative decline in human rights abuses, the Salvadoran security forces continued their persecution of opponents—both insurgent and civilian. Their complicity in death-squad murders, disappearances, and human rights violations tainted Duarte's administration at home and abroad. His inability to prevent further abuses by the security forces, reform the justice system to punish the perpetrators, or exert control over them constituted a major shortcoming of his tenure in office. The emergence of a depoliticized and neutral security force under civilian control—characteristic of legitimate governments—had to wait until the end of the war.

Duarte's inability to deliver necessary public services also damaged his standing with the public. Rampant government corruption stymied efforts to provide essential services. An official in the US Embassy summed up the issue aptly, noting, "In this highly polarized, war-torn country, one of the few things upon which most Salvadoran[s] agree is that their government does not work very well." The embassy official also noted that many people publicly blamed Duarte's party, and "most privately admit[ted] that the problem was almost as bad [as] in the 1960's and 1970's."[152] Arguably, the most notorious agency was CONARA, charged with administering civic action and development programs across the country.

The Salvadoran government's failure to deliver essential services or halt corruption also proved a considerable obstacle to the establishment of legitimacy. El Salvador's near-total reliance on US largesse also undermined Duarte politically. Although he was not Washington's puppet, his country's dependence on the United States made him susceptible to pressure from the White House and insurgent propaganda. If the rug had been pulled out from under Duarte, not only would the Salvadoran economy have collapsed but also its military would have been hard-pressed to sustain the fight against the FMLN.[153] Ahmed Eqbal made a similar point decades earlier. Even though Eqbal was discussing South Vietnam, his words ring true: "No foreign power has the ability to equip a native government with legitimacy. . . . Identification with a foreign power erodes the legitimacy of a regime."[154]

Building viable political institutions in the middle of conflict, a military occupation, or both is hardly conducive to the creation of long-lasting stability. Generally, insurgents and their supporters do not participate—or are not welcomed—in elections. Their omission is fatal because these actors have credibility with the population. If they did not, the insurgency would eventually wither away. The continued exclusion of the FMLN and FDR from electoral politics accentuated the lack of political legitimacy in El Salvador. In theory, although members of the Salvadoran left were free to participate if they laid down their arms, there were no guarantees to ensure their safety. Given the previous history of El Salvador, they had sufficient reasons not to trust Duarte or the military. The establishment of political legitimacy, in which all parties were allowed to participate, free of violence, would ultimately take several more years.

Politically, US policy was in trouble, especially after Duarte was diagnosed with stomach cancer. Furthermore, his party was in the process of splintering and limping toward the constituent elections in 1988. In spite of the optimism, the following year, the conflict would irrevocably change.

5

Terminating the Bloodletting, 1989–1992

Since 1980, Salvadorans had fought a brutal civil war that had devastated the countryside, caused widespread suffering, and led to massive emigration of Salvadorans both across the border to Honduras and to the United States. Throughout the previous eight years, the war ebbed and flowed, moving through periods of insurgent and government gains and stalemates. Despite being labeled as a low-intensity conflict, for those experiencing the war firsthand, it was anything but low intensity. One constant in the war had been unwavering US support for the government from the White House. Over the next few years, however, that commitment came increasingly under question.

Arguably, as the war entered a new year, few Salvadoran observers could have predicted that 1989 would be a decisive year in the conflict. Conventional wisdom held that however slowly, the Salvadoran military had improved significantly and would eventually win. Nevertheless, several key events challenged prevailing assumptions about the war. Among them, new occupants emerged in both the White House and La Casa Presidencial, the Salvadoran presidential mansion, who according to most accounts were more interested in ending the bloodshed than continuing it. For the previous few years, the FMLN had concentrated on small-scale attacks, seeking to prolong the conflict until US aid was terminated. Simultaneously, the insurgents had also been actively preparing one last large-scale demonstration of force. An insurgent offensive in 1989 changed both US and Salvadoran perceptions of the conflict and undermined many of the key assumptions behind US support for El Salvador. These events also took place while the cold war was winding down. As the decade-old struggle meandered to its conclusion, the various conflicts that had ravaged the region during the 1980s were also moving toward their denouement. Ultimately, the end of the Salvadoran Civil War did not culminate in a military victory but in a negotiated settlement.

This chapter begins in 1989 and concludes with the signing of the Chapultepec Accords, which terminated the Salvadoran Civil War in January 1992. Rather than focusing on US-backed pacification efforts to defeat the FMLN, this chapter will address how the insurgents forced both sides to negotiate and challenged prevailing notions about the conflict. Even though the Salvadoran government did not launch any nationwide pacification efforts, aspects of US COIN strategy persisted. After the FMLN launched a large offensive, the war shifted from focusing on winning military victories to engaging in negotiations.

New Occupant

In January 1989, George H. W. Bush assumed the US presidency. The new president was a stark contrast from his predecessor, especially in his temperament. According to contemporary accounts of the newly elected president, he shared none of his predecessor's charisma. US commentators often portrayed Bush as a "wimp," an allegation that hounded his election campaign and the first year of his presidency. The new president also differed from his predecessor in an important way rarely noticed by critical reporters: Bush was not nearly as committed to pursuing war in El Salvador as Reagan had been.

The Bush administration aimed to restore bipartisanship between the executive and legislative branches. Secretary of State James Baker III, a man of sharp political instincts, recognized the need to have a healthy and functioning relationship with Congress and the US media.[1] During Reagan's eight-year tenure, his Central American policy, and the zeal with which he pursued it, had poisoned relations with Congress. The Bush administration had a particularly pressing issue before it: improving relations between the United States and the Soviet Union and ending the cold war. Without congressional support, the administration feared it would be much harder to accomplish its goals. As Baker noted in his memoirs, "I knew we had to find a way to get Central America behind us if we were to be able to deal aggressively with the decline of Soviet power. Moreover, it was an obstacle to the continued growth of democracy in all Latin America. Without a doubt, it was my first priority."[2]

Whereas his predecessor had made Central America a priority, Bush shared few of Reagan's proclivities and little of his ideological fervor. Unlike Reagan, Bush seemed not to harbor any deep feelings toward the region.[3] In eschewing Reaganite zealotry, Bush and Baker instead favored quiet pragmatism.[4] Nevertheless, although El Salvador did not rank as high on Bush's agenda, nor did Central America for that matter, his administration's goals in El Salvador were similar to those of Reagan's. US policy toward the country remained predicated on preventing the overthrow of the government by either the extreme left or right. Nevertheless, its subordinate place on the president's agenda meant that he was not willing to pay heavy political costs to achieve these aims.[5]

Thus if the goals were the same, the policy was new. Rather than pursuing a military and political victory in El Salvador, the White House sought simply to end the conflict on the best possible terms. Several factors influenced Bush's Salvadoran policy. First, by 1989 the likelihood of an insurgent victory seemed remote. After a large-scale, insurgent offensive roiled San Salvador in November of that same year, the administration realized the need for a different approach. Successive elections in the country had provided for greater political stability, and the demise of the Warsaw Pact and eventually the Soviet Union greatly affected anticommunism as a factor influencing US Central American policy.[6] The implosion of the Communist bloc as well as the termination of the aid pipeline to Cuba removed the primary exporters of revolution—according to US policy makers—in the hemisphere. Freed of the supposed threat from Moscow and Havana, the Bush administration pursued a more flexible approach to the conflict not moored to the cold war struggle.

Although the Bush administration's goal might have been ending the various wars that plagued the region, the White House did not have an overarching vision for extricating the United States from Central America.[7] Even though the White House might have lacked a strategic plan for ending the region's wars, it pursued a negotiated settlement rather than a military victory. It forged a bipartisan policy that made continued US assistance contingent on El Salvador's willingness to conduct good-faith negotiations with the rebels. In Hal Brands's opinion, the message from the Bush administration was blunt: negotiate or face the FMLN without US support.[8]

Dark Clouds

For the previous several years, US aid and training for the Salvadoran military had kept the FMLN off balance and prevented it from launching any large-scale offensives that threatened the Salvadoran government's existence. In early 1989, various sectors of the US government believed this trend would continue. Conventional wisdom assumed that the Salvadoran military was progressing toward a military victory over the FMLN. Military studies conducted by several US government agencies, including the CIA, Department of Defense, and MILGP asserted that the United States was well on its way to achieving its goals.[9]

In spite of the apparently diminished risk of insurgent victory, CIA intelligence analysts identified several recent developments posing a challenge to US interests in El Salvador. The discouraging political signs became a source of concern. The PDC, which had won the Constituent Assembly and presidential elections in 1982 and 1984, respectively, risked losing the presidency to the ARENA. As José Napoleón Duarte slowly succumbed to stomach cancer, his party fractured. By 1989, the PDC had weakened itself with infighting, incompetence, and corruption. Demoralized and alienated from its base, it nearly disintegrated over choosing a successor to Duarte.[10] Their political fortunes seriously diminished, the Christian Democrats limped toward the next presidential election.

A series of austerity measures launched under pressure from the United States to revive the economy had cost the Christian Democrats support. Preaching the gospel of the free market and slashing social spending, Duarte's measures succeeded in weakening the PDC's traditional base of support.[11] Unable to pass a tax increase to raise revenues because of rightist opposition, he was forced to cut spending, thus increasing unemployment. The cumulative damage from capital flight, guerrilla sabotage, and the 1986 earthquake left the country with 50 percent unemployment and underemployment, 40 percent inflation, and a decreasing standard of living. US economic aid could keep the country afloat, but economic recovery could not begin until the war was finished.[12]

From 1985 onward, the PDC had also failed to end the war. Duarte's inability to produce results weakened support for his party across El Salvador. As one of the FMLN's leading strategists noted, it was part of a vicious cycle: "The war requires more funds, and that forces them to take unpopular economic measures. Popular discontent as a result of the economic measures deepens the crisis and intensifies the war, and as the war intensifies more aid and government military spending are needed."[13]

These debilitating factors benefitted the PDC's main rival, the ARENA. The previous year, the Christian Democrats had lost the Constituent Assembly elections, allowing their main political competitor to gain the majority. In the upcoming March 1989 presidential election, the CIA forecast that the ARENA candidate, Alfredo Cristiani, would win. Although he was considered a moderate within the ARENA, intelligence analysts were concerned that his party's extremists—specifically Roberto D'Aubuisson—might advocate policies inimical to US interests.[14]

US policy makers continued to be concerned over the poor state of the Salvadoran economy. The GDP of El Salvador had grown at an average of less than 1 percent between 1984 and 1989. During this same time frame, per capita GDP was down 16 percent from 1980. Agricultural production had also stagnated; between these same years it fell 32 percent, and per capita food production had fallen to 85 percent of the 1980 levels.[15] As James LeMoyne, an experienced *New York Times* reporter in El Salvador, noted, "In spite of more than $2 billion in American economic aid, infant mortality has risen, access to potable water has fallen and most rural health clinics do not have medicine."[16] Even though the US government had provided its ally hundreds of millions of dollars in aid, it had done little to improve the Salvadoran economy or alleviate the suffering of the majority of the people—the very individuals whose support the US and Salvadoran governments were trying to win.

CIA analysts also fretted over recent insurgent activities. Since the beginning of the year, the FMLN had intensified its military, political, and diplomatic activities in a bid to undermine US support for the government and enhance its own credibility. To create the conditions necessary for the strategic counteroffensive, the FMLN carried out assassinations, strikes, and work stoppages. In January 1989, a strike led by construction workers paralyzed 177 businesses, leaving approximately 40,000 people out of work.[17] A January CIA assessment suggested that the insurgents' efforts were also part of a much larger strategy to negotiate from a stronger position and achieve more favorable returns at the conference table.[18] This assessment was not far off the mark.

In 1989, the insurgents continued their policy of *ajusticiamientos*, summary executions of former allies and combatants, civilians, and government officials.[19] For the first half of the year, the FMLN killings of civilians, when deaths from mines were included, "outstripped assassinations by uniformed government forces for the first time in the course of the war."[20] In early January, the FMLN resumed its campaign of assassinating mayors. According to an article in the *Washington Post*, this effort threatened to leave more than one-third of the nation without local authorities.[21] According to a US Embassy telegram, the head of the ERP continued to view the mayors as "legitimate targets."[22] The following month, insurgents assassinated Miguel Castellanos, *nom de guerre* of Napoleon Romero García, a former FMLN guerrilla who had defected and written a prominent memoir about his experiences.[23] After the election, the FMLN also murdered other individuals including Francisco Peccorini; José Roberto García Alvarado, Cristiani's attorney general; and José Antonio Rodrigo Porth, Cristiani's chief of staff. According to different sources, the continued killing of civilians cost the FMLN broader public support.[24]

Recent insurgent attacks in El Salvador's main population centers had also provoked a response from right-wing extremists. In particular, concern existed among US officials that this would lead to a resurgence of death-squad activity. For the previous several years, these shadowy units had been relatively quiet and had not resumed the large-scale bloodletting that had characterized the early part of the decade. President Cristiani's lack of emphasis on death-squad activity during the elections and an expectation among right-wing Salvadorans that the new president would relax human rights standards encouraged their reappearance.[25] In a January 1989 telegram, Ambassador William Walker noted that the human rights situation was rapidly deteriorating and called into question claims that abuses were being curtailed.[26] By late 1989, human rights observers identified nine death squads operating in the country, including the Revolutionary Anticommunist Action for Extermination (ARDE), which published a list of targeted opposition leaders, a practice eerily similar to earlier methods used by D'Aubuisson.[27] Although these units operated quite openly and regularly during the early portion of the conflict, their activity after 1984 had become less noticeable. As a CIA memorandum cautioned, their resurgence could discredit the government and increase sympathy for the FMLN.[28]

Even though the Salvadoran rebels' recent activities might have unnerved US intelligence analysts, the CIA was not overly concerned because US strategy had reduced the size and effectiveness of the FMLN forces. Reports estimated that the insurgents had lost between 15 percent and 19 percent of their forces and predicted that this trend would continue, further reducing the FMLN by an additional one-third over the next three to five years. Nevertheless, despite the decrease in its overall size, the report cautioned that it was likely the FMLN would be able to carry out its strategy of prolonged war, depending even more heavily on terrorism, sabotage, and small-scale attacks.[29]

CIA assessments of insurgent strengths and weaknesses made one substantial error: they claimed that the FMLN did not have the ability to launch a "political-military offensive along the lines of its proposed strategic counteroffensive in 1989. The FMLN has not greatly increased the pace of its purely military operations nor has it been able to bring about a lasting strategic dispersion of government forces; FMLN front groups and penetrations of the armed forces are not able to foment a popular or military insurrection."[30] The memo was confident that the US government was well on its way toward achieving its objectives in the country. Several months later US representative Dave McCurdy (D-OK) also sounded a note of optimism, claiming, "The growing political isolation of the hard left appears to be matched, contrary to popular wisdom, by its declining military capability."[31] By the end of the year, the FMLN contradicted these cheery assessments as the war entered a new and final stage.

Changing of the Guard

In March 1989, the ARENA candidate, Cristiani, won the Salvadoran presidential election, running on a campaign of promises of economic recovery and negotiating with the FMLN. The election left the ARENA as the dominant political force in El Salvador. Months earlier, the CIA believed that Cristiani's election marked the collapse of the PDC, and with it, a decade of US policy. Concern also existed in both the congressional and executive branches that an ARENA government might lift the constraints imposed on the death squads and that repression would receive a green light.[32] Nevertheless, the United States soon embraced a political party it had spent a significant portion of the decade vilifying.

Cristiani's victory at the polls also signified the triumph of the moderate reformist sector of the ARENA over its founders and the reactionary wing of the party. In the late 1980s, the "agro-industrial elite," which the newly elected Salvadoran president represented, gained increasing prominence within the ARENA and sidelined the agrarian interests, D'Aubuisson's primary backers. Their triumph over the hardline elements should not be underestimated because it made the Chapultepec Accords possible as well as the transition to democracy in El Salvador.[33]

Over time, the relationship that had dominated El Salvador for almost half a century—between the military and oligarchy—had become increasingly fractured. The cracks in this alliance also proved important to the end of the conflict. To be fair, the affiliation between these two groups was never as smooth as portrayed. Throughout the twentieth century, reformist military officers concerned about the dominance of the oligarchy had tried to implement small reforms to stave off revolution, including in 1979. Unfortunately, their efforts were defeated either by the hostility of the Salvadoran elite or by their own conservative military peers.

Over time, the military began to see its former ally as concerned above all else with profit. Perhaps naturally, a similar view was shared by the oligarchy, who regarded military officers as dangerous economic competitors and bristled at the unfair advantages they enjoyed, including no municipal taxes and preferential business deals.[34] The reformist sectors of the ARENA also viewed the military as an obstacle to peace and thus to the rehabilitation and expansion of the Salvadoran economy.

The internal dynamics within the ARENA also mirrored larger changes in the economic elite's situation. By the end of the 1980s, the coffee growers had ceased to be the dominant economic force within El Salvador. Nevertheless, despite losing their position on top of the economic ladder, they retained considerable influence within the ARENA. The moderate sectors of the ARENA did not rely on the military for their security as the traditional elites did. Those owners who relied less on land and the services typically provided by the Salvadoran military saw these government forces as a threat not only because of the fear they inspired but also because of the taxes they imposed for protecting their private property.[35] From their perspective, the military's power needed to be circumscribed, but they also believed that FMLN members should be given access to political participation as long as they laid down their weapons.[36]

A Salvadoran Tet?

On November 8, 1989, a daily intelligence estimate noted that the Salvadoran military reported unusual insurgent activity. According to the Salvadoran military, the FMLN was planning to launch an attack soon, "possibly this week," indicated by an "unusual concentration of rebels in and around San Salvador."[37] According to General Orlando Zepeda, military intelligence had recognized that the insurgents were planning a major offensive.[38] Salvadoran intelligence operatives correctly perceived the unusual movements; they represented the first phase of an insurgent offensive that aimed at infiltrating troops, weapons, and equipment into the capital city.[39] For the Salvadoran government and military, it was not a question of *if* but *when* they would strike.

Over the previous several months, repression against center-left party activists, including labor unions, had escalated throughout the country's cities. These activities culminated in the bombing of the Federación Nacional Sindical de Trabajadores Salvadoreños (FENASTRAS).[40] While the FMLN and Salvadoran government had been negotiating, a bomb struck the office of FENASTRAS on October 31, 1989. It was the third time the organization had been targeted that year. Whereas the previous incidents did not result in the loss of life, this attack killed nine people, including the union's secretary general, Febe Elizabeth Velásquez, and wounded forty others. Following the bombing, the FMLN suspended peace negotiations with the government. The explosion was one of the primary motives for launching the offensive.[41] Although the attacks were initially blamed on the guerrillas, that was unlikely. FENASTRAS had been critical of the government for decades and was closely linked with the FARN, one of the five groups of the FMLN. As the UN Truth Commission noted, this incident occurred in the context of a number of attacks against the Salvadoran Army and opponents of the government. Before the bomb exploded at its headquarters, members of FENAS-TRAS had received death threats for months, and some had disappeared after their arrest.[42]

On November 11, 1989, one day after the fall of the Berlin Wall, the FMLN brought the war to the nation's capital. Simultaneously, the Salvadoran insurgents also launched large, urban offensives in Santa Ana, Zacatecoluca, Usulután, and San Miguel, but these were minor engagements compared with the campaign directed at San Salvador. This major operation represented the culmination of a strategy the insurgents had carried out for the previous several years aimed at producing a decisive battle and massive uprising. This offensive, also known as *Hasta el tope* ("to the breaking point" offensive) or *Ofensiva fuera los fascistas, Febe Elizabeth vive* (out with the fascists offensive, Febe Elizabeth lives; named for the murdered FENASTRAS secretary general), shook the government's confidence and profoundly affected the peace negotiations. For the next several weeks, the army struggled to evict the insurgents from San Salvador.

The FMLN launched the offensive in 1989 because its leaders believed that events provided an opportune moment.[43] According to Facundo Guardado, there were two goals behind the attack, at best to take power by sparking an insurrection, or at a minimum to sustain combat in the cities for seventy-two hours to produce a favorable change in the correlation of forces.[44] The election of Cristiani's government, which had no political experience handling the international implications of the conflict, was seen as a weakness by the Salvadoran guerrillas. In addition, the FMLN believed that it could count on the support of its allies in Latin America: Cuba, Mexico, Venezuela, and Panama.[45] By November 1989, the FMLN had been fully rearmed. Weapons imported from the Soviet bloc enabled the FMLN to launch the offensive and to sustain combat for an additional two years.[46]

The offensive also aimed at bolstering the FMLN's position for political concessions at the peace talks.[47] Although Cristiani's representatives had held negotiations with the FMLN, they had failed to offer any significant concessions. Mario Lungo concurs, arguing that the offensive was not designed to defeat the nation's armed forces. Rather, the uprising sought to provoke a qualitative change in the correlation of forces that would help start the stalemated negotiations process, which would lead to a negotiated settlement.[48] Nevertheless, there were some sectors of the FMLN that still held out hope for a decisive victory. Unfortunately for subscribers to this theory, the massive uprising never occurred. For the previous several years, the insurgents had been building and expanding their network of rearguards for this very occasion. The underlying idea was that the presence of the FMLN forces would provoke an insurrection by important social groups that would take up arms against the government.[49]

The offensive caught the US Embassy completely off guard. The previous night, the embassy had hosted the Marine Corps ball, an event that would never have happened had they been aware an attack was coming.[50] The next morning, the embassy staff rose to very sobering news—both literally and figuratively—the capital was under attack. Perhaps more importantly, for the next few days after the rebels had attacked the capital city, the situation in San Salvador was precarious. The biggest fear within the US Embassy was that the poor would rise with the FMLN. Even though they did not, the fear was palpable. The offensive also struck fear in the Salvadoran high command. According to Ambassador Walker, their mood was "panic stricken." As the days progressed, the embassy lost confidence in senior Salvadoran military officers. Eventually, the high command's fear and paranoia led it to commit arguably one of the biggest mistakes in the war.[51]

The FMLN initially occupied the working-class neighborhoods on the outskirts of the city. As the offensive spread, however, insurgents assumed positions in the wealthier suburbs, bringing the conflict to the doorsteps of the nation's wealthiest individuals. As LeMoyne noted prior to the offensive: "The affluent elite is cloistered from the war inside high-walled mansions watched by bodyguards. . . . Young men of monied families dance in the discos all night, secure in the knowledge that they will never have to fight in the war that has killed more than 25,000 peasant soldiers, most of them draftees."[52] This offensive was the first time in several years that the wealthy had experienced the full burden of war. For one wealthy Salvadoran, his experience with the insurgents, who occupied his home briefly, was not a traumatizing experience. In fact, according to him, the rebels treated him with respect and did not steal or vandalize his property.[53] Previously, the FMLN had carried out selective assassinations of prominent individuals in the capital, such as members of the government or defectors, but now this sector of society experienced firsthand the reach of the FMLN.

To dislodge the FMLN from their temporary sanctuaries, the Salvadoran Air Force bombed the working-class neighborhoods. The casualty figures caused by the attacks have been hotly disputed.[54] As one adviser lamented, these attacks gave critics the impression that the "Air Force was bombing indiscriminately without regard for civilian casualties or property damages."[55] Bush administration officials, such as Assistant Secretary of State for Inter-American Affairs Bernard Aronson, strongly disagreed, averring that "President Cristiani gave explicit orders to the Air Force" to prevent indiscriminate bombing and that the Salvadoran government "bent over backwards to avoid injuring civilians."[56]

The Bush administration tried to minimize the political impact of the offensive and depicted it as an act of desperation. Secretary of State Baker called it a "desperation move" and insisted that "there is no threat to the Salvadoran government."[57] As Aronson noted, "The FMLN failed totally in this offensive," losing "between fifteen and twenty percent of their forces."[58] *El Diario de Hoy*, a conservative Salvadoran newspaper, trumpeted on November 14 that the "terrorist offensive" was under control. In the same article, the newspaper castigated the FMLN for having a "total disregard" for human rights by launching indiscriminate attacks throughout the nation's capital.[59] One US diplomat disagreed with these assertions, telling a reporter, "This is not your average tin cup guerrilla group playing army in the hills. That's a serious force."[60] Indeed, the FMLN's offensive did not represent the actions of a desperate actor. Rather, it was the culmination of years of work intended to produce results favorable to the FMLN.

Murder

In the midst of the rebel offensive, a murder committed by the Atlacatl Battalion further damaged the credibility of Cristiani's government as well as its international reputation. On November 16, the Atlacatl Battalion entered the Universidad Centroamericana (UCA) campus and murdered the Jesuit priests Ignacio Ellacuría, rector of the university; Ignacio Martín-Baró, vice rector; Segundo Montes, director of the Human Rights Institute; and Amando López, Joaquín López, and Juan Ramón Moreno. After killing the Jesuit priests, the Atlacatl Battalion found their housekeeper and her daughter and murdered them as well. The most professional battalion in the Salvadoran military attempted to cover up the crime by staging a fake machine-gun fight and attributing the slaying to the FMLN by writing on a piece of cardboard, "FMLN executed those who informed on it. Victory or death, FMLN."[61]

The murdered Jesuit priests had been viewed with both suspicion and distrust by the Salvadoran military. Even prior to the outbreak of the civil war, Roman Catholic priests and clergy had been persecuted by the military and the security forces for their "subversive" activities. These "nefarious acts" included educating civilians that their fate in life was not predetermined and organizing *campesinos* in the countryside. Salvadoran elites viewed this as a dangerous intrusion into politics and especially as a challenge to their prerogatives and way of life. Several priests, notably Father Rutilio Grande, paid with their lives. According to a former US adviser, the higher-ranking Salvadoran military believed that if enough "peasants were killed along with the Jesuit priests who planted communist ideas in their minds everything would go back as it had been."[62] During the war, members of the armed forces called UCA a "refuge of subversives." According to reports, Colonel Inocente

Montano, vice minister for public security, publicly declared that the Jesuits were "fully identified with subversive movements." Former colonel Orlando Zepeda believed that the murder of a public prosecutor had been planned within the university's confines and referred to UCA as a "haven of terrorist leaders from which a strategy of attacks against Salvadoran citizens is planned and coordinated."[63]

Throughout the conflict, the Jesuit priests at UCA had maintained contact with the FMLN, especially Father Ellacuría, who had met several times with Joaquín Villalobos, the leader of the ERP. The Salvadoran military viewed the continuing contacts between the two as suspicious and as blatantly favoring the insurgents. Even if the Jesuits supported some of the FMLN's aims, they could be critical, especially over the kidnapping and killing of civilians and mayors. For example, the Jesuit magazine *Estudios Centroamericanos* published articles critical of the insurgents, including their lack of broad support. According to the magazine, "The growing misery is attributed more today to the war than structural injustice, and the war is attributed more to the FMLN than to the armed forces or the United States."[64] Throughout the war, Father Ellacuría sought to persuade Villalobos to become more flexible toward a political settlement.[65] From 1985 onward, the priest harbored doubts over the possibility of a FMLN military victory.[66] Instead, he urged the head of the ERP to negotiate.

As the UN Truth Commission for El Salvador established, the decision to murder the Jesuits was reached at a meeting on November 15. The unit chosen to carry out the order was the Atlacatl Battalion.[67] One of the participants in that meeting, Zepeda, flatly denied that any order was given to murder the Jesuit priests.[68] Despite the initial denials and cover-up, it was quickly discovered that the US-trained unit was behind the massacre.

In the aftermath of the murders, US policy toward El Salvador underwent a fundamental reevaluation. Allegations of foot dragging and obstruction of justice within the country angered members of Congress. The accusations embarrassed the Bush administration and made it increasingly difficult to convince Congress to continue bankrolling El Salvador. Consequently, the Jesuit murders brought into question whether these allegations were true, and perhaps more importantly, it demonstrated to skeptical members of Congress and the US public that despite all the US aid, it had made a marginal impact.

After the news of the murders reached Washington, Congress moved toward suspending aid, a move protested by the Bush administration, which claimed that Congress would send the "wrong signals."[69] As Congress debated reducing US aid, administration officials tried to persuade members to avoid turning off the funding pipeline. Aronson argued against such a move, reminding skeptical members that US aid had prevented "the FMLN from taking over the country and imposing a Marxist dictatorship." The consequences of suspending or reducing aid would also lead to a rapid and immediate escalation in violence as both "sides attempt to maximize their current resources." Aronson also echoed a claim that members of the Reagan administration routinely offered: "The FMLN is responsible for much of the savagery" in El Salvador, a claim later disputed by the UN Truth Commission.[70]

Since 1984, Congress had consistently funded El Salvador's war effort. Initially it condemned the insurgent offensive in strident terms. After repeated allegations of obstruction of justice and corruption over the Jesuits' murder and subsequent investigation of the case, the legislative body had seen enough. Further fuel was provided by *Barriers to Reform: A Profile of El Salvador's Military Leaders*, a study written by the staff of the US Senate Arms Control and Foreign Policy Caucus in May 1990. Although the study did not have concrete evidence linking Salvadoran military leaders to a variety of human rights abuses, *Barriers to Reform* noted that fourteen of fifteen of El Salvador's military leaders had presided over commands implicated in a series of troubling actions, including murder, rape, torture, and forced disappearances. Of those fourteen, twelve had received US training, "some for many years."[71] Ultimately, Congress passed an amendment that cut aid to El Salvador by half. It contained language, however, that allowed the president to reinstate the other half of the suspended aid if the FMLN negotiated in bad faith or launched another offensive that threatened the Cristiani government's survival.[72] In January 1991, President Bush restored full aid to El Salvador after a series of insurgent attacks.

In spite of launching a massive attack against the nation's capital, the offensive had lost steam by the end of November. The popular uprising envisioned by the Salvadoran rebels had failed to materialize. Although it had brought the war into the nation's most important city and made its presence felt among the nation's elite, it also demonstrated something very important and arguably disconcerting for the FMLN: there was not as much support for the armed struggle among the population as the rebels had hoped. Arguably, the offensive convinced all actors — the FMLN, Washington, and the Salvadoran military and government — that the only way to peace in the country was through dialogue.

Sober Conclusions

In a postoffensive analysis, the CIA reached sobering conclusions that contradicted the prognosis it had made months earlier. According to the assessment, although it failed to "inflict a crippling blow" and defeat the Salvadoran Armed Forces, "the fighting has probably caused many Salvadorans — particularly the elite, who previously were more insulated from the war — to question the government's ability to provide for their most basic requirement: security. . . . The rebels also have benefitted from apparent Army complicity in the Jesuit murders, which have damaged San Salvador's credibility and could threaten critical foreign support if the guilty are not brought to justice."[73] Comandante Raúl Mijango agreed with the CIA's analysis. As he noted, the Sheraton Hotel hostage crisis in the midst of the offensive also carried troubling implications for the Cristiani government. According to him, it demonstrated the incapacity of the Salvadoran Army to provide security to the social sectors and important individuals it protected.[74]

Even though the FMLN did not achieve its goal of overthrowing the government, and failed militarily, it scored a political victory. The CIA agreed, noting, "The rebels' clearest victory was in the war of perceptions. They demonstrated a military prowess that has boosted their credibility and focused international attention on El Salvador. The FMLN probably believes its offensive helped to depict the war as 'unwinnable,' bolstering the argument that US assistance to the government has been ineffective and encouraging additional international pressure to make concessions during future negotiations."[75] In particular, the CIA lamented the negative effects of the offensive, including that it had shifted attention away from the violence caused by the FMLN to the government, which altered Salvadoran domestic perceptions about the government's credibility and authority. Perhaps even more jarring, the government lost some of the legitimacy it had gained over the previous few years. Beyond US domestic opinion, in the eyes of the international community, the Salvadoran military suffered a total loss of credibility.[76] The "rebels' seeming ability to operate with impunity throughout the capital shook the faith of many Salvadorans—particularly those directly affected by the violence—in the government's ability to provide security." As the memo cautioned, this could lead to further elite emigration, capital flight, and low investment, undermining the democratic process and hindering efforts to build political consensus.[77]

The offensive also demonstrated to Washington that the insurgents retained the capability to carry out a daring offensive when most analyses claimed they did not. The strength and tenacity of the offensive shattered the illusion that the Salvadoran Army was winning the war, and its response shattered the illusion "that the trappings of Salvadoran democracy constrained the men in uniform."[78] The military's subsequent cover-up and obstruction of justice also demonstrated to critics that the armed forces' progress under US tutelage of respecting human rights and adhering to the rule of civilian political institutions was illusory.[79]

For several *comandantes*, the 1989 offensive demonstrated that the FMLN still remained a powerful force.[80] Their efforts also acted as a catalyst for negotiations.[81] For one former FMLN insurgent, the offensive marked the beginning of the end of the conflict.[82] Although some might have continued to harbor visions of a military victory, the FMLN leaders increasingly began to see the end of the war as resulting from a negotiated settlement. This sentiment was also echoed in the White House and among the ruling elite in El Salvador.

After the offensive, the US military also harbored doubts. For the previous several years, senior US military commanders publicly proclaimed that the Salvadoran military had made major strides in improving its battle prowess and that the war was heading in the right direction. Although some of the comments were rosy, none of them approached General William Westmoreland's infamous quote in November 1967 that the United States had reached a point in El Salvador where "the end begins to come into view."[83] The offensive, however, changed the message. The senior US military officer responsible for Latin America believed that negotiations were the only way to settle the conflict. During testimony on Capitol Hill, General Maxwell Thurman, head of SOUTHCOM, was asked about the likelihood of the Salvadoran government defeating the FMLN. Thurman bluntly replied, "I think they will not be able to do that."[84]

The 1989 offensive also altered the calculus in the White House. Rather than seeking a military victory, administration officials looked to the negotiating table to end the war.[85] Secretary of State Baker continued to view the offensive as a military defeat for the guerrillas. Yet, Baker also viewed the event as a catalyst for negotiations. As he noted in his memoirs, "On the one hand, it ended any illusions among the guerrillas that the civilian population was ready to follow their call, but it also shattered the military's hopes that the guerrillas were a spent force. And, the Jesuit massacre galvanized Congress as never before to cut off aid."[86] In order to pursue negotiations, the US government relied on Mexico, Venezuela, Spain, and Colombia to relay messages to the guerrillas. The maneuvering also involved a delicate balance: sending signals to the Salvadoran military that it must support a negotiated peace—and purge its officers guilty of human rights violations—or risk losing support. At the same time, the administration also had to convince the more hardline FMLN *comandantes* that if they continued the war, the United States would not abandon the government.[87] It was a formula that required a nuanced and balanced approach. Nevertheless, the message from the White House had changed.

One of the leading proponents for negotiations within the Bush administration was Aronson. Addressing the murder of the Jesuits on Capitol Hill, Aronson declared, "Many will try to exploit Father Ellacuría's memory and name," but the only "fitting memorial" was to "mobilize whatever resources and pressures can be brought to bear to negotiate an end to the conflict in El Salvador and guarantee safe space in the democratic process for all." Aronson's statement marked the first time a US official had explicitly acknowledged favoring a settlement to the war through political negotiations.[88] Months later, in testimony before the House Subcommittee on Western Hemisphere Affairs in January 1990, Aronson declared, "El Salvador needs peace and the only path is at the negotiating table. . . . We don't think the country can afford the years of suffering that it will take for a military victory. We don't think that is what the Salvadoran people want."[89] Such statements would have been unthinkable under the Reagan administration. Aronson's message indicated that the White House was not going to seek a military victory in El Salvador.

President Cristiani also became one of the most outspoken advocates for terminating the war. Unlike his predecessor, the new Salvadoran president had the requisite leverage to compel the recalcitrant military to negotiate. The military's poor handling of the offensive and the subsequent murder of the Jesuits strengthened Cristiani's hand. Equally important, he had the backing of the right.[90] According to the US Embassy, the Salvadoran president believed that economic and political progress required peace. Cristiani also viewed a military victory as impossible, and quite possibly, his interest in ending the conflict could be the result of a desire within his party to lessen El Salvador's dependence on the United States.[91] The Salvadoran president also grasped something else equally essential: there was growing war weariness within the country and a desire for peace.[92] For a country that had endured a war for more than a decade, there was simply not much of an appetite for continuing the conflict.

By 1989, actors in both the United States and El Salvador realized that neither side could achieve a military victory. The FMLN's foreign backers had also been applying pressure to negotiate, which along with the offensive's failure to spark a nationwide uprising and topple the government made the insurgents more amenable to negotiations.[93] International events also demonstrated that as the cold war was slowly ending, the need for a sustained and expensive US COIN effort to prevent the collapse of El Salvador was unnecessary. Put another way, the basis of the previous years of US policy toward the country now appeared anachronistic.

International Context

The end of the Salvadoran Civil War occurred in the midst of far-reaching international events. By 1989, the cold war was slowly moving toward its conclusion as both sides worked to ratchet down the rhetoric and improve relations between the superpowers. When Mikhail Gorbachev assumed the helm of the Soviet Union, he made improved relations with the West an important component of his efforts to restructure Soviet society. Gorbachev's "new thinking" also extended to the realm of international affairs. In particular, the Soviet leader stressed that US-Soviet security must be mutual and based on political, not military, instruments. Unfortunately for him, his actions unleashed a Pandora's box neither he nor the leaders of the Soviet leadership could contain.

When the new chair assumed command of the world's other superpower, the Soviet economy had stagnated, and grumblings of discontent simmered beneath the surface. Gorbachev sought to relieve the burden facing the Soviet economy by reducing foreign aid, including military, to his country's various allies. His policy of *perestroika* redirected Soviet foreign policy, especially toward its allies in Eastern Europe and the rest of the globe. Nonetheless, Gorbachev did not move immediately toward distancing his country from his revolutionary allies in Latin America. For example, in 1987, Gorbachev brokered a full-scale rearmament with the FMLN and pledged "solidarity with the struggle waged by Nicaragua against the aggressive intrigues of imperialism." Nevertheless, economic and geopolitical realities forced the Soviet chair to scale back involvement in the hemisphere.[94]

In 1989, the Soviet empire began slowly disintegrating. In dramatic and startling fashion, member states of the Soviet bloc collapsed one after another. These events culminated in the fall of the Berlin Wall in November 1989. By the end of the year, the international arena was not favorable or conducive to the FMLN's interests. The following year, the situation actually worsened, and the FMLN could no longer count on support from either of its reliable patrons, Cuba and Nicaragua.

Regional events also loomed large. In January 1990, the FMLN received a jolt from neighboring Nicaragua—the Sandinistas lost the national elections. The Nicaraguan leadership fully expected to win the election in spite of a poor economy and the continuing covert war initially sponsored by the Reagan administration. In a closely contested election, the opposition leader, Violeta Chamorro, whose husband was murdered by Somoza and who received lavish funding from the United States, defeated the Sandinistas. As one disappointed US activist noted,

"After nine years of what Pentagon strategists call 'low-intensity warfare' against the Sandinistas, the Nicaraguan people 'cried uncle.'"[95]

The Sandinistas' defeat affected the FMLN in several ways but especially politically. According to Comandante Balta, it represented more than a psychological loss; the loss at the polls removed the possibility of a revolutionary victory in El Salvador.[96] The failure of the FMLN allies removed a significant political partner that provided sanctuary for the guerrillas' high command. Moreover, the defeat also left an even more important mark: it demonstrated to the FMLN that it needed to avoid the same mistakes made by the Sandinistas and be more inclusive politically.

Despite being voted out of power, the Sandinistas retained key posts within the Nicaraguan military and continued to support the FMLN clandestinely. For example, they provided deadly new weapons, especially SAMs—antiaircraft missiles—to the FMLN to continue fighting.[97] Nevertheless, although the Salvadoran insurgents might have received military support from the Nicaraguan Army, the loss of political support and a close ally demonstrated that the writing was on the wall.

The winding down of the cold war also meant that Washington was no longer as concerned about "winning" in El Salvador. As regional and international players moved toward ending the region's wars, the Bush White House abandoned its predecessor's goal of achieving a decisive victory. Although an FMLN victory was still unacceptable, the administration was willing to tolerate a negotiated settlement under the changed international context.

Negotiations

For approximately the next two years, the Salvadoran belligerents worked toward negotiating an end to the stalemate. Essentially, the FMLN asked for a thorough reorganization of the Salvadoran Army and the security forces and purging of officers accused or implicated in human rights abuses. The Salvadoran insurgents also demanded strengthening civilian control over the military and transferring "police functions out of the armed forces." Throughout the deliberations, tensions between the Salvadoran executive branch and the military existed. According to a State

Department memorandum, it was crucial for the US government to maintain the "confidence of the armed forces to help Cristiani persuade them to support difficult concessions at the bargaining table." This same document also characterized Cristiani's position as "far reaching and de-stabilizing." It noted, "No nation in Latin America has offered these kinds of concessions to end a guerrilla insurgency—particularly asking major reductions of its army in the middle of a war."[98]

In 1990, the ERP launched another offensive to change the calculus at the negotiating table. That year, the FMLN inflicted more than 2,000 casualties on the armed forces and police, an almost 0.5 percent casualty rate.[99] Unlike previous offensives, this one was solely aimed at improving the FMLN's negotiating stance. Its objectives were to search for a decisive battle and attack the morale of the army.[100] Launched in November 1990, the Final Offensive also featured the use of antiaircraft missiles. According to the US Embassy, the introduction of these missiles "has all but neutralized the tactical advantage of the air force, affected the morale of the ground forces, and reduced the aggressiveness of ground operations. Additionally, aircraft modifications necessary to counter the threat are extremely costly and have diverted already scarce security assistance funding from other much needed sustainment programs."[101]

During the offensive the FMLN used the advanced antiaircraft weapons it received from Nicaragua against its enemy. These weapons forced helicopters to fly lower to avoid the missiles, making them susceptible to ground fire. They also reduced the number of sorties and limited air support to Salvadoran troops. One of the casualties included three US servicemen executed by FMLN insurgents after their helicopter was shot down.[102] US concerns about these weapons falling into the hands of the FMLN dated back to at least 1985, when Nicaragua procured several missiles from the Soviet Union. As Ambassador Edwin Corr noted, if these weapons fell into FMLN hands, it would force the Salvadoran Air Force to "make major adjustments in air mobile and close-air-support tactics." This would negatively affect the war because the government's growing airpower had been a major factor in forcing the guerrillas to switch tactics the previous year.[103]

Until 1989, the Salvadoran Air Force's best aircraft had been immune. Now, they were in striking distance of the antiaircraft missiles.[104] The CIA worried that the introduction of these weapons could potentially "degrade the government's counterinsurgency effort" and "give the guerrillas freer control over larger areas of the country."[105] The introduction of the antiaircraft missiles positively affected the morale of the insurgents, who "felt that the ESAF morale is down . . . that there is a chance for power-sharing concessions from GOES."[106] Another former insurgent agreed, claiming that the destruction of several A-37s severely affected the army's morale. After the introduction of the antiaircraft missiles, the Salvadoran military did not assume an aggressive posture for the remainder of the conflict and avoided contact with the insurgents.[107]

In 1991, Secretary of State Baker authorized Aronson to make direct contact with representatives from the FMLN. One of the first contacts came when Ambassador Walker visited the Guazapa Volcano, an insurgent-dominated area outside of the capital. Walker followed these efforts by visiting another insurgent camp, Santa Marta, the repatriation camp for guerrillas who sought refuge during the early years of war.[108] His visit to the insurgent stronghold was not proposed either by the Bush administration or by his superiors in the State Department. Rather, it was the result of personal invitations and diplomatic protocol. The US ambassador visited the camp twice. During the second meeting, Walker and his entourage met with Comandante Hercules, a guerrilla commander of the Resistencia Nacional (RN). The talks between the enemies were very cordial and productive. It was also during this visit to Santa Marta that the ambassador came to believe the war would end.[109] Such contacts would have been unthinkable years before. These visits changed the ambassador's as well as Commander of MILGP Mark Hamilton's opinions about the FMLN. Nevertheless, the former ambassador was not sure how Washington viewed his exploits.[110]

This was a crucial event, in retrospect, because in the minds of the FMLN it established a link with the US Embassy, with which they previously had no contact.[111] According to ERP head Villalobos, the ambassador's trips signaled a willingness to treat the rebels as legitimate participants in Salvadoran life.[112] The ambassador's visit strengthened the hand of those who favored a unilateral cease-fire. In Villalobos's words,

We were discussing the possibility of a unilateral cease-fire, a key step to push negotiations forward. . . . Some were opposed to taking such a definitive step, but when we saw Walker in Santa Marta, we felt conditions were really different. We knew the trip made the military furious, but we were impressed. But had we known it was an individual gesture, not a policy statement, I doubt we would have called the cease-fire.[113]

As the ambassador noted, he did not learn about the importance of his visit to Santa Marta until after the conflict.[114] These actions also affected events at the United Nations, where, according to one US official, "the FMLN started treating us as part of the solution."[115]

The negotiations that ended the conflict often took a winding and sometimes tortuous path.[116] By May 1991, the FMLN and the Salvadoran government had agreed upon establishing a UN Human Rights monitoring group, a package of constitutional reforms strengthening civilian control of the military, transfer of police functions out of the armed forces, reform of the electoral and judicial systems, and establishment of the Truth Commission to study and report on outstanding human rights cases.[117] The most troubling agreements related to civilian control of the military and reform of the armed forces. In September 1991, talks that involved Cristiani and all five of the FMLN's general command broke the deadlock over military reform. Under significant pressure from Washington, Cristiani agreed to reduce the armed forces by half and create an independent civilian commission to investigate human rights abuses. In return, the insurgents accepted participation in the newly created civilian police force rather than the armed forces. By the end of September, all the significant issues between the two sides had been resolved. However, the implementation of these agreements, especially the cease-fire, still required further discussion.[118] Nonetheless, both sides continued to talk, and by December 1991 their efforts finally paid off.

In spite of delays and disagreements over particular negotiating points, on January 16, 1992, representatives of the Salvadoran government and the FMLN signed a peace agreement that officially ended the war. The announcement was celebrated heavily throughout El Salvador. The end of the Salvadoran Civil War also occurred as the region's various other conflicts ended. For approximately twelve years, Salvadorans committed horrific violence against each other, causing at least 70,000 deaths and large-scale emigration. The following month, an official cease-fire was established that, although there were several tense moments in the FMLN's demobilization effort, was never broken. Now, instead of fighting each other, the former enemies had to resolve their differences peacefully and take up the task of rebuilding and governing the country.

Since the end of the conflict, El Salvador continues to move forward with its experiment in democracy and free-market capitalism. In some instances, former enemies have stopped viewing each other as such, particularly former FMLN *comandantes* and Salvadoran officers. Political reconciliation, however, lags behind. In the 2014 Salvadoran presidential election, the ARENA candidate, Norman Quijano, protested the results, claiming that the FMLN had committed electoral fraud, and demanded a full recount, rejected by the electoral authorities. The frustrated candidate also raised the specter of intervention by the Salvadoran Armed Forces, putting the nation on edge.[119] Quijano subsequently denied he ever made such claims.[120] Fortunately, the Salvadoran Armed Forces issued a statement supporting the electoral results.[121] As the recent election demonstrates, fears of civil war and military intervention still exist in polarized El Salvador.

Victory?

After the signing of the Chapultepec Accords, all sides in the conflict claimed victory. Nearly every actor claimed some sort of benefit from the termination of hostilities. The list included peace, the establishment of democracy, and reconciliation. Although all the belligerents could claim victory, some actors were more successful than others were.

Arguably, the FMLN emerged from the conflict as a victor. Several FMLN *comandantes* viewed the end of the war in such terms. None of the insurgents interviewed characterized it as a military success for their side. During the civil war, the FMLN had created the most effective guerrilla army in the region's history.[122] For twelve years the Salvadoran insurgents had battled the government to the verge of collapse, and then to a stalemate, yet they never inflicted a decisive defeat against their enemy. Nevertheless, there were other notable and more tangible gains.

For example, according to Villalobos, "If looked at from the point of view of the dreams, we lost. However, being realists we clearly won. We generated constitutional changes in justice, in the police, in the electoral system, and we were able to get the army to return to the barracks. Furthermore, the Front is now the second political force in the country."[123] That was before the FMLN became the first political force in El Salvador and captured the presidency in 2009. To paraphrase the former *comandante*, although the FMLN might not have achieved all of its goals, especially overthrowing the government, all was not lost. In fact, there were several important results in which the former guerrillas could take pride.

Several *comandantes* remarked on the political gains achieved not only by the FMLN but also by the Salvadoran people. For Guardado, the struggle instituted political changes in El Salvador, including ending the government's previous exclusionary policies. In prewar El Salvador, political space was extremely narrow and tightly controlled. Subsequently, political parties denied access to political life were allowed to organize and run for office. In his opinion, the war was responsible for these improvements. He also characterized the war as creating the first social pact in the country's history signed between the government and its people.[124] The accords created a new Salvadoran constitution that required the government to be responsive to its citizens. Arguably, the end of the conflict marked the beginning of political legitimacy in El Salvador. Another former guerrilla concurred with Guardado's assessment and noted that it was also a victory for the nation's political structure because it provided a mechanism to resolve disagreements peacefully.[125] In particular, the ability of the FMLN to participate legally in elections was heralded among former guerrillas.

Arguably the institution most affected by peace was the Salvadoran military. The FMLN demanded during the peace negotiations to reduce the military's size, reeducate or reorient its central mission, and redefine itself as an institution. For most observers, the peace treaty accomplished those very goals. Moreover, it not only reduced the size of the Salvadoran military but also abolished the BIRI units. Although these units had been considered essential by the US military advisers for US-style COIN efforts, their role and notoriety for committing human rights abuses during the conflict meant that they were no longer necessary in postwar El Salvador. For one former guerrilla, peace broke the power of the most powerful institution in the country — the Salvadoran military.[126] Nevertheless, not all scholars agree with such rosy pronouncements. Philip Williams and Knut Walter have noted that several dimensions of the military's power were not addressed or touched: the military's position within the state, the network of social control in *el campo,* and the military's institutional and political autonomy. Although they praise the accords for laying the groundwork for a significant reduction of the military's prerogatives, Williams and Walter argue that the agreements did not go far enough in ensuring civilian supremacy over the armed forces. Despite the changes, the Salvadoran Armed Forces emerged from the conflict with much of their autonomy intact.[127]

In spite of the supposedly successful application of US COIN in El Salvador, the conflict produced several negative consequences as well. First, it generated a massive emigration of Salvadorans across the border to Honduras and to the United States. For example, in 1987, Salvadoran and US officials believed more than 400,000 had fled to the United States since 1982. As the *New York Times* noted, the migration represents one of the most determined and concentrated migrations of any national group to the United States in recent history.[128] The conflict also poisoned relations between the executive and congressional branches of the US government, especially under Reagan, which led the president to circumvent Congress. There are moral concerns as well, especially with the large-scale violations of human rights that occurred during the conflict. As with other cases of the fear of communist expansion during the cold war, one could reasonably ask if the fear of communism justified US support of a corrupt and brutal government. Blaming the various human rights abuses on wartime exigencies is not only mistaken but a distortion. During the conflict, violence was a fundamental aspect of the Salvadoran approach to battling the FMLN, and in the eyes of some critics, approved by the Reagan administration. Of course, this does not absolve the Salvadoran insurgents of killing civilian government officials and other rebels, kidnapping wealthy businesspeople, or sabotaging the nation's electrical supply. When compared with the human rights violations committed by the government, however, the number is small. The

UN Truth Commission attributed at least 85 percent of the violent acts investigated to the Salvadoran government, including the military, the security forces and their allies, and the death squads.

Since the end of the conflict, El Salvador has held numerous presidential elections. Initially, the first several of these contests were dominated by the ARENA. Nevertheless, Mauricio Funes's election in 2009 represented the first transfer of political power from the ARENA to the FMLN. Recently, the FMLN's candidate and former vice president, Salvador Sánchez Cerén, won a closely contested presidential election over his ARENA rival. Prior to his election, Reaganite Elliot Abrams sounded the alarm should the former guerrilla win.[129] Sánchez Cerén's victory not only marks the first time that his party has won two consecutive presidential elections but also that a former high-ranking insurgent was elected. The closely contested nature of the election also demonstrates the continuing political polarization in El Salvador. One can imagine that US and Salvadoran leaders who tried to defeat the FMLN, including President Reagan, Senator Jesse Helms, and Roberto D'Aubuisson, are rolling over in their graves.

The Salvadoran Civil War left a very bloody and troubling legacy not only from a moral standpoint but also as a model for defeating insurgency. US tacticians have argued that El Salvador not only represents a successful application of COIN but also that it should be used as a case model for similar contingencies. A meticulous study of the conflict should give them cause for concern.

The US experience in El Salvador confirms that outside intervention in civil wars exacerbates an already volatile situation and extends the bloodshed. US aid prolonged the conflict by encouraging a military solution to defeating the FMLN, not a political or diplomatic resolution. The majority of US funding prioritized the military dimension instead of addressing the root causes of discontent. Even if the White House supported Duarte's negotiations with the FMLN, it continued to hold out for a decisive military victory. The generous funds provided by the US government buoyed the Salvadoran government and military and fueled the notion that they would eventually wear down their enemy and destroy them. US military support, especially combat aircraft, also further contributed to the devastation of El Salvador by destroying the countryside and depopulating its inhabitants. Arguably, FMLN external supporters Cuba and Nicaragua could also be faulted, although relevant sources from these countries are necessary to evaluate fully the significance of their support. If anything, this project confirms the necessity of an international approach to the topic.

The Salvadoran Civil War caused an appalling level of destruction, especially for a country of its size. In General William Tecumseh Sherman's words, "War is cruelty." However, COINdinistas have portrayed counterinsurgency interventions differently from their conventional counterparts. Recently, they have presented such tactics to the US public as thoughtful and humane strategies that respect the lives and rights of civilians. Proponents such as Colonel John Nagl have characterized COIN as a more sophisticated form of warfare. An inane epigraph in *FM 3-24* informs its readers, "Counterinsurgency is not just thinking man's warfare—it is the graduate level of war."[130]

COIN is often used interchangeably with winning "hearts and minds." In El Salvador, government forces attempted to woo the population by instituting traveling fairs, giving pep talks, providing dental and medical care, and implementing grassroots development efforts. Typically, the Salvadoran military played the leading role instead of the appropriate civilian agencies. Its involvement in civic action programs and other pacification efforts not only led to a militarization of aid but also designated civilians as targets for retaliation and retribution. The historical record provides several examples of the use of brute force and coercion to acquire the civilians' allegiance or to provide protection. As El Salvador and other US experiences with battling insurgency demonstrate, COIN interventions are often as destructive as conventional conflicts.

Anthropologists and other social scientists have traced the destructiveness of the conflict to the theoretical underpinnings of US COIN doctrine. Often referred to as the National Security Doctrine, its tenets were disseminated at US military academies throughout the Western Hemisphere, especially after Fidel Castro's victory in 1959. Included among these countries was El Salvador, which with US help established a formidable intelligence apparatus and paramilitary organization that targeted people with "questionable" political affiliations. More importantly, the threat posed to the Salvadoran state by communist insurgents in the 1960s was minimal; the military machinery created was designed to tackle an invisible enemy. The doctrine's broad and general language stretched the definition of a "subversive" to include individuals and organizations involved in political opposition or even ecclesiastical activities deemed hostile to the state. Although US advisers probably did not overtly urge their patrons to murder, torture, and commit human rights abuses, the various methods and doctrine taught by US military personnel to their clients and the security apparatus they created were often used to commit the very acts the United States supposedly abhorred. At the least they also contributed to the ferocity of the conflict and the no-holds-barred approach taken by the Salvadoran military during the early stages of the civil war.

Throughout the war US policy makers and military strategists attempted to convince their Salvadoran counterparts to reform or potentially face the possibility of a reduction or suspension of aid. These efforts included ending human rights abuses, curbing the power of the right, and reforming El Salvador's judicial system. Supporters of the US approach also assumed that massive aid and support gave the United States leverage over its client. As the conflict demonstrated, when it is apparent that the donor is committed to the survival of its client, the recipient nation is more unlikely to carry out the necessary reforms. Even though Congress restricted the White House's policy in El Salvador, it did not want to, or have the courage to, fundamentally alter it out of fear of a FMLN victory. Potentially, Democrats feared the political damage associated with "losing" another ally to communism.

US COIN strategists tried to change the Salvadoran military's behavior and convince its leaders of the necessity of focusing less on body counts and technology and more on addressing the root causes of the conflict. They faced a formidable opponent in the Salvadoran high command, which was not interested in applying US COIN tactics. Among the junior officer corps, MILGP made more progress. The older and more conservative officers had their own reservations about US advice. The high command believed not only that its strategy was sound but also that it had worked successfully for decades. Conceivably, the Salvadoran military could have distrusted US advice because quite simply it was very similar to the strategies used by the United States in Vietnam. In the end, although the Salvadoran military accepted military aid, its leaders pursued their own strategy to defeat the FMLN, which minimized the importance of civilians.

Some fault must also lie with the message disseminated by US advisers. Although they had a sophisticated understanding of the threat they faced, the socioeconomic measures promoted by the United States offered very little in the way of real reform or addressing the issues that caused the conflict. Even if the senior officers had wholly embraced their allies' COIN strategy, it is unlikely the conflict would have ended any differently. Simply placing blame on Salvadorans for failing to adopt US advice is misguided. It is eerily reminiscent of US officials who blamed "primitive" locals for the failure of modernization in the 1960s.

From a strategic and military perspective, the expensive and resource-intensive COIN operations envisioned by US tacticians were impractical and unrealistic. It would have been difficult even in the best of times for a country confronted by an insurgency, high unemployment, and a deteriorating economy to launch a nationwide civic action program for several months. The entire effort was dependent on US funding—Duarte's government did not have the appropriate funds. Compounding these matters, the Salvadoran bureaucracy was both unwilling and unable to share the burden. In other words, the government infrastructure and its lack of adequate funds assured failure. Even more importantly, the various policies used to woo popular support—civic action and development efforts—never altered the strategic or political balance. They were based on the premise that people wanted simple alteration of the existing socioeconomic political system, not drastic reform. In spite of their failure in both El Salvador and other conflicts, such as Vietnam and Afghanistan, these practices continue to be fundamental elements of US COIN strategy.

In many ways, supporters of US COIN strategy have also drawn the wrong lessons. The ability to keep the number of Americans in danger low, or maintain a "light footprint," is often portrayed as a positive outcome. In reality, there was nothing low-key about the US effort in El Salvador, including its massive and heavily fortified embassy in San Salvador. Keeping a minimal military presence was mandated by Congress;

however, the fifty-five-adviser limit was routinely abused but not in such an egregious fashion to warrant congressional intervention. Another key factor keeping US ground troops out of El Salvador included opposition from the broad US public and the nation's top military brass. The latter was unwilling to risk its massive budget increase on another messy and protracted war. Instead, its priorities were focused on fighting an enemy and a battle that (thankfully) never took place.

US aid not only greatly increased the size of the Salvadoran military but also helped prevent the likelihood of a FMLN military victory. Even though US aid might have built a larger and more professional force, it could not overcome the government's inability to end the war and improve the majority of the people's well-being. Simply put, US COIN doctrine in El Salvador did not end the war or result in a decisive victory. What emerged was a negotiated settlement because the belligerents realized that they could not feasibly continue the war indefinitely.

US policy makers continue to view the United States in the words of former secretary of state Madeleine Albright as the "indispensable nation." A recent manifestation of this view can be glimpsed in Hillary Clinton's farewell speech as she stepped down from her position as the president's top diplomat in 2013. In Clinton's words, "We are the force for progress, prosperity, and peace."[131] Throughout the cold war, and indeed until present, the US government has not only fashioned itself as a force for good but also asserted that it has the right to intervene globally and that when it does, its actions are not only positive but also central to the resolution of the crisis. As this chapter has demonstrated, the end to the conflict had very little to do with US COIN doctrine, its tactics, or US funding. Nonetheless, the fiction still survives.

Coda: "The Salvadoran Option" in Iraq

Shortly after the US-led invasion of Iraq in 2003, the security situation rapidly deteriorated. It quickly became evident that not only were the George W. Bush administration and US military's postwar occupation plans insufficient but also both had failed to adequately plan for the aftermath of the invasion. Within months of the termination of major combat operations, an insurgency quickly developed, exploiting the existing security vacuum. Officials in Washington originally dismissed the attacks and the perpetrators, labeling them "regime dead-enders." Secretary of Defense Donald Rumsfeld downplayed the level of violence, equating the casualties with everyday violence in US cities.[1]

As US fatalities in Iraq continued to mount, violence among Kurds, Shias, and Sunnis threatened the disintegration of the Iraqi state. Grisly reports of sectarian killings; kidnappings; beheadings of foreigners, including journalists and aid workers; large-scale relocation of Iraqis to relatively ethnically homogenous neighborhoods; and suicide bombings dominated the headlines. By the end of 2004, Iraq was sliding toward the precipice of disaster. Unable to halt the escalating violence or secure order, US policy makers became increasingly desperate for solutions.

In early 2005, officials from the Pentagon and Bush administration met in the nation's capital to devise a strategy to defeat the insurgency in Iraq. To address the deteriorating security situation, they proposed what became known as the Salvadoran Option. According to reports, this policy advocated using US Special Forces commandos to train either Shia militia members or Kurdish Peshmerga fighters to target Sunni insurgent leaders. In addition to assassinating insurgents, the plan also raised the possibility of launching raids into Syria to capture high-profile individuals.[2]

The Salvadoran Option in Iraq also included nonviolent measures. To move forward with the supposed democratization of Iraq, the Bush administration decided to hold parliamentary elections in 2005. Elections were also meant to diminish the appearance that US forces were illegitimate occupiers of Iraq and provide a veneer of legitimacy to the floundering Iraqi government. As with El Salvador, critics claimed that holding elections in the midst of violence amounted to little more than a propaganda charade. General John Abizaid, head of US Central Command, made the case while appearing on *Meet the Press.* As he told the show's host, "I can't predict 100 percent that all areas will be available for complete, free, fair, and peaceful elections. . . . That having been said, if we look at our previous experiences in El Salvador, we know that people who want to vote will vote."[3]

During a vice-presidential debate between Vice President Dick Cheney and Senator John Edwards in 2004, Cheney also discussed the 1982 constituent elections held in El Salvador.[4] Cheney had visited El Salvador as an electoral observer on behalf of Congress. The vice president recounted how fearless Salvadorans had defied the "terrorists" who shot up polling stations because they would not be denied the right to vote. According to Cheney, the United States should conduct elections in both Iraq and Afghanistan—as it did in El Salvador, approximately twenty-two years earlier—despite the violence that continued to ravage those nations. Holding elections, Cheney argued, would result in a decisive defeat for the insurgents and demonstrate that democracy was on the march.

Not everyone was enamored with the portrayal of El Salvador offered by administration and defense officials. Critics alleged that these units were modeled after the Salvadoran death squads, groups composed of members of El Salvador's security and paramilitary forces. The death squads were especially active during the first four years of the conflict, murdering suspected insurgents and sympathizers, leftists, members of trade unions, and even Archbishop Oscar Arnulfo Romero. Among the most vociferous critics were former journalists who covered the Salvadoran Civil War. To one nationally syndicated magazine, returning to

El Salvador–style tactics should be repudiated, not encouraged.[5] Former journalists who covered the civil war saw eerie parallels between the proposed Iraqi units and the Salvadoran death squads, which operated largely with impunity in the civil war. As Christopher Dickey, a journalist from *Newsweek*, remarked, "When I hear talk of a Salvador Option, I can't help but think about *El Playón* . . . one of the killers' favorite dumping grounds. I've never forgotten the sick-sweet stench of carnal refuse there, the mutilated corpses half-devoured by mongrels and buzzards, the hollow eyes of a human skull peering up through the loose-piled rocks, the hair fallen away from the bone like a gruesome halo."[6]

When asked about the Salvadoran Option, Rumsfeld stopped short of categorically denying the plan's existence and refused to comment further.[7] Weeks after Rumsfeld's denial, investigative journalist Seymour Hersh published an essay in the *New Yorker* that contradicted his claims. According to the interviews conducted by Hersh, this policy had ramifications beyond Iraq. Several months before, President George W. Bush had authorized secret commando groups and Special Forces units to conduct covert operations in the Middle East. As an unidentified intelligence source informed Hersh, "The new rules will enable the Special Forces community to set up what it calls 'action teams' in the target countries overseas which can be used to find and eliminate terrorist organizations. Do you remember the right-wing execution squads in El Salvador? We founded them and we financed them. . . . The objective now is to recruit locals in any area we want. And we aren't going to tell Congress about it."[8]

Prior to the January 2005 meeting described above, the United States had arguably already implemented various aspects of the Salvadoran Option. As early as 2003, officials in Washington realized the need to do something drastic—and quickly. An unidentified neoconservative official explained how to tackle the problem to investigative journalist Robert Dreyfuss. "It's time for 'no more Mr. Nice Guy.' . . . All those people shouting 'Down with America' and dancing in the street when Americans are attacked? We have to kill them."[9] Beginning in May 2004, Washington initiated the creation of paramilitary forces to hunt down remnants of Saddam Hussein's regime and target Sunni insurgents.[10]

Journalists viewed the appointments of former officials involved in the various "dirty wars" in Latin America during the cold war as evidence that Washington had implemented the Salvadoran Option. They also viewed them as an ominous harbinger of dark times ahead. These individuals included Colonel James Steele, commander of the US MILGP in El Salvador (1984–1986) and Ambassador to Iraq John Negroponte. Both of these individuals had checkered pasts that included alleged support for death squads. In Steele's case, he had been involved in activities prohibited by US law.

Negroponte has been accused of covering up human rights violations committed by the Honduran military during his tenure as US ambassador to Honduras. As a 1995 article in the *Baltimore Sun* described, "Hundreds of [Honduran] citizens were kidnapped, tortured, and killed by a secret army unit trained and supported by the Central Intelligence Agency." That unit, Battalion 316, supposedly operated with his connivance. His predecessor in Honduras, Ambassador Jack R. Bins, claimed that Negroponte discouraged reporting abductions and other abuses to Washington. As Bins told the *New York Times*, his successor "tried to put a lid on reporting abuses" and "was untruthful to Congress about those activities."[11] The former ambassador has denied all of the accusations leveled against him. In 2004, Negroponte told the *Washington Post* these claims "were old hat" and snidely added, "I want to say to those people: Haven't you moved on?"[12]

In October 2003 Steven Casteel, a former DEA operative involved in the hunt for Colombian drug lord Pablo Escobar, arrived in Iraq as the senior adviser to the Iraqi minister of the interior. According to journalist Max Fuller, Casteel laid the foundation for the creation of Iraqi paramilitary units.[13] To oversee their training, Rumsfeld deployed Steele—as a civilian—to Iraq in 2003.[14] These paramilitary units played a prominent role in the US COIN strategy by acting as "force multipliers" and arresting, interrogating, and/or killing suspected insurgents. In the process they also created a climate of terror. One of the groups created by US advisers, the Special Police Commandos, headed by Adnan Thabit, carried out nighttime raids that generated terror among Iraqis.[15] From May 2004, Washington increasingly recognized the utility of these unconventional forces for destroying the insurgency.

Similar to those in El Salvador, the commando units either funded or trained by the US military advisers were accused of perpetrating human rights violations, political murders, and torture. Critics also accused the Iraqi Interior Ministry of allowing death squads to operate with the connivance of senior Iraqi officials.[16] According to an investigation launched by the British newspaper the *Guardian*, Colonel Steele and another American, Colonel James H. Coffman, trained and oversaw Iraqi units that conducted some of the worst acts of torture during the US occupation. Several eyewitnesses claimed that Steele and Coffman were either aware of or present during these violations.[17]

Counterinsurgency enthusiasts, especially General David Petraeus, also resurrected the US intervention in El Salvador in *FM 3-24*. Petraeus and like-minded officers hoped to change the way the military waged war and adopt a new approach toward combating the insurgency in Iraq. Within two months of its publication the manual had been downloaded approximately two million times and the University of Chicago Press published a subsequent edition. *FM 3-24* portrays the Salvadoran effort as a success that helped prevent a revolutionary victory. There is no mention of the complicity of US-trained forces in human rights abuses or the death and destruction spread by US policy. The text thus offers its readers a misleading and sanitized depiction of the conflict. Its authors, including Petraeus, were keen to minimize the use of violence and coercion in counterinsurgency to promote the manual to skeptical congressional representatives and the US public.

The United States reapplied the concept of elimination from its intervention in El Salvador. This should not have come as a surprise. Throughout the twentieth century, the US military established elite commando forces, including "hunter-killer" teams in the Philippines and the Phoenix Program in Vietnam. In both cases, these units targeted high-profile insurgents and either arrested and/or killed them. Human rights abuses, including torture and political assassinations, were common. Questions also remain regarding their overall effectiveness. In Vietnam, US intelligence officials and their South Vietnamese counterparts used the latest technology—they fed dossiers into an IBM-1401 computer—to compile lists of targets. As analysts accumulated more names, pressure mounted to achieve quotas. Programs such as Phoenix also served as models for the US program in El Salvador and the Salvadoran option in Iraq.

David Kilcullen, a prominent counterinsurgency enthusiast, recently reaffirmed the need for a "disaggregation strategy" resembling the "unfairly maligned (but highly effective) Vietnam-era Phoenix Program."[18] The US military has recently targeted high-level insurgent leaders in both Afghanistan and Iraq. Although this strategy has produced a massive body count, including Abu Musab al-Zarqawi, the insurgents have replenished their leadership. Quite often, the slain leader's successor has been more ruthless than his predecessor, including Abu Ayyub al-Masri.[19] In spite of General David Petraeus's musings about protecting civilians, current US COIN doctrine continues to, and probably always will, emphasize the necessity of killing. Instead of referring to the practice of elimination in these terms, military parlance uses sterile euphemisms such as "disaggregation" to obfuscate the emphasis on taking human lives.

Terror and violence remained an integral component of the war used by the Salvadoran security forces, the Treasury Police, the National Guard, and the Salvadoran military. One common thread linking the conflict to the various other guerrilla wars in Latin America is the prevalence of paramilitary units as well as official conventional soldiers combating revolution through terror. The intensity of violence was a result not simply of the ideology of the left or its supposed revolutionary extremism but also of the threat to traditional interests from various revolutionary movements in the hemisphere, including the FMLN.[20] In El Salvador, death squads and paramilitary units such as the ORDEN attempted to destroy insurgent networks and their sympathizers throughout the country. In addition to killing individuals, state-sponsored violence (or that committed by private groups sanctioned by the government) has also been aimed at instilling a climate of fear. The ultimate goal is to make citizens discontinue supporting or tolerating insurgents out of fear for their own personal safety or that of their family.

The brutal violence unleashed by the Salvadoran death squads and the government's security forces attempted to terrorize civilians and destroy the revolutionary challenge. Whereas these units were notorious human rights abusers, the Salvadoran military's strategies of indiscriminate aerial bombing against rebel areas and instituting large military sweeps accomplished the same feat in the Salvadoran *campo*, uprooting tens of thousands of *campesinos* and instilling an environment of fear. The terror unleashed during the late 1970s and early 1980s (including the vicious response after the 1981 Final Offensive) decimated the FMLN's urban networks. Under this policy of brutality, the government killed thousands of insurgents, members of their affiliated popular fronts, and/ or people sympathetic to their aims. Innocent civilians were also caught in the death squads' crosshairs as well. For the first several years of the Salvadoran Civil War, a maelstrom of murder and repression engulfed the country's urban population centers.

Neil Livingstone, a former consultant to Oliver North, unsuccessful candidate for governor of Montana in 2012, and "counterterrorism expert," claimed that "as many as half of the approximately 40,000 victims in the current conflict in El Salvador were killed by death squads. . . . In reality, death squads are an extremely effective tool, however odious, in combating revolutionary challenges."[21] RAND analyst Benjamin Schwartz also reached similar conclusions, noting that "U.S. military advisers and intelligence officers" who served in the conflict understood that the murder of thousands of people, not reform, prevented an FMLN victory.[22]

Paradoxically, FMLN members enjoyed their greatest success when death-squad violence and massacres were at their peak. Correspondingly, between 1980 and 1983 the insurgents were at the height of their power. The military's approach of *tierra arrasada* (scorched earth) strengthened the FMLN links with *campesinos* and caused considerable outrage among their sympathizers in the United States. Faced with congressional and public opposition, the Reagan administration in certain instances blatantly lied to Congress and the public to continue providing aid. This policy ultimately poisoned relations between the executive and legislative branches. Lastly, it enabled the rebels to fill their ranks with new recruits from among the victims' relatives and others who lost what little faith they had in the government's legitimacy.

Although killing the enemy is central to warfare, history provides examples of counterrevolutionary forces trying to out-terrorize the insurgents and losing or achieving only a stalemate. After rebels have established themselves as a legitimate force or made effective use of international forums as did the FLN in Algeria, it becomes extremely difficult for counterinsurgent forces simply to destroy their enemies through brute force and murder. Perhaps even more importantly, the likelihood is diminished that an infusion of token political reform and development will reverse their gains—or convince a skeptical population that its former abusers are now its friends—and result in a decisive victory.

Continued reliance on paramilitary forces represents an example of shortsighted policy making. Junior and senior policy makers are often under considerable pressure from their superiors and the US public to produce dramatic results in a remarkably short period. In such a demanding and tense environment, moral considerations and/or long-term ramifications are often secondary; what is more important is to produce results—fast. Jonah Goldberg, a journalist from the *National Review*, aptly summed up this line of reasoning. As Goldberg attested, "I have no principled problem with the U.S. doing whatever it can to capture and, preferably, kill the terrorists in Iraq. The El Salvador Option sounds like the Chicago way to me, and that's fine. If American-trained Kurds and Shia can do it better than the Americans, that's cool with me."[23]

Whether for economic, political, or even professional expediency (or because these units are believed effective), supporting clandestine forces that act with decisiveness and speed, but also with great brutality, is a hallmark of US third-world foreign policy and of its response to insurgency. Even though this policy may succeed in the short term, its reliance on such shadowy units typically produces more damaging long-term effects, including the development of a fractured civil society, an increasingly intractable opposition, and wide political polarization, none of which, of course, bodes well for establishing good governance. In Iraq, these schisms are the direct consequence of the US invasion and the Bush administration's disastrous policy making after the fall of Saddam Hussein.

As former vice president Cheney acknowledged, another similarity between El Salvador and Iraq was the practice of holding elections in the midst of a civil war. The United States also supported elections in Afghanistan, where several presidential elections (including the most recent in 2014) were marred by electoral fraud. Washington has repeatedly relied on this strategy to convince skeptical congressional representatives to continue funding the war effort, demonstrate that the United States is consolidating democracy and establishing a legitimate government, and demonize the nonvoters as illegitimate actors.

In several instances, such as the Salvadoran constituent elections in 1982 and Iraqi parliamentary elections in 2005, voter turnout was high. Insurgent threats to disrupt the elections and retaliate against civilians who voted were, for the most part, prevented. However, in El Salvador and Iraq, significant segments of the population refrained from voting. The Iraqi parliamentary elections to draft a new constitution in January 2005 featured a Sunni boycott and the rise of Shia political parties that were not only religious but allied with Iran.[24] Rather than uniting the country, the parliamentary elections of 2005 demonstrated the sectarian nature of Iraq and the deep political divides between the various religious and ethnic groups. Technically, today Iraq is a democracy that provides its citizens more opportunities for political expression than had existed under Saddam Hussein. None of the governments elected in subsequent years has created a legitimate and politically viable central government that can overcome sectarian distrust (or one sincerely committed to political reconciliation).

Unfortunately for Washington, in Afghanistan and Iraq voters have more recently elected candidates, such as Hamid Karzai and Nouri al-Maliki, who lack legitimacy or have failed to produce political reconciliation and stability. Former US ambassador to Afghanistan Karl Eikenberry, who opposed a US troop increase to bolster Karzai's government, registered his disapproval with the policy and his lack of faith in the Afghani president's leadership by infamously remarking in a leaked cable that Karzai was not "an adequate strategic partner."[25] As these governments entrenched themselves in power, US leverage over them diminished. In spite of billions of dollars' worth of US aid to these countries and US officials heralding them as paragons of democracy, neither government is closer to achieving political reconciliation or stability. In the case of Iraq, the Islamic State's (IS) gains not only caused substantial consternation over the implosion of Iraq but also forced President Barack Obama to deploy US advisers to Iraq and initiate air strikes against IS in Iraq and Syria.[26] As Secretary of Defense James Mattis recently acknowledged, US troops will remain in Iraq for "a while." Indeed, the Donald Trump administration appears to be increasing the number of US troops and potentially loosening their restrictions.

That US policy makers suggested El Salvador as a potential model for Iraq is curious. During the Salvadoran Civil War, the United States relied on a relatively small group of Special Forces soldiers and civilians; it did not deploy more than 100,000 combat troops to Central America or use a variety of private contractors, including the notorious security firm Blackwater. The main purpose was to avoid another costly imbroglio, a Vietnam in the Americas. Keeping a small footprint in Iraq was impossible, especially with the presence of hundreds of thousands of US soldiers and citizens and the construction of a massive fortified embassy—the largest and most expensive in the world. Using a conflict modeled on a limited number of advisers and a supposedly minimal US presence was also incompatible with the Bush administration's larger effort of remaking Iraq—and potentially the Middle East.

Reusing the same strategies and tactics from a conflict characterized by such human rights abuses and expecting them to be avoided in Iraq demonstrates wishful thinking at best, and a complete disregard for the ethical and moral dimensions of policy making at worst. Additionally, expecting a proud and nationalist country simply to do the bidding of Washington is indicative of cultural arrogance, ignorance, and a flawed historical understanding of Washington's previous experiences in El Salvador.

Using El Salvador as a model for Iraq is also flawed for a very important and ignored reason: the insurgency developed as a reaction to the US invasion and occupation. In El Salvador, Washington did not have to contend with managing an occupation or the presence of hundreds of thousands of foreigners. The Bush administration and its political appointees blundered early and often, including L. Paul Bremer's fateful decision to disband the Iraqi Army and the US military's aggressive policies of kicking down doors and humiliating the source of patriarchal authority, male heads of household. In El Salvador, the Reagan White House and Pentagon intervened to reform the Salvadoran state; although Washington was often viewed as the master pulling the strings, San Salvador could plausibly avoid the label of "made in the

USA." Murdering the Iraqi central government's enemies as part of the Salvadoran Option could not overcome the more important task: building a legitimate government. Constructing legitimacy, the raison d'être of COIN, was impossible with tens of thousands of foreign troops occupying Iraq. Their very presence ensured a continuation of insurgent violence toward the United States because of the perception of Baghdad as a puppet government.

The United States faced a far more favorable scenario in El Salvador than it did in Iraq. That US strategists reapplied their approach to El Salvador in Iraq is striking because of the discrepancies in population, territory size, and respective sociohistorical context and historical development. El Salvador's population in 1980 is typically estimated at approximately 4.6 million in a country the size of Massachusetts. In stark contrast, Iraq is almost three times as large as New York State, with a population of more than 33 million. Salvadoran forces could easily reach most destinations in El Salvador by helicopter within a few hours, and its dense population saturation made it a more ideal candidate for the population-centric COIN preferred by the US military.

Unlike in El Salvador, there are major religious fault lines in Iraq as well as complex tribal and clan hierarchies. These political and religious cleavages remain significant obstacles to developing a legitimate state in the Fertile Crescent. In contrast, Salvadoran culture, including its language and religion, was also more familiar to US operatives than that of Iraq or Vietnam. US advisers also viewed their counterparts in El Salvador more affectionately than they did their peers in Vietnam, including former veterans who served in both conflicts. Practically all of the Special Forces soldiers who served in El Salvador spoke Spanish, some fluently. Thus, US advisers and soldiers did not face an unfamiliar, alien culture, and in the view of some, an inferior and uncivilized one. Simply put, US military strategists confronted a far more complex situation in Iraq. If the United States could not succeed under such favorable conditions in El Salvador, it is little wonder the same policies have fared poorly in Afghanistan and Iraq.

It is beyond doubt that US aid and training affected the Salvadoran Civil War, but it was primarily from a military standpoint, not a political one. For former FMLN *comandantes*, the massive infusion of US funds and adoption of US tactics improved their enemy's effectiveness and fighting prowess. In particular, the BIRIs, PRALs, and helicopters caused considerable damage to the Salvadoran insurgents' military capabilities.[27] Nevertheless, there was divided opinion among former *comandantes* as to whether US aid prevented an FMLN victory. Even though there might be a lack of consensus on this issue, none believed that the US COIN effort ended the conflict.

Conversely, the socioeconomic reforms inspired or supported by San Salvador and/or Washington failed to alter El Salvador's inequitable economic and political system. The various programs enacted, including agrarian reform and elections, were meant to address the roots of the conflict. However, they had an even higher aim—establishing a moderate democracy in the heart of Central America. To cite one example, agrarian reform (promulgated by the first Salvadoran junta) did not circumscribe the power of the elites because its most important phase was cancelled out of fear its effects would be too far reaching. Essentially, this act ripped the guts out of agrarian reform because the program and organizations created to implement it lacked the capability to transform dramatically one of the most pressing issues in El Salvador, land ownership.

Overall, the various socioeconomic grievances that fueled discontent have not been satisfactorily resolved despite approximately twelve years of war, billions of dollars in US aid, and the establishment of peace. In El Salvador today, access to opportunity and wealth remains concentrated in the hands of the few—as it has historically. The economic measures enacted by the ARENA and the PDC with support from Washington, both during the war and after, have created more inequality. These disparities have important consequences, including a continuing exodus of Salvadorans to the United States, the economy's reliance on their remittances, and the rising number of young people involved in *las maras* (gangs, such as Mara Salvatrucha, MS-13, and Calle 18).

Gang-related violence has also plagued El Salvador since the termination of the conflict. The country's homicide rate continues to be among the highest in the region and the world.[28] Murder statistics in El Salvador dropped in 2012 after the country's two leading gangs signed a truce. According to observers, the central government brokered the deal; the details of the agreement remain a closely guarded secret. Two years later, the murder rate was again on the rise. In May 2014, the country recorded 356 murders compared with 174 for the same month of the previous year. In one weekend alone, a staggering 81 people lost their lives.[29] As the country's security situation deteriorates, the Salvadoran government's ability to provide essential services and address the conditions that make gang membership desirable or inevitable will become increasingly difficult. Thus, the state's inability to tackle these issues will arguably pave the way for the cycle of violence to continue.

From a political standpoint, the results are more ambiguous. The frequent elections held in the midst of the civil war have been heralded by Washington as a dramatic turning point in the conflict. The White House repeatedly claimed credit, insisting that US aid had allowed democracy to take root. However, none of the left-wing political parties participated in any of the elections, either out of fear for their lives or because they viewed them as illegitimate. Moreover, to ensure the election of its ally, the CIA funneled millions of dollars to its proxy to prevent the ARENA candidate from winning. Instead of US aid, the spread of democracy in El Salvador happened as the direct consequence of the FMLN war against the Salvadoran state. Even though it might have been prevented from overthrowing José Napoleón Duarte and Alfredo Cristiani, its efforts forced the state to allow *all* political parties to participate, not just those favored by Washington or its allies in San Salvador.

In the future it is very likely that an outbreak of insurgency will again threaten a US ally somewhere in the world. It is also entirely conceivable that US policy makers might once again turn to the US COIN intervention in El Salvador for solutions. As this book has demonstrated, the notion that El Salvador represents a "successful" model for pacifying insurgency rests on shaky ground. When Washington's efforts are viewed from a holistic perspective—and not from a short-term military vantage point—such claims are not only historically inaccurate but also wrong. Rather than being heralded as an exemplar of US nation-building, Washington's efforts in El Salvador should be viewed as an expensive effort that prolonged the conflict, led to the further devastation of the country, and failed to address the roots of the insurgency, which still reverberate in El Salvador today.

NOTES

INTRODUCTION

1. *Daily Show with John Stewart,* August 23, 2007. Comedy Central website, http://www.cc.com/episodes/loeu7m/the-daily-show-with-jon-stewart-august-23-2007-john-nagl-season-12-ep-12111.

2. William LeoGrande, *Our Own Backyard: The United States in Central America, 1977–1992* (Chapel Hill: University of North Carolina Press, 1998), 6.

3. Stephen Rabe, *The Killing Zone: The United States Wages Cold War in Latin America* (New York: Oxford University Press, 2011), xxx.

4. John Caldwell, memorandum, March 28, 1972, Record Group 286, Records of AID, Office of Public Safety, Latin American Branch Country File, El Salvador 1956–1972, Box 59, IPS 1-2/CASP/El Salvador, National Archives and Records Administration (NARA), College Park, Maryland.

5. Some of the notable exceptions are Alan McPherson, *The Invaded: How Latin Americans and Their Allies Fought and Ended U.S. Occupations* (Oxford, UK: Oxford University Press, 2014); Jeremy Kuzmarov, *Modernizing Repression: Police Training and Nation-Building in the American Century* (Amherst: University of Massachusetts Press, 2012); Martha Huggins, *Political Policing: The United States and Latin America* (Durham, NC: Duke University Press, 1998); J. Patrice McSherry, *Predatory States: Operation Condor and Covert War in Latin America* (Lanham, MD: Rowman and Littlefield, 2005); and Greg Grandin and G. M. Joseph, eds., *A Century of Revolution: Insurgent and Counterinsurgent Violence during Latin America's Long Cold War* (Durham, NC: Duke University Press, 2010).

6. Mark Peceny and William D. Stanley, "Counterinsurgency in El Salvador," *Politics and Society* 38, no. 1 (2010): 38–67; Tommy Sue Montgomery, "Fighting Guerrillas: The United States and Low-Intensity Conflict in El Salvador," *New Political Science* 9, no. 1 (Fall–Winter 1990): 21–53; Benjamin Schwartz, *American Counterinsurgency Doctrine and El Salvador: The Frustrations of Reform and the Illusions of Nation Building* (Santa Monica, CA: RAND, 1991); Andrew Bacevich, *American Military Policy in Small Wars: The Case of El Salvador* (Cambridge, UK: Pergamon Brassey's, 1988); Richard Alan White, *The Morass: United States' Intervention in Central America* (New York: Harper and Row, 1984); Michael McClintock, *The American Connection*, vol. 1 (London: Zed, 1985).

7. Kalev Sepp, "Best Practices in Counterinsurgency," *Military Review* (May–June 2005): 8–12.

8. H. Hayden, "Revolutionary Warfare: El Salvador and Vietnam—a Comparison," *Marine Corps Gazette* (July 1991): 50–54; Victor M. Rosello, "Lessons from El Salvador," *Parameters* (Winter 1993–1994): 100–108; Alfred Valenzuela

and Victor Rosello, "Expanding Roles and Missions in the War on Drugs and Terrorism: El Salvador and Colombia," *Military Review* (March–April 2004): 28–35.

9. Richard W. Stewart, gen. ed., *American Military History,* vol. 2: *The United States Army in a Global Era, 1917–2003* (Washington, DC: US Army Center of Military History, 2009), 393–395.

10. Greg Grandin, *Empire's Workshop: Latin America, the United States, and the Rise of the New Imperialism* (New York: Metropolitan, 2006), 108.

11. James Hallums, email interview with author, March 5, 2013.

12. David E. Spencer argues that without external aid, especially from Nicaragua, the Salvadoran insurgents could not have continued the war. David E. Spencer, "External Resource Mobilization and Successful Insurgency in Cuba, Nicaragua, and El Salvador, 1959–1992" (PhD diss., George Washington University, 2002). Andrea Oñate emphasizes the importance of Cuban support for the FMLN. See Oñate, "The Red Affair: FMLN-Cuban Relations during the Salvadoran Civil War, 1981–1992," *Cold War History* 11, no. 2 (May 2011): 133–154. Americans and Europeans who traveled with the FMLN dispute such claims, arguing that most of their weapons were derived from the Salvadoran military and often reflected on the poor state of their military preparedness. Charles Clements, *Witness to War: An American Doctor in El Salvador* (Toronto, ON: Bantam, 1984); Wendy Shaull, *Tortillas, Beans, and M16s: Behind the Lines in El Salvador* (London: Pluto, 1990); Philippe Borgois, "What U.S. Foreign Policy Faces in El Salvador," *Monthly Review* 39, no. 1 (May 1982). Some Salvadoran insurgents also dispute the importance of external support.

13. Wilson Center Digital Archive, "Ordnance: Chronology of Historical Events," vol. 2 (Hanoi, South Vietnam: People's Army Publishing House, 1999). Translated for the Cold War International History Project by Merle Pribbenow, http://www.quansuvn.net/index.php?topic=4117.0; http://digitalarchive.wilsoncenter.org/document/110535.

14. Ted Galen Carpenter, *The Fire Next Door: Mexico's Drug Violence and the Danger to America* (Washington, DC: CATO Institute, 2012).

15. Jonathan Brown, "To Make the Revolution: Solidarity and Divisions among Latin American Guerrillas in the 1960s," *Asian Journal of Latin American Studies* 28, no. 1 (2015): 1–25.

16. Cynthia McClintock, *Revolutionary Movements in Latin America: El Salvador's FMLN and Peru's Shining Path* (Washington, DC: US Institute of Peace Press, 1998), 245.

17. Joint Chiefs of Staff, "Department of Defense Dictionary of Military and Associated Terms, Joint Publication 1-02," http://www.dtic.mil/doctrine/new_pubs/jp1_02.pdf.

18. David Kilcullen, "Counter-insurgency Redux," *Survival: Global Politics and Strategy* 48, no. 4 (Winter 2006): 111–130, 2.

19. Ibid.

20. This definition is an amalgamation of several different definitions, including those of Scott Moore and David Kilcullen. See Scott Moore, "The Basics of Counterinsurgency" (Washington, DC: US Joint Forces Command, J9, Joint Urban Operations Office, n.d.), 14; Kilcullen, "Counter-insurgency Redux."

21. One notable exception was Plan Colombia, initiated under President Bill Clinton. This initiative aimed at combating the drug war and guerrilla organizations in Colombia through diplomatic and military measures. However, it appears that the vast majority of funds were devoted to the latter. Over the course of a decade, the United States spent approximately $8 billion. More recently, supporters of Plan Colombia have argued that Washington should replicate the program in Central America to address the region's pressing immigration and security issues. For example, see Luis Alberto Moreno, "Plan Colombia Worked. Why Not Try Something Similar in Central America?" *Miami Herald,* August 11, 2014; Daniel Runde, "Addressing the U.S. Border Emergency: Building a 'Plan Colombia' for Central America," Center for Strategic and International Studies website, August 8, 2014, http://csis.org/publication/ad dressing-us-border-emergency-building-plan-colombia-central-america. Two US military officers also recommended exporting the Salvadoran experience to Colombia, primarily through the deployment of small military training teams. See Alfred Valenzuela and Victor Rosello, "Expanding Roles and Missions in the War on Drugs and Terrorism: El Salvador and Colombia," *Military Review* (March–April 2004): 28–35.

1. HISTORICAL ANTECEDENTS

1. Journalist Thomas Ricks, critical of the US effort in Iraq prior to "the Surge," wrote a fawning piece profiling several of the theorists behind the most recent manifestation of COIN. In particular, he lauds the efforts of David Petraeus, the subject of his second book on the Iraq War. See "The COINdinistas," *Foreign Policy* (December 2009).

2. Most of the information gleaned from decades of counterinsurgency and occupation was codified in the *Small Wars Manual,* produced by the US Marines in 1940. Its publication, a year before US entry into World War II, was soon forgotten. COINdinistas have bemoaned its lack of publicity and influence on military doctrine. Authors such as Max Boot have implied that if the United States had dusted off its cover and applied the various strategies contained within its pages, the United States would not have suffered defeat in Vietnam—not only a counterfactual but also a dubious proposition. See Boot, *The Savage Wars of Peace: Small Wars and the Rise of American Power* (New York: Basic Books, 2003); US Marine Corps, *Small Wars Manual* (Washington, DC: US Government Printing Office, 1940).

3. Walter L. Williams, "United States Indian Policy and the Debate over the Philippine Annexation: Implications for the Origins of American Imperialism," *Journal of American History* 66, no. 4 (March 1980): 810.

4. Many of these officers served in the Civil War as well. Boot, *Savage Wars of Peace*, 127.

5. *General Orders 100: The Lieber Code*, art. 82, Avalon Law Project, http://www.avalon.law.yale.edu/19th_century/lieber.asp.

6. Ibid.

7. Stanley Karnow, *In Our Image: America's Empire in the Philippines* (London: Century, 1990), 173.

8. Michael Hunt and Steve Levine, *Arc of Empire: America's Wars in Asia from the Philippines to Vietnam* (Chapel Hill: University of North Carolina Press, 2012), 43.

9. Aguinaldo did not seek to win a decisive victory. Rather, conscious that many Americans were opposed to the acquisition of the Philippines, Aguinaldo sought to undermine the US will to fight. Andrew Birtle, *U.S. Army Counterinsurgency and Contingency Operations Doctrine, 1860–1941* (Washington, DC: US Army Center of Military History, 1998), 112; Boot, *Savage Wars of Peace*, 112; Karnow, *In Our Image*, 177.

10. Richard E. Welch, "American Atrocities in the Philippines: The Indictment and the Response," *Pacific Historical Review* 43, no. 2 (May 1974): 237–238.

11. Ibid., 241.

12. The US Army did not launch any significant concentration campaigns until after the US presidential election of 1900. The issue was so sensitive that when a large-scale center plan was proposed, the leader of the US forces told his subordinate to "hand it to the Secretary to read and then destroy it. I don't care to place on file in the Department any paper of the kind, which would be evidence of what may be considered in the United States as harsh measures of treatment of the people." Birtle, *U.S. Army Counterinsurgency and Contingency Operations Doctrine, 1860–1941*, 131.

13. Quoted in Glenn May, "A Filipino Resistance to American Occupation: Batangas, 1899–1902," *Pacific Historical Review* 48, no. 4 (November 1979): 550.

14. Brian McAllister Linn, *The U.S. Army and Counterinsurgency in the Philippine War, 1899–1902* (Chapel Hill: University of North Carolina Press, 1989), 155.

15. Boot, *Savage Wars of Peace*, 124.

16. Theodore Roosevelt, "Proclamation 483: Granting Pardon and Amnesty to Participants in Insurrection in the Philippines," July 4, 1902, American Presidency Project, http://www.presidency.ucsb.edu/ws/index.php?pid=69569.

17. Karnow, *In Our Image*, 195.

18. Mary A. Renda, *Taking Haiti: Military Occupation and the Culture of U.S. Imperialism, 1915–1940* (Chapel Hill: University of North Carolina Press, 2001). Renda offers a vivid description of the program and the resistance it engendered.

19. Walter LaFeber, *Inevitable Revolutions: The United States and Central America* (New York: Norton, 1993), 67.

20. Richard Millet, *Searching for Stability: The U.S. Development of Constabulary*

Forces in Latin America and the Philippines (Fort Leavenworth, KS: Combat Studies Institute, 2010). Two of the more notorious examples were Rafael Trujillo in the Dominican Republic and Anastasio Somoza García in Nicaragua.

21. Kyle Longley, *In the Eagle's Shadow: The United States and Latin America* (Wheeling, IL: Harlan Davidson, 2009), 161.

22. Michael J. Schroeder, "The Sandino Rebellion Revisited: Civil War, Imperialism, Popular Nationalism, and State Formation Muddied Up Together in the Segovias of Nicaragua, 1926–1934," in *Close Encounters of Empire: Writing the Cultural History of U.S.–Latin American Relations,* ed. Gilbert Joseph, Catherine LeGrand, and Ricardo Salvatore (Durham, NC: Duke University Press, 1998), 210.

23. See David C. Brooks, "U.S. Marines, Miskitos, and the Hunt for Sandino: The Río Coco Patrol in 1928," *Journal of Latin American Studies* 21, no. 2 (May 1989): 314. Brooks also notes that this strategy often has serious consequences for such groups, especially if they are losers.

24. Describing one aerial raid, Major Ross "Rusty" Rowell noted that the Nicaraguans "threw away their rifles, jumped over fences, and raced wildly through the streets. . . . I never saw such a wild rout, and probably never will again." Quoted in Boot, *Savage Wars of Peace,* 238.

25. Michael J. Schroeder, "Social Memory and Tactical Doctrine: The Air War in Nicaragua during the Sandino Rebellion, 1927–1932," *International History Review* 29, no. 3 (September 2007): 512.

26. Max Boot disagrees with this assertion, arguing that several veterans of Nicaragua later served with distinction in the war against Japan, including Lewis "Chesty" Puller, Herman Hanneken, and "Red Mike" Edson. According to Boot, these marines gained invaluable experiences participating in small-unit operations, jungle fighting, and close air support. He even makes the preposterous claim, "It might be said with equal justice that the Pacific campaign in World War II was won in the jungles of Nicaragua." Boot, *Savage Wars of Peace,* 252.

27. John J. Tierney, *Chasing Ghosts: Unconventional Warfare in American History* (Washington, DC: Potomac, 2006), 201–202.

28. Leslie Bethell, ed., *The Cambridge History of Latin America,* vol. 7: *1930 to the Present* (Cambridge, UK: Cambridge University Press, 1990), 326.

29. Longley, *In the Eagle's Shadow,* 167.

30. Birtle, *U.S. Army Counterinsurgency and Contingency Operations Doctrine, 1860–1941,* 246.

31. There were differences and similarities between the two US interventions. First, unlike the previous revolt in the Philippines, the Huk Rebellion was mostly confined to the island of Luzon, including the central and southern regions. More significantly, the United States did not deploy troops to the country, nor did it actively control the country. At the time of the second US counterinsurgency effort, the Philippines was not a US colony. However, similarly, the

Huks operated in remote areas—in the jungles, mountains, and inaccessible terrain.

32. A series of prewar groups that had fought the Japanese and their collaborators during World War II coalesced around communist front organization the Hukbalahaps (Huks) after fraudulent elections and repression pushed them into revolt. The Huks pursued a two-stage strategy: first, a terror campaign against supporters of the government designed to demonstrate the inability of the government to protect its citizens, and aggressive indoctrination of the peasants to sow dissatisfaction with the US-supported regime and shift their allegiance to the Huks. Matthew Phares, "Combating Insurgency: Can Lessons from the Huk Rebellion Apply to Iraq?" (master's thesis, US Marine Corps Command and Staff College, 2008), 6.

33. Within the COIN literature, an important requirement for a successful counterinsurgency effort is leadership. According to studies of the conflict, Magsaysay was a credible leader. For an example of the importance of leadership in COIN, see Mark Moyar, *A Question of Command: Counterinsurgency from the Civil War to Iraq* (New Haven, CT: Yale University Press, 2009).

34. Some of the measures US advisers argued were necessary were changing the conventional focus of the Filipino Army, improving troop discipline, outlawing the Communist Party, and suspending habeas corpus for insurgents. Andrew Birtle, *U.S. Army Counterinsurgency and Contingency Operations Doctrine, 1942–1976* (Washington: US Army Center of Military History, 2003), 61–62. The US advisory group also deployed US officers versed in "guerrilla and anti-guerrilla operations and particularly involving Communist-led forces." Michael McClintock, *Instruments of Statecraft: U.S. Guerrilla Warfare, Counterinsurgency, and Counter-Terrorism, 1940–1990* (New York: Pantheon, 1992), 106.

35. He also established means for citizens to address their grievances to him and established committees to hear civilians' complaints.

36. Jonathan Nashel, *Edward Lansdale's Cold War: Culture, Politics, and the Cold War* (Amherst: University of Massachusetts Press, 2005), 29.

37. Quoted in McClintock, *Instruments of Statecraft*, 110.

38. Birtle, *U.S. Army Counterinsurgency and Contingency Operations Doctrine, 1942–1976*, 64.

39. McClintock, *Instruments of Statecraft*, 113.

40. Daniel Immerwahr, *Thinking Small: The United States and the Lure of Community Development* (Cambridge, MA: Harvard University Press, 2015), 109.

41. Some authors have argued that EDCOR was successful because it eroded the peasants' support for the Huks. For an example of this argument, see Napoleon Valeriano, *Counter-Guerrilla Operations: The Philippine Experience* (New York: Praeger, 1962), Introduction by Kalev Sepp. The Central Intelligence Agency (CIA) also supported this reasoning, stating that some four hundred people were resettled. CIA, "Reintegration of Insurgents into National Life," December 20, 1965, CIA Freedom of Information Act Reading Room, https://www

.cia.gov/library/readingroom/docs/CIA-RDP80B01676R002900100013-8
.pdf. As another writer noted, "The lesson to be derived is in the effect the
program had on the population and in the consequent loss of support suffered
by the insurgents. This success was realized largely because the people began
to trust the government to deliver on its promise and to question the overall
message of the insurgency and its leadership." Quoted in Phares, "Combating
Insurgency," 17. On the negative side, the program failed to meet demands or
expectations. Simply put, it was more of a propaganda tool than a meaningful
experiment in land reform. As the conflict continued, fewer and fewer families
were settled. Birtle, *U.S. Army Counterinsurgency and Contingency Operations Doctrine, 1942–1976*, 65; as one official involved with the US COIN effort
noted, "As a resettlement program, EDCOR did not accomplish a great deal.
I doubt if more than perhaps 300 families of Huks were resettled under that
program. But I will guarantee you that at least 3,000 Huks surrendered." See
McClintock, *Instruments of Statecraft*, 114.

42. McClintock, *Instruments of Statecraft*, 112.
43. Arguably the most successful item was the "Eye" leaflet, a picture with a large
   eye staring intently at its observers. Lawrence M. Greenberg, *The Hukbalahap
   Insurrection: A Case Study of a Successful Anti-Insurgency Operation in the
   Philippines, 1946–1955* (Washington, DC: US Army Center of Military History, 1987), 117–118.
44. Sometimes, rehabilitated Huks served in these units. They provided government forces intelligence, information about insurgent strategy, and locations of
   guerrilla bases. Ibid., 71; McClintock, *Instruments of Statecraft*, 119.
45. Valeriano, *Counter-Guerrilla Operations*, 79.
46. Quoted in McClintock, *Instruments of Statecraft*, 121.
47. Valeriano, *Counter-Guerrilla Operations*, 79.
48. Ibid., 79–80.
49. McClintock, *Instruments of Statecraft*, 120.
50. Birtle, *U.S. Army Counterinsurgency and Contingency Operations Doctrine,
   1942–1976*, 64; Greenberg, *Hukbalahap Insurrection*, 144. Greenberg, however, also notes that US indifference and shortsighted policies helped put the
   Philippine government in jeopardy from 1945 to 1950. Other important elements were that the Huks did not have cross-border sanctuaries and there was
   no large-scale aid from either China or the Soviet Union. Their decision to create a supply network based in Manila was also foolhardy and led to the arrest
   of senior leaders by an informant. Karnow, *In Our Image*, 352.
51. Magsaysay pursued a policy that not only beat back the insurgents but also
   reincorporated them into the body politic. He did so both because the structure
   of the government made it possible and because the nature of the insurgency
   required it. D. Michael Shafer, *Deadly Paradigms: The Failure of U.S. Counterinsurgency Policy* (Princeton, NJ: Princeton University Press, 1988), 239. David
   Fitzgerald also concurs, noting that the success was the result of a "confluence
   of luck and skill that would not easily be replicated." Fitzgerald, "Learning

to Forget? The US Army and Counterinsurgency Doctrine and Practice from Vietnam to Iraq" (PhD diss., University College Cork, June 2010), 11.

52. Andrew Mumford, *Puncturing the Counterinsurgency Myth: Britain and Irregular Warfare in the Past, Present, and Future* (Carlisle, PA: Strategic Studies Institute, 2011), 15.

53. David French, in his study of ten COIN operations in which the British participated, notes that coercion was a prominent feature of British COIN policy to sever the link between the insurgents and civilians. In Malaya and other theaters of conflict, British conduct was not governed by its manuals but by locally enacted emergency regulations. These not only defined when police could use lethal force but also allowed them wide discretion as to when to apply it. French also notes that although the amount of violence employed by the British was less than that of other colonial powers, it should not be underestimated. French, "Nasty Not Nice: British Counterinsurgency Doctrine and Practice, 1945–1967," *Small Wars and Insurgencies* 23 (October–December 2012): 751.

54. David French, *The British Way in Counterinsurgency, 1945–1967* (Oxford, UK: Oxford University Press, 2011),

55. Thomas Rid, "The Nineteenth-Century Origins of Counterinsurgency Doctrine," *Journal of Strategic Studies* 33, no. 5 (October 2010): 750. Rid argues that much of the theory behind contemporary COIN doctrine reflects French strategy during the nineteenth century. David Galula, a heavily cited French author in recent COIN strategy, is the joint that connects the nineteenth century to the twenty-first century. David Fitzgerald also concurs with Rid's overall argument, noting that the French strategy of a combined politico-military approach, in which soldiers would be administrators and educators as well as police, is reflected in the *Small Wars Manual.* Fitzgerald, "Learning to Forget," 6.

56. Robert Thompson, *Defeating Communist Insurgency: Experiences from Malaya and Vietnam* (London: Chatto and Windus, 1966), 51–60.

57. John Nagl's study compares the British operation in Malaya with the US experience in Vietnam. He argues that the British had a more flexible military organization that allowed them to react to threats and change their tactics accordingly. Nagl, *Counterinsurgency Lessons from Malaya and Vietnam.*

58. Mumford, *Puncturing the Counterinsurgency Myth,* 15.

59. Bernard B. Fall, *The Two Viet-Nams: A Political and Military Analysis* (New York: Praeger, 1967). Another author agreed with Fall's analysis but also noted that the operational environments were dissimilar. Unlike in the South Vietnamese Mekong Delta, the jungles of Malaya did not provide nearly as much food or sustenance. See Milton E. Osborne, *Strategic Hamlets in South Viet-Nam: A Survey and Comparison* (Ithaca, NY: Cornell University Press, 1965).

60. The most recent US COIN field manual states that the "Malaya insurgency provides lessons applicable to combating any insurgency." See *FM 3-24.* Anthony James Joe has identified seven traits of British COIN that has enabled

it to be successful: (1) Employ conventional military force sparingly and selectively, (2) Emphasize the central role of police and civil administration in COIN, (3) Establish close cooperation among the military, police, and civil government, especially in regard to sharing intelligence, (4) Regroup exposed civilian settlements into secure areas, (5) Deny the guerrillas a reliable supply of food, (6) Harass the guerrillas with a small, flexible force, and (7) Identify and ameliorate major socioeconomic irritants. Joe, *Resisting Rebellion: The History and Politics of Counterinsurgency* (Lexington: University Press of Kentucky, 2004).

61. Douglas Porch, "The Dangerous Myths and Dubious Promise of COIN," *Small Wars and Insurgencies* 22, no. 2 (May 2011): 247.

62. British COIN is also similar to existing French and Portuguese doctrines, including the oil-spot strategy, in coercing locals and securing the population. It is inaccurate to present a sharp dichotomy between British strategy of winning "hearts and minds" and French and Portuguese tactics based on "terror and coercion." See Bruno C. Reis, "The Myth of British Minimum Force in Counterinsurgency Campaigns during Decolonisation, 1945–1970," *Journal of Strategic Studies* 34, no. 2 (April 2011): 272.

63. This quotation is derived from the title of David French's article, "Nasty Not Nice: British Counterinsurgency Doctrine and Practice."

64. The British experience in Kenya trying to quell the Mau Mau Rebellion was marked by atrocities. Two of the more commonly cited texts are David Anderson, *Histories of the Hanged: Britain's Dirty War in Kenya and the End of Empire* (London: Weidenfield and Nicolson, 2005) and Caroline Elkins, *Britain's Gulag: The Brutal End of Empire in Kenya* (London: Jonathan Cape, 2005). Elkins's study, however, especially her statistics regarding the numbers of deaths, has been highly criticized, as was another book written by Daniel Goldhagen, *Worse Than War: Genocide, Eliminationism, and the Ongoing Assault on Humanity* (New York: PublicAffairs, 2009). For a variety of criticisms, see David Elstein, "Daniel Goldhagen and Kenya: Recycling Fantasy," *Open Democracy,* April 7, 2011, http://www.opendemocracy.net/david-elstein/daniel-goldhagen-and-kenya-recycling-fantasy.

65. In Kenya, the number of those held in detention without trial was 4,575 per 100,000 of a "target" population. In Malaya, the number was 405, and in French Algeria, 750.

66. Wade Markel, "Draining the Swamp: The British Strategy of Population Control," *Parameters* (Spring 2006): 36.

67. Douglas Porch, *Counterinsurgency: Exposing the Myths of the New Way of War* (Cambridge, UK: Cambridge University Press, 2013), 260.

68. One of the notable exceptions is Daniel Branch, *Defeating Mau Mau, Creating Kenya: Counterinsurgency, Civil War, and Decolonization* (New York: Cambridge University Press, 2009). Branch claims that almost as many Ken-

yans fought with the British as against them. In contrast to other authors, Branch relies more heavily on interviews with loyalists (supporters of the British) than with those who supported the Mau Mau. Huw Bennett's recent work discusses the role of indiscriminate violence and dismisses the notion that the British military focused on winning the affections of Kenyan civilians. See Bennett, *Fighting the Mau Mau: The British Army and Counter-Insurgency in the Kenya Emergency* (Cambridge, UK: Cambridge University Press, 2013).

69. Jeet Heer, "Counterpunch Revisionists Argue That Counterinsurgency Won the Battle against Guerrillas in Vietnam, but Lost the War. Can I Do Better in Iraq?" *Boston Globe*, January 4, 2004.

70. One military analyst has complained about the amount of attention French COIN doctrine received in *FM 3-24*. As the critic noted, "We should study the insurgent war in Algeria, but when it comes to including lessons drawn from it in our (read US) counterinsurgency doctrine—if the choice of lessons to include is so thin, and the best lessons overlooked—we might do better to just to leave it out altogether." Geoff Demarest, "Let's Take the French Experience in Algeria out of US Counterinsurgency Doctrine," *Military Review* (July–August 2010): 23.

71. *Regroupment* was carried out in three stages: first, remove civilians from vulnerable locations to well-defended positions; second, indoctrinate the villagers to establish a degree of self-administration and the active participation of the community in its own defense; and last, after political and military indoctrination have been completed, have the villagers assume the role of self-defense. Peter Paret, *French Revolutionary Warfare from Indochina to Algeria: The Analysis of a Political and Military Doctrine* (New York: Praeger, 1964), 43–44.

72. Jason Norton, "The French-Algerian War and *FM 3-24*: Counterinsurgency—a Comparison" (master's thesis, US Army Command and General Staff College, 2007), 45.

73. David Galula, *Pacification in Algeria, 1956–1958* (Santa Monica: RAND, 2006), xx. Roger Trinquier concurs because they also could be used to identify political preferences. See Trinquier, *Modern Warfare: A French View of Counterinsurgency* (New York: Praeger, 1964), 35. A recently leaked US Special Forces manual also discusses the benefits of the census during cordon-and-search operations and during the second phase of "consolidation operations," which correspond to the "hold" phase of current US COIN doctrine. US Army, *FM 31-20-3: Foreign Internal Defense Tactics, Techniques, and Procedures for Special Forces* (Washington, DC: US Army, 1994).

74. Lou DiMarco, "Losing the Moral Compass: Torture and Guerre Révolutionnaire in the Algerian War," *Parameters* 36, no. 2 (Summer 2006): 68.

75. Paret, *French Revolutionary Warfare from Indochina to Algeria*, 51.

76. Philippe Francois, "Waging Counterinsurgency in Algeria: A French Point of View," *Military Review* (September–October 2008): 7.

77. Matthew Connelly, *A Diplomatic Revolution: Algeria's Fight for Independence and the Origins of the Post–Cold War Era* (Oxford: Oxford University Press, 2002), 4.

78. Alistair Horne, *A Savage War of Peace: Algeria, 1954–1962* (New York: New York Review of Books, 2006), 135.

79. Paul Aussaresses, *The Battle of the Casbah: Terrorism and Counter-Terrorism in Algeria, 1955–1957* (New York: Enigma, 2002). The author, a former intelligence officer who served during the conflict, argued not only that torture was effective and justified but that if faced with the same situation again, he would not hesitate to use the same tactics again.

80. Henry Butterfield Ryan, *The Fall of Che Guevara: A Story of Soldiers, Spies, and Diplomats* (New York: Oxford University Press, 1998), 97.

81. James Siekmeier, *The Bolivian Revolution and the United States, 1952 to the Present* (University Park: Pennsylvania State University Press, 2011), 117.

82. Ibid., 111.

83. Ryan, *Fall of Che Guevara*, 43.

84. Nancy Tucker, "Vietnam, the Never-Ending War," in *The Vietnam War as History*, ed. Elizabeth Errington and B. J. C. McKercher (New York: Praeger, 1990).

85. There are several contours to this debate, but the major dispute within the counterinsurgency literature breaks down into a dichotomy between conventional strategists and counterinsurgents. Harry G. Summers's book *On Strategy*, an excellent example of the former, fired the first salvo with its publication. Summers believed that the Viet Cong guerrillas were a mere sideshow in the war; what was really important was to go after the main nerve center: Hanoi. Summers, *On Strategy: A Critical Analysis of the Vietnam War* (Novato, CA: Presidio, 1982). Recently, numerous authors have suggested that the United States lost in Vietnam because it did not adopt an adequate COIN strategy soon enough. Some of these authors include Boot, *Small Wars;* Lewis Sorley, *A Better War: The Unexamined Victories and Final Tragedy of America's Last Years in Vietnam* (New York: Harcourt, Brace, 1999); Nagl, *Counterinsurgency Lessons from Malaya and Vietnam;* and Andrew F. Krepinevich, *The Army and Vietnam* (Baltimore, MD: Johns Hopkins University Press, 1988). Krepinevich's work places the blame for failure on the shoulders of General William Westmoreland, who mistakenly continued to pursue conventional tactics in the face of the more important threat emanating from the guerrillas. However, many authors have contested this idea as well, noting that the problems with pacification were much deeper and that General Westmoreland, US commander in Vietnam, was justified in pursuing a conventional strategy: Dale Andradé, "Westmoreland Was Right: Learning the Wrong Lessons from the Vietnam War," *Small Wars and Insurgencies* 19, no. 2 (2008): 145–181; Birtle, *US Army Counterinsurgency and Contingency Operations Doctrine, 1942–1976;* Richard Hunt, *Pacification: The American Struggle for Vietnam's*

Hearts and Minds (Boulder, CO: Westview, 1995); Jeffrey Race, *War Comes to Long An: Revolutionary Conflict in a Vietnam Province* (Berkeley: University of California Press, 1972).

86. Willard Foster Barber and C. Neale Ronning, *Internal Security and Military Power: Counterinsurgency and Civic Action in Latin America* (Columbus: Ohio State University Press, 1966), 77–78.

87. Dale Andradé, *Ashes to Ashes: The Phoenix Program and the Vietnam War* (Lexington, KY: Lexington, 1990), 35.

88. The Agrovilles were launched without notifying the United States and were based on French strategic thinking. Joseph Zasloff, *Rural Resettlement in Vietnam: An Agroville in Development* (Lansing: Michigan State University Press, 1961); Hunt, *Pacification*, 20–21; Birtle, *U.S. Army Counterinsurgency and Contingency Operations Doctrine, 1942–1976*, 319.

89. John Prados, *Vietnam: The History of an Unwinnable War, 1945–1975* (Lawrence: University Press of Kansas, 2009), 69.

90. As one contemporary observer noted, "Many of the problems which later plagued the Strategic Hamlets were experienced during the development of the Agrovilles." Osborne, *Strategic Hamlets in South Viet-Nam*, 23.

91. Robert Thompson believed that the Strategic Hamlets were implemented too hastily, the program lacked strategic direction, the villages were overextended, and the government did not establish secure base areas where it could begin expanding the settlements. Thompson, *Defeating Communist Insurgency*, 138.

92. Race, *War Comes to Long An*, 133.

93. Hannah Gurman, "Vietnam: Uprooting Revolution—Counterinsurgency in Vietnam," in *Hearts and Minds: A People's History of Counterinsurgency*, ed. Hannah Gurman (New York: New Press, 2013), 86.

94. US Army, *FM 31-20-3*.

95. Dale Andradé and James H. Willbanks, "CORDS/Phoenix: Counterinsurgency Lessons from Vietnam for the Future," *Military Review Special Edition: Counterinsurgency Reader* (October 2006): 85.

96. Its detractors have viewed it as a massive assassination program and instrument of torture. Douglas Valentine, *The Phoenix Program* (New York: William Morrow, 1990). Phoenix has its defenders, such as Mark Moyar, who argue that depictions such as Valentine's are mistaken. See *Phoenix and the Birds of Prey: Counterinsurgency and Counterterrorism in Vietnam* (Annapolis, MD: Naval Institute Press, 1997). Dale Andradé has claimed the program decimated the VCI leadership by using a quotation from General Tran Do, communist deputy commander in the South, who admitted that Phoenix was "extremely destructive." Andradé, *Ashes to Ashes*, 279.

97. William Rosenau and Austin Long, *The Phoenix Program and Contemporary Counterinsurgency* (Santa Monica, CA: RAND, 2009), vii.

98. Fitzgerald, "Learning to Forget," 3.

99. Social scientists have debated what ultimately prompts people to take up arms

against the state. There are several theories including that clandestine revolutionary parties foment revolution, certain structurally weak governments are susceptible to revolution, and a lack of political space leaves revolution the only apparent outlet for change. Two of the leading works are Timothy P. Wickham-Crowley, *Guerrillas and Revolution in Latin America: A Comparative Study of Insurgents and Regimes since 1956* (Princeton, NJ: Princeton University Press, 1992) and Theda Skocpol, *States and Social Revolutions: A Comparative Analysis of France, Russia, and China* (New York: Cambridge University Press, 1979).

100. David H. Price, *Weaponizing Anthropology: Social Science in Service of the Militarized State* (Oakland, CA: Counterpunch and AK Press, 2011).

101. William R. Polk, *Violent Politics: A History of Insurgency, Terrorism, and Guerrilla War, from the American Revolution to Iraq* (New York: HarperCollins, 2007), 187.

102. Gian Gentile, *Wrong Turn: America's Deadly Embrace of Counterinsurgency* (New York: New Press, 2013), 8.

103. Bard E. O'Neill has argued that if a country has porous borders or neighbors sympathetic to the insurgents' cause, it will make defeating the insurgency much more difficult. See O'Neill, *Insurgency and Terrorism: From Revolution to Apocalypse* (Washington, DC: Potomac, 2005). As the experience of Cambodia demonstrates, however, attacking cross-border sanctuaries had unintended and destructive consequences, especially for its inhabitants. Invading Cambodia's territory did not defeat the Viet Cong (VC) nor seriously hinder its war-fighting capabilities. Although the US bombing might have temporarily disrupted the VC supply system, it did not greatly affect the outcome of the war. As some authors have argued, the US intervention destabilized Cambodia, leading to the rise of Pol Pot. See William Shawcross, *Side-Show: Kissinger, Nixon, and the Destruction of Cambodia* (New York: Cooper Square, 2002).

104. Edward Luttwak, "Dead End: Counterinsurgency Warfare as Military Malpractice," *Harper's* (February 2007).

105. See Greg Grandin, *Empire's Workshop: Latin America, the United States, and the Rise of the New Imperialism* (New York: Metropolitan, 2006).

2. THE DEVELOPMENT AND IMPLEMENTATION OF US COUNTERINSURGENCY STRATEGY IN EL SALVADOR AND LATIN AMERICA, 1961–1979

1. Reformers within the military seriously pursued economic reforms to avoid the specter of revolution. Héctor Lindo-Fuentes and Erik Ching, *Modernizing Minds in El Salvador: Education Reform and the Cold War, 1960–1980* (Albuquerque: University of New Mexico Press, 2012).

2. Aaron Bell, "Transnational Conservative Activism and the Transformation of the Salvadoran Right, 1967–1982" (PhD diss., American University, January 2016).

3. Quoted in Oliver Stone and Peter Kuznick, *The Untold History of the United States* (New York: Gallery, 2012), 290.

4. Martha Huggins, *Political Policing: The United States and Latin America* (Durham, NC: Duke University Press, 1998), 80.

5. Roger Hilsman, *To Move a Nation: The Politics of Foreign Policy in the Administration of John F. Kennedy* (Garden City, NJ: Doubleday, 1967).

6. National Security Action Memorandum (NSAM) 2, February 3, 1961, Federation of American Scientists, http://www.fas.org/irp/offdocs/nsam-jfk/nsam2.jpg.

7. National Security Action Memorandum (NSAM) 182, US Overseas Internal Defense Policy, n.d., Archives Unbound, http://gdc.gale.com/archivesunbound/.

8. David Fitzgerald, "Learning to Forget? The US Army and Counterinsurgency Doctrine and Practice from Vietnam to Iraq" (PhD diss., University College Cork, June 2010), 42.

9. Robert H. Holden, *Armies without Nations: Public Violence and State Formation in Central America, 1821–1960* (Oxford, UK: Oxford University Press, 2004), 163–164.

10. Ibid., 172.

11. MAP typically provided direct grants of arms and equipment, such as tanks, to foreign militaries. IMET focused on training foreign military personnel, generally outside of the United States, as well as promoting democracy and increasing cooperation between the United States and other countries. This program was thought the most cost effective among all three. And finally, FMS provided credit to militaries to buy US military supplies, including arms and defense equipment.

12. Michael Klare and Cynthia Arnson, *Supplying Repression: U.S. Support for Authoritarian Regimes Abroad* (Washington, DC: Institute for Policy Studies, 1977), 44.

13. J. Patrice McSherry, "Operation Condor as a Hemispheric 'Counter-Terror Organization,'" in *When States Kill: Latin America, the U.S., and Technologies of Terror,* ed. Cecilia Menjívar and Néstor Rodriguez (Austin: University of Texas Press, 2005), 30.

14. More recently, the controversy gathered momentum after the US Department of Defense declassified seven interrogation manuals used in the School of the Americas between 1987 and 1991. Dana Priest, "U.S. Instructed Latins on Executions, Torture; Manuals Used 1982–1991, Pentagon Reveals," *Washington Post,* September 21, 1996; others have seen patterns of prisoner abuse in Iraq that can be traced back to the 1960s and include tactics used in Latin America during the cold war. National Security Archive, *Prisoner Abuse: Patterns from the Past—Electronic Briefing Book 122.* These manuals were also distributed in El Salvador.

15. This figure is derived from Don Etchinson, *The United States and Militarism in Central America* (New York: Praeger, 1975), 105, Table 9.
16. Leslie Gill, *The School of the Americas: Military Training and Political Violence in the Americas* (Durham, NC: Duke University Press, 2004), 106.
17. United Nations, *From Madness to Hope: The Twelve Year War in El Salvador, Report of the Commission on the Truth for El Salvador,* http://www.usip.org /files/file/ElSalvador-Report.pdf.
18. The economic aspect of civic action is aimed at development, especially in rural areas. Military uses of civic action include stationing troops in strategic locations, securing the population and isolating it from the insurgents, and securing vital intelligence. Politically, civic action has been used to improve the government's or military's image with the population and extend the government's influence into remote areas. Finally, the social aspect of civic action has often focused on health and education.
19. Industrial College of the Armed Forces (ICAF), "The Role of AID in Counter-insurgency," in *Insurgency and Counterinsurgency: An Anthology,* ed. Richard M. Leighton and Ralph Sanders (Washington, DC: Industrial College of the Armed Forces, 1962), 328; out of print but found in Box 13, Edward Lansdale Collection.
20. According to the *Counterinsurgency Planning Guide* published by the US Special Warfare School in the 1960s, "The initial priority should be given to select high-impact projects aimed at establishing the credibility of the civic action program. If longer-range projects are undertaken, they should be accomplished in stages to permit partial use and allow intermediate evaluation of their effectiveness." See Willard Foster Barber and C. Neale Ronning, *Internal Security and Military Power: Counterinsurgency and Civic Action in Latin America* (Columbus: Ohio State University Press, 1966), 184.
21. Etchinson, *The United States and Militarism in Central America,* 75.
22. Barber and Ronning, *Internal Security and Military Power,* 61.
23. Cole Blasier, *The Hovering Giant: U.S. Responses to Revolutionary Change in Latin America, 1910–1985* (Pittsburgh, PA: University of Pittsburgh Press, 1985), Table 11.
24. Stephen G. Rabe, *The Most Dangerous Area in the World: John F. Kennedy Confronts Communist Revolution in Latin America* (Chapel Hill: University of North Carolina Press, 1999), 144.
25. Klare and Arnson, *Supplying Repression,* 17.
26. The CIA or Department of Defense could also train troops. The decision depended upon the nature of the threat, the type of force to be assisted, and the client country's preferences. Throughout OPS's history, the CIA was intimately involved with the organization. One of its main tasks was to recruit police agents who could furnish intelligence. Huggins, *Political Policing,* 89. A. J. Langguth also noted that police agents often were prime candidates for

enrollment as CIA employees. Langguth, *Hidden Terrors* (New York: Pantheon, 1978).

27. Douglas S. Blaufarb, *The Counterinsurgency Era: U.S. Doctrine and Performance, 1950 to the Present* (New York: Free Press, 1977), 85.

28. Klare and Arnson, *Supplying Repression*, 23.

29. Jeremy Kuzmarov, *Modernizing Repression: Police Training, Political Violence, and Nation-Building in the American Century* (Amherst: University of Massachusetts Press, 2012).

30. Stephen Rabe, "Controlling Revolutions: Latin America, the Alliance for Progress, and Cold War Anti-Communism," in *Kennedy's Quest for Victory: American Foreign Policy, 1961–1963*, ed. Thomas G. Paterson (New York: Oxford University Press, 1989), 118.

31. Michael McClintock, *Instruments of Statecraft: U.S. Guerrilla Warfare, Counterinsurgency, and Counter-Terrorism, 1940–1990* (New York: Pantheon, 1992), 189.

32. Cynthia Arnson, "Beefing Up the Salvadoran Military Forces: Some Components of U.S. Intervention," in *El Salvador: Central America in the New Cold War*, ed. Marvin Gettleman (New York: Grove, 1987), 222–223.

33. Quoted in Kuzmarov, *Modernizing Repression*, 223.

34. Walter LaFeber, *Inevitable Revolutions: The United States in Central America* (New York: Norton, 1993), 173.

35. Fuentes and Ching, *Modernizing Minds in El Salvador*, 73.

36. Byron Engle to Earl Sears, Chief Public Safety Officer, April 13, 1964, Box 59, IPS1/General/El Salvador Folder, 1956–1960, Records of AID, Office of Public Safety Latin American Branch Country File, El Salvador 1956–1972, Record Group 286, NARA.

37. According to one account approximately 15 percent to 20 percent of cadets' studies were dedicated to anticommunist indoctrination. Etchinson, *The United States and Militarism in Central America*, 109–110.

38. Philip J. Williams and Knut Walter, *Militarization and Demilitarization in El Salvador's Transition to Democracy* (Pittsburgh, PA: University of Pittsburgh Press, 1997), 52.

39. Tommy Sue Montgomery, "Fighting Guerrillas: The United States and Low-Intensity Conflict in El Salvador," *New Political Science* 9, no. 1 (Fall–Winter 1990): 24.

40. Allan Nairn, "Behind the Death Squads: An Exclusive Report on the U.S. Role in El Salvador's Official Terror," *Progressive* (May 1984): 23.

41. Medrano was also on the CIA's payroll and was assassinated by insurgents in March 1985.

42. Julie Mazzei, *Death Squads or Self-Defense Forces? How Paramilitary Groups Emerge and Challenge Democracy in Latin America* (Chapel Hill: University of North Carolina Press, 2009), 148.

43. The FMLN would also make a concentrated effort to attack and kill the

informers. This was a policy referred to as *ajusticimientos*. "Documento 40: plan de guerra," July 1980, Folder 3, Box 5, David E. Spencer Collection, Hoover Institution, Stanford University, Palo Alto, California.

44. Nairn, "Behind the Death Squads," 22.

45. Andrew Birtle, email correspondence with the author, February 26, 2013. The figures he provided are located in the 8th Special Forces Group, Special Action for Latin America, Historical Report, 1965, US Army Center for Military History.

46. The total cost of training Latin American militaries between 1951 and 1967 was approximately $91 million. Brian Smith, "U.S.-Latin American Military Relations since WWII," in *Human Rights and Basic Needs in the Americas*, ed. Margaret Crahan (Washington, DC: Georgetown University School of Language, 1982), 269–270.

47. Joaquín M. Chávez, "The Pedagogy of Revolution: Popular Intellectuals and the Origins of the Salvadoran Insurgency, 1960–1980" (PhD diss., New York University, 2010), 31.

48. Ibid., 39.

49. Telegram, October 20, 1960, IPS1/General/El Salvador Folder, 1956–1960, Box 59, Records of the Office of Public Safety, Latin America Branch Country File, El Salvador 1956–1972, Record Group 286, NARA.

50. Michael McClintock, *The American Connection: State Terror and Popular Resistance in El Salvador* (London: Zed, 1985), 199.

51. Donald P. Downs, telegram, "Recommendations for an Assistance Program to the Public Security Forces of El Salvador," May 19, 1961, IPS1/General/El Salvador Folder, 1961, Box 59, Records of the Office of Public Safety, Record Group 286, NARA.

52. Department of Defense, "Status of Military Counterinsurgency Programs, Part V," September 18, 1963, Archives Unbound.

53. Cited in LaFeber, *Inevitable Revolutions*, 174.

54. Etchinson, *The United States and Militarism in Central America*, 59.

55. Aldo Laura-Santiago, "The Culture and Politics of State Terror and Repression in El Salvador," in *When States Kill: Latin America, the U.S., and Technologies of Terror*, ed. Cecilia Menjívar and Néstor Rodriguez (Austin: University of Texas Press, 2005), 94.

56. William Deane Stanley, *The Protection Racket State: Elite Politics, Military Extortion, and Civil War in El Salvador* (Philadelphia, PA: Temple University Press, 1996).

57. The ultimate number will probably never be known. One of the more popularly cited numbers is 10,000. See Thomas P. Anderson, *Matanza: El Salvador's Communist Revolt of 1932* (Lincoln: University of Nebraska Press, 1971). The causes and effects of this massacre have been a topic of recent debate. Jeffrey L. Gould has questioned several key aspects of the massacre, including the leadership of the rebellion by the Salvadoran Communist Party, the ethnic

composition of the participants in the massacre and how the Communist Party and FMLN subsequently downplayed their ethnic character, and the key role of urban skilled workers. See Gould and Aldo Lauria-Santiago, *To Rise in Darkness: Revolution, Repression, and Memory in El Salvador, 1920–1932* (Durham, NC: Duke University Press, 2008); Gould, "Revolutionary Nationalism and Local Memories in El Salvador," in *Reclaiming the Political in Latin American History*, ed. Gilbert Joseph (Durham, NC: Duke University Press, 2001), 138–171. Other scholars have noted how changing political conditions have affected how both the right and left in El Salvador have interpreted the massacre. See Héctor Lindo-Fuentes, Erik Ching, and Rafael Lara-Martínez, *Remembering a Massacre in El Salvador: The Insurrection of 1932, Roque Dalton, and the Politics of Historical Memory* (Albuquerque: University of New Mexico Press, 2007). For an account of the massacre, see Roque Dalton, *Miguel Mármol* (Willimantic, CT: Curbstone Press, 1987).

58. Gould and Lauria-Santiago, *To Rise in Darkness.*
59. Jeffery M. Paige, *Coffee and Power: Revolution and the Rise of Democracy in Central America* (Cambridge, MA: Harvard University Press, 1997).
60. H. E. Vanden, "Terrorism, Law, and State Policy in Central America: The Eighties," *New Political Science* 18 (Fall–Winter 1990): 60.
61. James Petras, "The Anatomy of State Terror: Chile, El Salvador, and Brazil," *Science and Society* 51, no. 3 (Fall 1987): 330.
62. Paul Almeida, *Waves of Protest: Popular Struggle in El Salvador, 1925–2005* (Minneapolis: University of Minnesota Press, 2008).
63. Philip J. Williams and Knut Walter, *Militarization and Demilitarization in El Salvador's Transition to Democracy* (Pittsburgh, PA: University of Pittsburgh Press, 1997), 95.
64. Almeida, *Waves of Protest,* 114.
65. Ching and Lindo-Fuentes also noted an earlier example, when General Maximiliano Hernández Martinez surrendered to landowner pressure to allow plantation stores to reopen.
66. There are many excellent secondary sources that document the 1970s and the outbreak of the Salvadoran Civil War. These include Enrique Baloyra, *El Salvador in Transition* (Chapel Hill: University of North Carolina Press, 1982); Tommie Sue Montgomery, *Revolution in El Salvador: Origins and Evolution* (Boulder, CO: Westview, 1982); James Dunkerley, *The Long War: Dictatorship and Revolution in El Salvador* (London: Junction, 1982); and Raymond Bonner, *Weakness and Deceit: U.S. Policy and El Salvador* (New York: Times, 1984).
67. Baloyra, *El Salvador in Transition,* 64.
68. Ibid., 66.
69. These various groups had an armed wing and their own popular organization that interacted with the masses. They recruited members, spread propaganda, organized Salvadorans, and represented the legal, open wing of the armed

groups. Working with the clandestine guerrillas, these organizations sought to harness popular support to link their struggle with the armed insurgents and overthrow the regime. As the chaos and violence deepened, these groups began actively arming themselves and seeking to achieve power through violence. The various front groups were the Bloque Popular Revolucionario (BPR), affiliated with the FPL; Las Ligas Populares de 28 Febrero (LP-28), associated with the ERP; and Resistencia Nacional (RN), the front organization of the FARN. Members of these groups were routinely targeted and many were arrested, tortured, or killed by Salvadoran security forces or death squads. As the repression intensified, those who escaped the carnage eventually fled to the countryside to take up arms against the government. Later in the civil war, the guerrillas would try to rebuild the networks they had previously established.

70. Chávez, "Pedagogy of Revolution," 266.

71. The name of this section is derived from the title of Rafael Menjívar Ochoa, *Tiempos de Locura: El Salvador, 1979–1981* (San Salvador: FLACSO, 2006).

72. Ambassador Frank Devine noted that after 1977 the United States had poor contact with the Salvadoran military. Consequently, distrust existed between US advisers and their Salvadoran counterparts. The situation was most likely considered poor. In the same cable, representatives from SOUTHCOM noted that inspections of the Salvadoran military produced "alarming results," but they did not elaborate. See Devine to Secretary of State, telegram, December 11, 1979, El Salvador Online Collections, National Security Archives (hereafter NSA). A cable on December 13, 1979, from Devine to the secretary of state discussing the military and political situation in El Salvador and possible US aid remains classified.

73. Robert Pastor to Zbigniew Brzezinski, memorandum, October 13, 1979, CREST Files, NLC-132-78-1-2-6, Jimmy Carter Library, Atlanta, Georgia.

74. Montgomery, *Revolution in El Salvador,* 10.

75. Frank Devine to Secretary of State, telegram, October 24, 1979, El Salvador Online Collections, NSA.

76. Zbigniew Brzezinski to Jimmy Carter, memorandum, January 20, 1980, El Salvador Online Collections, NSA.

77. Robert Pastor to Zbigniew Brzezinski, memorandum, February 15, 1980, CREST Files, NLC-24-65-9-1-4, Jimmy Carter Library, Atlanta, Georgia.

78. Memo, "Talking Points for Use with Congress," n.d., Box 42, El Salvador II Document Collection, Part 21G: US Aid to El Salvador 1979 to 1981, El Salvador Human Rights Cases, Record Group 59, NARA.

79. The various countries would perform different tasks. The Salvadoran government wanted the Colombians to send experts in guerrilla warfare, the Spanish were asked to provide training to the National Guard, and the United States was supposed to help with surveillance and interception and provide equipment and civic action techniques to the military. Oddly, the West German role was not discussed. Robert Pastor to Zbigniew Brzezinski, memorandum,

February 21, 1980, CREST Files, NLC-24-20-11-4-7, Jimmy Carter Library, Atlanta, Georgia.

80. Zbigniew Brzezinski to David Aaron and Les Denend, October 30, 1980, CREST Files, NLC-17-141-6-5-6, Jimmy Carter Library, Atlanta, Georgia.

81. "Choice Land Is Grabbed by El Salvador: Government Imposes Form of Martial Law," *Miami Herald,* March 7, 1980.

82. Roy L. Prosterman, Jeffrey M. Riedinger, and Mary N. Temple, "Land Reform and the El Salvador Crisis," *International Security* 6, no. 1 (Summer 1981): 59–60.

83. The telegram also noted that the JRG was "dealing with a two-edged sword" that could alienate both the military and the moderate left if it was delayed. "JRG Appears Ready for First Steps in Agrarian Reform," November 28, 1979, El Salvador Online Collections, NSA.

84. Telegram, "Millionaires' Murder Inc.," January 1981, El Salvador Online Collections, NSA.

85. United Nations, *From Madness to Hope.*

86. Shirley Christian, "Salvadorans Battle Erosion of Land Reform," *Miami Herald,* July 13, 1982.

87. Richard V. Culahan to William C. Doherty, memorandum, "Violence against Agrarian Reform Beneficiaries and Workers Pertaining to Real Properties," November 12, 1980, El Salvador Online Collections, NSA.

88. LaFeber, *Inevitable Revolutions,* 249.

89. Zbigniew Brzezinski to Jimmy Carter, memorandum, March 13, 1980, CREST Files, NLC-17-39-1-1, Jimmy Carter Library, Atlanta, Georgia.

90. David Aaron to Robert White, telegram, January 1, 1981, CREST Files, NLC-16-128-4-11-7, Jimmy Carter Library, Atlanta, Georgia.

91. Ibid.

92. One of the civilians on the junta, José Morales Erlich, told Ambassador White that he was opposed to them. Robert White, telegram, August 14, 1980, CREST Files, NLC-16-123-4-20-2, Jimmy Carter Library, Atlanta, Georgia.

93. Robert Pastor to Zbigniew Brzezinski, December 21, 1980, CREST Files, NLC-17-44-8-5-2, Jimmy Carter Library, Atlanta, Georgia.

94. Hector Dada Press Conference, March 17, 1980, Special Collection of Records Relating to El Salvador HR Cases, Box 59, Part 5, Possible MTTs to ES-1980, E830, El Salvador Human Rights Collection, NARA.

95. Archbishop Óscar Arnulfo Romero to President Jimmy Carter, February 17, 1980, Box 42, Part 21C, El Salvador Human Rights Collection, NARA.

96. Cyrus Vance to Archbishop Romero, March 11, 1980, Box 42, Part 21C, El Salvador Human Rights Collection, NARA.

97. Annual Security Assistance Assessment, telegram, El Salvador, June 2, 1980, Box 42, Part 21D, U.S. Aid to ES 1979–1981, El Salvador Human Rights Cases, Record Group 59, NARA.

98. Report, July 19, 1979, CREST Files, NLC-20-25-1-1-0, Jimmy Carter Library,

Atlanta, Georgia. Between September 1978 and August 1979, the United States had turned down requests for pistols and revolvers, ammunition, tear gas, CH-47 helicopters, and night-vision goggles. "A Selective and Representative List of Conventional Arms Transfer Cases which were Turned Down or Turn[ed] off for Policy Reasons from September 1, 1978, through August 31, 1979," ND, CREST Files, NLC-15-49-2-12-7, Jimmy Carter Library, Atlanta, Georgia. However, in October 1979, Secretary of State Cyrus Vance authorized the US ambassador to provide El Salvador tear gas and other related, nonlethal material. Cyrus Vance to Jimmy Carter, memorandum, November 8, 1979, CREST Files, NLC-128-14-13-6-4, Jimmy Carter Library, Atlanta, Georgia.

99. Telegram, February 12, 1980, El Salvador Online Collections, NSA.

100. Warren Christopher to Jose Zalaquett, letter, August 8, 1980, El Salvador 06/04/1981 General Folder, Box 4, Edwin Meese Collection, Ronald Reagan Library.

101. Ibid.

102. Nevertheless, the Unified Revolutionary Directorate (DRU) proclaimed in September 1980 that the people's struggle was nearing an end. According to the DRU, the insurgents had made numerable achievements, especially regarding military strategy. See DRU, Comunicado de la Dirección Revolucionaria Unificada al Pueblo Salvadoreño, Septiembre 1, 1980, CEDEMA, http://www .cedema.org/index.php?ver=mostrar&pais=19&nombrepais=Elpercent20Sal vador.

103. David Spencer, "External Resource Mobilization and Successful Insurgency in Cuba, Nicaragua, and El Salvador, 1959–1992" (PhD diss., George Washington University, 2002), 252.

104. Patricia Derian to Secretary of State, memorandum, December 4, 1980, El Salvador Online Collections, NSA.

105. Warren Christopher to William Bowdler, telegram, November 29, 1980. El Salvador Online Collections, NSA.

106. This claim was not held just by the Salvadoran military; UN ambassador designate Jeanne Kirkpatrick suggested that the deceased were not nuns but FMLN political activists. Secretary of State Alexander Haig infamously called them "pistol-packing nuns" and suggested that the vehicle they were in might have run a roadblock. LaFeber, *Inevitable Revolutions*, 277. A State Department spokesperson later responded in a letter to William Ford, brother of one of the slain women, that Haig's remarks had been "misinterpreted" and that his suggestion that the attempt to run a roadblock was "only one theory and not a fact." Bonner, *Weakness and Deceit*, 76.

107. This assessment also argued that the offensive was launched because the government had strengthened its political bases and increased pressure from the Salvadoran armed forces, with which most secondary sources disagree. Memorandum to Brzezinski, January 9, 1981, CREST Files, NLC-1-18-3-20-6, Jimmy Carter Library, Atlanta, Georgia.

108. Quoted in William M. LeoGrande, *Our Own Backyard: The United States in Central America, 1977–1992* (Chapel Hill: University of North Carolina Press, 1998), 68; Bonner, *Weakness and Deceit,* 223–224.
109. One of the leading comandantes in the FMLN, Cayetano Carpio, was opposed to launching the Final Offensive. A proponent of PPW, Carpio insisted the timing was not yet right; nevertheless, he acquiesced. Brian J. Bosch, *The Salvadoran Officer Corps and the Final Offensive of 1981* (Jefferson, NC: McFarland, 1999), 75.
110. Jenny Pearce, *Promised Land: Peasant Rebellion in Chalatenango, El Salvador* (London: Latin America Bureau, 1986), 193.
111. Spencer, "External Resource Mobilization," 265.
112. El Salvador on the Threshold of a Democratic Revolutionary Victory: A Call by the General Command of the FMLN to Initiate the General Offensive, Box 43, Part 21H: U.S. Aid to El Salvador, 1979–1981, El Salvador Human Rights Cases, Record Group 59, NARA.
113. Quoted in Montgomery, *Revolution in El Salvador,* 139.
114. Max Manwaring and Courtney Prisk, *El Salvador at War: An Oral History of Conflict from the 1979 Insurrection to the Present* (Washington, DC: National Defense University Press, 1988), 68.
115. Zbigniew Brzezinski to Jimmy Carter, memorandum, January 14, 1981, CREST Files, NLC 15-99-1-4-2, Jimmy Carter Library, Atlanta, Georgia.
116. Ibid.
117. Telegram, "Resupply of Salvadoran Armed Forces," January 11, 1981, Box 43, Part 21H: U.S. Aid to El Salvador, 1979–1981, El Salvador Human Rights Cases, Record Group 59, NARA.
118. Quoted in W. Scott Thompson, "Choosing to Win," *Foreign Policy* 43 (Summer 1981): 78. Thompson at the time of this article was also an ardent supporter of Reagan's foreign policy in El Salvador and a member of the Committee for the Free World, which announced its support of the new president's policies in an advertisement in the *New York Times* on April 6, 1981.
119. "Final Offensive by FMLN," briefing paper, January 10, 1981, Box 40, Part 17, El Salvador Human Rights Cases, Record Group 59, NARA.

3. THE REAGAN ADMINISTRATION ENTERS THE MAELSTROM, 1981–1984
  1. US Congress, *Presidential Certification on El Salvador,* vol. 1, Hearings before the Subcommittee on Inter-American Affairs of the Committee on Foreign Affairs, House of Representatives, 97th Congress, 2nd sess. (February 2, 23, and 25, 1982, and March 2, 1982).
  2. US Department of State, *American Foreign Policy Current Documents: 1984* (Washington, DC: Department of State, 1984).
  3. "LBJ Goes to War, 1964–1965," *American Experience,* Public Broadcasting Service, http://www.pbs.org/wgbh/amex/vietnam/series/pt_03.html.

4. Most scholars who have studied the conflict sharply disagree. They have traced the outbreak of war to the country's history of economic exploitation, political stratification, and control of the political system by the military and oligarchy. See Enrique A. Baloyra, *El Salvador in Transition* (Chapel Hill: University of North Carolina Press, 1982); James Dunkerley, *The Long War: Dictatorship and Revolution in El Salvador* (London: Junction, 1982); Tommie Sue Montgomery, *Revolution in El Salvador: Origins and Evolution* (Boulder, CO: Westview, 1982); Jeffery M. Paige, *Coffee and Power: Revolution and the Rise of Democracy in Central America* (Cambridge, MA: Harvard University Press, 1997); William Deane Stanley, *The Protection Racket State: Elite Politics, Military Extortion, and Civil War in El Salvador* (Philadelphia, PA: Temple University Press, 1996); Alan L. McPherson, *Intimate Ties, Bitter Struggles: The United States and Latin America since 1945* (Washington, DC: Potomac, 2006), 89.

5. L. Paul Bremer III to Richard V. Allen, memorandum, Paper for the NSC Meeting on El Salvador, February 23, 1981, NSC0004 27 February 1981 (Poland, Caribbean Basin, etc.) Folder 2/4, Box 1, Executive Secretariat NSC: Meeting Files, Ronald Reagan Library, Simi Valley, California.

6. See Roger Burbach and Patricia Flynn, eds., *The Politics of Intervention: The United States in Central America* (New York: Monthly Review Press, 1984).

7. As Ronald Cox has demonstrated, differences in the business community existed as to how to respond to the Central American crisis. Labor-intensive businesses reliant on generous government concessions and, wanting to keep labor costs low, favored a more aggressive approach to combating potential threats. Ronald Cox, *Power and Profits: U.S. Policy in Central America* (Lexington: University Press of Kentucky, 1994).

8. William LeoGrande, *Our Own Backyard: The United States in Central America, 1977–1992* (Chapel Hill: University of North Carolina Press, 1998), 81.

9. Hal Brands, *Latin America's Cold War* (Cambridge, MA: Harvard University Press, 2010), 198–199.

10. Stephen Rabe, *The Killing Zone: The United States Wages Cold War in Latin America* (Oxford, UK: Oxford University Press, 2011), 158.

11. LeoGrande, *Our Own Backyard,* 90.

12. Quoted in Malcolm Byrne, *Iran-Contra: Reagan's Scandal and the Unchecked Abuse of Presidential Power* (Lawrence: University Press of Kansas), 2014, 10.

13. American Friends Service Committee (AFSC), "The U.S. Pacification Program in El Salvador," n.d., Folder 2.4, Box 2, Salvadoran Subject Collection, Hoover Institution Archives, Stanford University, Palo Alto, California.

14. Tommie Sue Montgomery, "Fighting Guerrillas: The United States and Low-Intensity Conflict in El Salvador," *New Political Science* 91 (Fall–Winter 1990): 29.

15. Andrew Bacevich, *American Military Policy in Small Wars: The Case of El Salvador* (Cambridge, UK: Pergamon Brassey's, 1988), v.

16. The limit was set at fifty-five advisers, mandated by Congress to avoid expanding US involvement. According to most sources, however, this number was routinely violated. Additional advisers often trained Salvadorans in Honduras, were classified as medical staff, or would simply fly out of the country and later return. Americans also were not allowed to accompany Salvadoran troops into the field, but they were occasionally involved in fighting. For an example, see John Terzian, "SF Advisors in El Salvador: The Attack on El Paraíso," *Special Warfare* 14, no. 2 (Spring 2001): 18–25.

17. Telegram, June 6, 1981, Guerrillas Folder, Box 6, Subject Files: Abrams—Christian Democratic Party, National Security Agency (hereafter NSA) Archival Collection.

18. "Report of the El Salvador Military Strategy Assistance Team," November 16, 1981, El Salvador Online Collections, NSA.

19. Roger Fontaine and Robert L. Schweitzer to Richard Allen, memorandum, August 19, 1981, C0046 El Salvador (047000-052999) Folder, Box 68, WHORM Subject Files (017091-145499), Ronald Reagan Library, Simi Valley, California.

20. Juan Orlando Zepeda, *Perfiles de la guerra en El Salvador* (San Salvador: New Graphics, 2008), 175.

21. Mark Danner, *The Massacre at El Mozote: A Parable of the Cold War* (New York: Vintage, 1994), 22–23.

22. Central Intelligence Agency, "Near-Term Prospects for El Salvador," December 14, 1983, CIA Freedom of Information Act Reading Room.

23. Alexander Haig to Ronald Reagan, memorandum, "The Risk of Losing in El Salvador and What Can Be Done about It," August 11, 1981, Folder NISC00030 17 August 1981 (East-West Trade, Central America, Strategic Forces), Box 2, Executive Secretariat: Meeting Files, Ronald Reagan Library, Simi Valley, California. Haig's opinion was also supported by Reagan's first national security director, Richard Allen.

24. L. Paul Bremer III to Richard V. Allen, memorandum, Paper for the NSC Meeting on El Salvador, February 23, 1981, Folder NSC0004 27 February 1981 (Poland, Caribbean Basin, etc.) 2/4, Box 1, Executive Secretariat NSC: Meeting Files, Ronald Reagan Library, Simi Valley, California.

25. L. Paul Bremer III to Richard Allen, memorandum, Paper for the NSC Meeting on El Salvador, February 17, 1981, El Salvador Online Collections, NSA.

26. In order to preempt concern, several White House officials argued that the administration should meet this threat head on by consulting informally with Congress. Most policy makers believed that the War Powers Resolution did not apply to the present circumstances. Ibid.

27. Bremer to Allen, Paper for the NSC Meeting on El Salvador, February 23, 1981.

28. US Department of State, *American Foreign Policy Current Documents: 1981* (Washington, DC: Department of State, 1981), 1258.

29. US Senate, Committee on Foreign Relations, *El Salvador: The United States*

in the Middle of a Maelstrom, Joint Committee Report (Washington, DC: US Government Printing Office, March 1982).

30. Kyle Longley, *In the Eagle's Shadow: The United States and Latin America* (Wheeling, IL: Harlan Davidson, 2009), 303.

31. Comptroller General of the United States, "US Military Aid to El Salvador and Honduras," August 22, 1985, U.S. Military Aid to El Salvador [and Honduras] Folder, Box 1, Oliver North Files, Ronald Reagan Library, Simi Valley, California.

32. "Report of the El Salvador Military Strategy Assistance Team," November 16, 1981, El Salvador Online Collections, NSA.

33. This was an assessment made by John Waghelstein, commander of the US MILGP in El Salvador, who was familiar with the report. Max Manwaring and Courtney Prisk, *El Salvador at War: An Oral History of Conflict from the 1979 Insurrection to the Present* (Washington, DC: National Defense University Press, 1988), 223–224.

34. "Report of the El Salvador Military Strategy Assistance Team," November 16, 1981.

35. The assessment also noted that this was a "fertile area for U.S. training assistance." "Report of the El Salvador Military Strategy Assistance Team," November 16, 1981.

36. The report called for maintaining and publishing, at sensitive points around the country and in nationally syndicated newspapers, a blacklist of insurgents' identities and their aliases.

37. "BG Woerner's Briefing on the El Salvador Military Situation," November 18, 1981, El Salvador, Oliver North, NSC Folder, Box 12, Oliver North Files, Ronald Reagan Library, Simi Valley, California; "Report of the El Salvador Military Strategy Assistance Team," November 16, 1981.

38. "BG Woerner's Briefing on the El Salvador Military Situation," November 18, 1981.

39. Ibid.

40. "Report of the El Salvador Military Strategy Assistance Team," November 16, 1981.

41. For Woerner's own discussion of the strategy, see Manwaring and Prisk, *El Salvador at War.*

42. Hugh Byrnes, *El Salvador's Civil War: A Study of Revolution* (Boulder, CO: Lynne Rienner, 1996), 80.

43. Quoted in Michael Childress, *The Effectiveness of U.S. Training Efforts in Internal Defense and Development: The Cases of El Salvador and Honduras* (Santa Monica, CA: RAND, 1995), 31.

44. Telegram, El Salvador/Status of the New Atlacatl Battalion, October 14, 1981, El Salvador Online Collections, NSA.

45. Memorandum, The Atlacatl Battalion and Alleged Human Rights Abuses,

Section: Atlacatl's Record and U.S. Policy, Barriers to Reform—Research Folder, Box 2, Records of the Arms Control and Foreign Policy Caucus, Caleb Rossiter Files, El Salvador, National Archives and Records Administration (NARA), Washington, DC.

46. Greg Walker, *At the Hurricane's Eye: US Special Forces from Vietnam to Desert Storm* (New York: Ivy, 1994), 93.

47. Inquiry from Senator Moakley about Atlacatl Battalion: Response from Carl W. Ford, Acting Assistant Secretary of Defense International Security Affairs, Caleb Rossiter Files, El Salvador, NARA.

48. Leigh Binford, *The El Mozote Massacre: Anthropology and Human Rights* (Tucson: University of Arizona Press, 1996), 146.

49. Ibid., 146.

50. After the conflict, the UN Truth Commission attributed more than 80 percent of all human rights abuses committed during the war to Salvadoran security forces, not insurgents or "unknown assailants."

51. Several authors have made this claim including Michael Childress, Benjamin Schwartz, and Andrew Bacevich, in Todd R. Greentree, *Crossroads of Intervention: Insurgency and Counterinsurgency Lessons from Central America* (Westport, CT: Praeger Security International, 2008).

52. Central Intelligence Agency, "Status of the Military Capabilities of the El Salvadoran Government to Stem Insurgency within That Country and Plans for a US Military Assistance Program for El Salvador," January 2, 1981, Declassified Documents Reference System (DDRS).

53. John T. Fishel, email interview with the author, September 21, 2016.

54. This also includes agrarian reform and other development projects such as Unidos para Reconstruir. Montgomery, "Fighting Guerrillas," 21–23; Richard Duncan Downie, *Learning from Conflict: The US Military in Vietnam, El Salvador, and the Drug War* (Westport, CT: Praeger, 1998), 132–133.

55. According to Diana Villiers-Negroponte, Carpio gave this name to himself. However, Sheldon B. Liss argued that others referred to Carpio as Ho Chi Minh because of his age. Villiers-Negroponte, *Seeking Peace in El Salvador: The Struggle to Reconstruct a Nation at the End of the Cold War* (New York: Palgrave Macmillan, 2012), 31; Liss, *Radical Thought in Latin America* (Boulder, CO: Westview, 1991), 81.

56. The FES units, the special forces of the FMLN, were modeled after the North Vietnamese sappers. These units carried out the most daring and spectacular raids of the conflict. Each faction within the FMLN had its own FES units; however, the ERP developed the largest and most sophisticated units. David E. Spencer, *From Vietnam to El Salvador: The Saga of the FMLN Sappers and Other Guerrilla Forces in Latin America* (Westport, CT: Praeger, 1996), 2–3.

57. Polemica Internacional, June 1980, Folder 1, Box 1, Salvadoran Subject Collection, Hoover Institution Archives, Stanford University, Palo Alto, California.

58. Joaquín Villalobos, "Popular Insurrection: Desire or Reality?" *Latin American*

Perspectives 16, no. 3 (Summer 1989): 5. Comandante Balta also agreed with Villalobos's statement.

59. Facundo Guardado, interview with the author, San Salvador, El Salvador, August 22, 2013.

60. Juan Ramón Medrano, a former FMLN comandante, and Facundo Guardado confirmed this in their interviews. William Pascasio (Comandante Memo), interview with the author, San Salvador, El Salvador, August 19, 2013. None of the former insurgents interviewed studied Algeria or mentioned it as a useful example.

61. These authors include T. X. Hammes, Mary Kador, and Philip Melinger. According to these critics, Clausewitz's conception of war is state-centric, or a military competition between two nations. A very concise introduction to these authors' critiques of Clausewitz is Bart Schuurman, "Clausewitz and the 'New Wars' Scholars," *Parameters* (Spring 2010). Christopher Daase, "Clausewitz and Small Wars," in *Clausewitz in the Twenty-First Century,* ed. Hew Strachan and Andreas Herberg-Rothe (Oxford, UK: Oxford University Press).

62. La Guerra Revolucionaria del Pueblo, 1987, Folder 2, Box 2, David E. Spencer Collection, Hoover Institution, Stanford University, Palo Alto, California.

63. José Moroni Bracamonte and David Spencer, *Strategy and Tactics of the Salvadoran FMLN Guerrillas: Last Battle of the Cold War, Blueprint for Future Conflicts* (Westport, CT: Praeger, 1995), 13.

64. Ibid., 20–21.

65. Pablo Parada Andino, interview with the author, San Salvador, El Salvador, August 20, 2013. It also lacked training on how to effectively and properly use the arms. Raúl Mijango, *Mi Guerra: Testimonio de toda una vida* (San Salvador: Laser Print, 2007), 143.

66. José Medrano, interview with the author, San Salvador, El Salvador, August 22, 2013.

67. Andino interview, August 20, 2013.

68. Documento: El Plan Puente, 1981, Folder 4, Box 5, David E. Spencer Collection, Hoover Institution, Stanford University, Palo Alto, California.

69. Mijango, *Mi Guerra,* 152, 265–269.

70. Documento 57: Plan Militar General DRU, February 1981, Folder 4, Box 5, David E. Spencer Collection, Hoover Institution, Stanford University, Palo Alto, California.

71. "Report of the El Salvador Military Strategy Assistance Team," November 16, 1981.

72. US Senate Committee on Foreign Relations, *El Salvador.*

73. See Max Manwaring and Courtney Prisk, *A Strategic View of Insurgencies: Insights from El Salvador,* McNair Papers, no. 8 (Washington, DC: Institute for National Strategic Studies, 1990).

74. Byrnes, *El Salvador's Civil War,* 106. Juan Ramón Medrano, interview with the author, San Salvador, El Salvador, August 19, 2013.

75. US Department of State, January 26, 1984, Unclass: El Salvador-1/26/1984–3/25/1984 Folder, Box 6, Constantine Menges Files, Ronald Reagan Library, Simi Valley, California.
76. "El Salvador: Domestic Troubles," December 11, 1985, El Salvador Folder, Box 1, Oliver North Files, Ronald Reagan Library, Simi Valley, California.
77. Medrano interview, August 19, 2013, San Salvador, El Salvador.
78. Quoted in Danner, *Massacre at El Mozote,* 42, 52.
79. Ibid., 53.
80. As Nick Turse has demonstrated, the US massacre at My Lai was not an unusual event but a minor portion of the larger US military strategy in Vietnam. Turse, *Kill Anything That Moves: The Real American War in Vietnam* (New York: Metropolitan, 2013).
81. Binford, *El Mozote Massacre,* 47.
82. United Nations, *From Madness to Hope: The 12-Year War in El Salvador—Report of the Commission on the Truth for El Salvador,* http://www.usip.org/sites/default/files/file/ElSalvador-Report.pdf.
83. See "Major Describes Move," *New York Times,* February 8, 1968; for an interesting follow-up article, see "Ruined Bentre, after 45 Days, Still Awaits Saigon's Aid," *New York Times,* March 15, 1968.
84. Comandante Balta, *Memorias de un Guerrillero* (San Salvador: New Graphic, 2006), 140.
85. LeoGrande, *Our Own Backyard,* 112–113.
86. Cynthia McClintock, *Revolutionary Movements in Latin America: El Salvador's FMLN and Peru's Shining Path* (Washington, DC: US Institute of Peace, 1998), 228.
87. LeoGrande, *Our Own Backyard,* 158.
88. Mijango, *Mi Guerra,* 156.
89. Telegram, "Country Team Assessment of Security Environment for Elections," March 18, 1982, FMLN Background 1980–1992, Records Relating to the UN Truth Commission, 1980–1993, Record Group 59, NARA.
90. Raymond Bonner, "For the Left, Big Setback: Rebels Failed to Bar Nation from Voting," *New York Times,* March 30, 1982.
91. Medrano interview, August 19, 2013.
92. Telegram, "FDR Publication," January 25, 1983, Box 1: FMLN File Indices, FMLN Background 5/84–6/84, FMLN Background January 1983–April 1984, Records Relating to the UN Truth Commission, 1980–1993, Record Group 59, NARA.
93. Alexander Haig to All Diplomatic and Consular Posts, telegram, April 1982, Folder Cable File—El Salvador, 04/01/1982–04/14/1982, Box 12, Roger Fontaine Files, Ronald Reagan Library, Simi Valley, California.
94. McClintock, *Revolutionary Movements in Latin America,* 125.
95. William Stanley and Mark Peceny, "Counterinsurgency in El Salvador," *Politics and Society* 38, no. 1 (2010): 68.

96. Central Intelligence Agency, "The Election Outlook in El Salvador," in *Salvadoran Human Rights*, vol. 1, Library of Congress.

97. Conservative opponents saw agrarian reform as the first step toward communism and thought all privately owned farms would be collectivized. Representing this viewpoint, Virginia Prewett, a conservative writer working with the Council for Inter-American Security, argued that the program was a terrible idea and had replaced private enterprise and agriculture with state control. Denouncing it as "instant Socialism" tailor made by President Carter, Prewett opined, "Supporting this attack on free enterprise, the U.S. had severely damaged El Salvador's prospects for political stability by undermining the productivity of its economy." Prewett, "Washington's Instant Socialism in El Salvador," Folder 1, Box 5, Salvadoran Subject Collection, Hoover Institution, Stanford University, Palo Alto, California; Checchi and Company, "Agrarian Reform in El Salvador," report to AID, December 1981, El Salvador Online Collections, NSA.

98. Tom Barry and Deb Preusch, "The War in El Salvador: A Reassessment," *Monthly Review* 38 (April 1987).

99. Checchi and Company, "Agrarian Reform in El Salvador."

100. Ibid.

101. Quoted in the World Bank Country Study, *El Salvador: Rural Development Strategy* (Washington, DC: World Bank, 1998), 196.

102. Checchi and Company, "Agrarian Reform in El Salvador."

103. LeoGrande, *Our Own Backyard*, 167.

104. US Embassy Briefing Book, n.d., Folder 2.1, Box 2, Salvadoran Subject Collection, Hoover Institution, Stanford University, Palo Alto, California.

105. Checchi and Company, "Agrarian Reform in El Salvador."

106. LeoGrande, *Our Own Backyard*, 168.

107. The report also noted that the "slash and burn" practiced by Salvadoran peasants, who relied on rotating the soil, would also rapidly deplete the quality of the soil of the land granted to them by Decree 207. "Difficulties with the Implementation of Decree 207 ('land to the tiller') in El Salvador's Agrarian Reform Program," n.d., El Salvador Online Collection, NSA.

108. Ibid.

109. Michael Sussman, *AIFLD: U.S. Trojan Horse in Latin America and the Caribbean* (Washington, DC: Epica, 1983), 17.

110. T. David Mason, *Caught in the Crossfire: Revolutions, Repression, and the Rational Peasant* (Lanham, MD: Rowman and Littlefield, 2004), 148.

111. Raymond Bonner, *Weakness and Deceit: U.S. Policy and El Salvador* (New York: Times, 1984), 194–195.

112. Quoted in ibid., 195.

113. Molly Todd, *Beyond Displacement: Campesinos, Refugees, and Collective Action in the Salvadoran Civil War* (Madison: University of Wisconsin Press, 2010), 33.

114. Ibid., 35.
115. Daniel Siegel and Joy Hackel, "El Salvador: Counterinsurgency Revisited," in *Low Intensity Warfare: Counterinsurgency, Proinsurgency, and Antiterrorism in the Eighties,* ed. Michael Klare and Peter Kornbluh (New York: Pantheon, 1988), 112–135.
116. Bureau of Intelligence and Research Analysis, "El Salvador: Brighter Prospects for Land Reform," March 17, 1983, El Salvador Folder, Box 1, Jaqueline Tillman Files, Ronald Reagan Library, Simi Valley, California.
117. LeoGrande, *Our Own Backyard,* 227.
118. Benjamin Schwartz, *American Counterinsurgency Doctrine and El Salvador: The Frustrations of Reform and the Illusions of Nation Building* (Santa Monica, CA: RAND, 1991), 49.
119. Ibid., vi.
120. Christine Wade, *Captured Peace: Elites and Peacebuilding in El Salvador* (Athens: Ohio University Press, 2016), 51.
121. Villiers-Negroponte, *Seeking Peace in El Salvador,* 4.
122. Ibid., 5.
123. Alan Riding, "López Portillo to Reagan on Central America: Don't," *New York Times,* January 4, 1981.
124. Longley, *In the Eagle's Shadow,* 311.
125. Walter LaFeber, *Inevitable Revolutions: The United States in Central America* (New York: Norton, 1993), 297.
126. LeoGrande, *Our Own Backyard,* 360.
127. Manwaring and Prisk, *El Salvador at War,* 233.
128. CIA, "Near-Term Prospects for El Salvador."
129. This same analysis also expected the ESAF to make "moderate progress against the guerrillas in the coming year." Defense Intelligence Agency, "El Salvador: Military-Guerrilla Balance," January 14, 1983, El Salvador, Oliver North, NSC Folder, Box 12, Oliver North Files, Ronald Reagan Library, Simi Valley, California.
130. AFSC, "U.S. Pacification Program in El Salvador."
131. Russell Watson and James LeMoyne, "A Plan to Win in El Salvador," *Newsweek,* March 21, 1983.
132. US Department of State, "Briefing Paper on El Salvador: Issues Include State of War in El Salvador; U.S. Military Assistance to El Salvador," June 10, 1983, DDRS.
133. Greentree, *Crossroads of Intervention,* 103.
134. US Department of State, "Combined Political, Economic, Military Plan," memorandum, January 1, 1983, El Salvador Online Collection, NSA.
135. Ibid.
136. Gobierno de El Salvador, *Comisión nacional de restauración de areas* (San Salvador: Gobierno de El Salvador, 1983). A copy is available at the Fundación Salvadoreña para el Desarrollo Económico y Social (FUSADES) library.
137. Bacevich, *American Military Policy in Small Wars,* 44.

138. James LeMoyne, "Salvador Candidate Suspected of U.S. Aid Misuse; He Is Reportedly Backed by Duarte's Son within the Governing Party," *New York Times*, March 6, 1988.

139. Telegram, August 20, 1983, Guerrillas Folder, Box 6, Subject Files: Abrams—Christian Democratic Party, NSA.

140. Ibid.

141. Bacevich, *American Military Policy in Small Wars,* 44.

142. Central Intelligence Agency, "The Salvadoran Military: A Mixed Performance," June 1, 1984, CIA Freedom of Information Act Reading Room, https://www.cia.gov/library/readingroom/docs/CIA-RDP85S00317R000100140001-4.pdf.

143. Defense Intelligence Agency, "Guatemala and El Salvador: Civil Defense as a COIN Tactic," November 1987, El Salvador Online Collection, NSA.

144. Bacevich, *American Military Policy in Small Wars,* 40.

145. Ibid., 41–42; AFSC, "U.S. Pacification Program in El Salvador."

146. Richard Alan White, *The Morass: United States' Intervention in Central America* (New York: Harper and Row, 1984), 165.

147. Defense Intelligence Agency, "Guatemala and El Salvador."

148. Ibid.

149. Montgomery, *Revolution in El Salvador*, 171; Robert J. McCartney, "El Salvador Confirms Loss of 100," *Washington Post*, January 4, 1984.

150. "Salvadoran Rebels Cut Vital Span," *Washington Post*, January 2, 1984.

151. Sam Dillon, "Salvadoran Rebels Carve Out Enclave," *Miami Herald,* November 27, 1983.

152. Robert Rivard, "El Salvador: The Rebels Show New Strength," *Newsweek*, December 5, 1983, 80.

153. Bacevich, *American Military Policy in Small Wars,* 44.

154. Greentree, *Crossroads of Intervention,* 99.

155. Bacevich, *American Military Policy in Small Wars,* 44.

156. Marta Harnecker, "De la Insurrection a la Guerra," entrevista con Joaquín Villalobos, noviembre–diciembre 1982, Biblioteca de Universidad Centroamericana.

157. Raúl Mijango, interview with the author, August 22, 2013, San Salvador, El Salvador.

158. FMLN, "Sobre el carácter y perspectiva de la guerra revolucionaria en el Salvador," January 1984, loose papers (no folder), Box 1, Nidia Díaz Collection, Hoover Institution, Stanford University, Palo Alto, California.

159. Memorandum, "A Low-Cost Tactical and Offensive Strategy for the Systematic Defeat of Urban and Rural Guerrilla Forces in El Salvador," El Salvador Military Issues 01/01/1983–07/31/1983 Folder, Box 11, Oliver North Files, Ronald Reagan Library, Simi Valley, California.

4. CHASING VICTORY, 1984–1988

1. Chris Hedges, "Salvador Army Morale Sinks after Losses," *Christian Science Monitor,* January 9, 1984.

2. Telegram, "Reaction to New Year's Strikes by Guerrillas," January 4, 1984,

Guerrilla Activity in El Salvador Folder (No. 2032), Box 9, National Security Agency (hereafter NSA).

3. US Senate, *Central American Migration to the United States,* June 21, 1989, Hearing before the Subcommittee on Immigration and Refugee Affairs, 101st Cong., 1st sess., 81.

4. James Corum, "The Air War in El Salvador," *Airpower Journal* (Summer 1998): 31.

5. Ibid., 33.

6. William LeoGrande, *Our Own Backyard: The United States in Central America, 1977–1992* (Chapel Hill: University of North Carolina Press, 1998), 266.

7. Jenny Pearce, *Promised Land: Peasant Rebellion in Chalatenango, El Salvador* (London: Latin America Bureau, 1986), 227.

8. Quoted in LeoGrande, *Our Own Backyard,* 266.

9. Charles Clements reportedly treated civilians with wounds consistent to the injuries produced by these bombs. See Clements, *Witness to War: An American Doctor in El Salvador* (Toronto, ON: Bantam, 1984).

10. Quoted in Kenneth Sharpe, "El Salvador Revisited: Why Duarte Is in Trouble," *World Policy Journal* 3, no. 3 (Summer 1986): 475.

11. Americas Watch Committee and the Lawyers Committee for International Human Rights, *Free Fire: A Report on Human Rights in El Salvador, August 1984* (New York: Americas Watch Committee, 1984).

12. United Nations, *From Madness to Hope: The 12-Year War in El Salvador—Report of the Commission on the Truth for El Salvador,* http://www.usip.org/sites/default/files/file/ElSalvador-Report.pdf.

13. This figure was cited by Sylvia Rosales-Fike during her testimony before the US Senate committee. US Senate, *Central American Migration to the United States,* 87.

14. Elisabeth Wood, "Civil War and Reconstruction: The Repopulation of Tenancingo," in *Landscapes of Struggle: Politics, Society, and Community in El Salvador,* ed. Aldo Lauria-Santiago and Leigh Binford (Pittsburgh, PA: University of Pittsburgh Press, 2004), 128.

15. US Senate, *Central American Migration to the United States,* 87.

16. David Haines and Karen Roseblum, eds., *Illegal Immigration in America: A Handbook* (Westport, CT: Greenwood, 1999), 234.

17. Ibid., 240.

18. Elisabeth Wood describes the repopulation of this village as part of efforts to reconstruct and to redefine civil society, including the relationships between the elite and the villagers. As Wood argues, the results were short-lived and limited. See Wood, "Civil War and Reconstruction," esp. 130–146.

19. Molly Todd, *Beyond Displacement: Campesinos, Refugees, and Collective Action in the Salvadoran Civil War* (Madison: University of Wisconsin Press, 2010), 217.

20. Facundo Guardado, interview with the author, August 22, 2013, San Salvador, El Salvador.

21. José Medrano, interview with the author, August 22, 2013, San Salvador, El Salvador.

22. Comandante Balta, *Memorias de un Guerrillero* (San Salvador: New Graphics, 2006), 257.

23. Quoted in Mark Danner, *The Massacre at El Mozote: A Parable of the Cold War* (New York: Vintage, 1994), 91.

24. Kyle Longley, *In the Eagle's Shadow: The United States and Latin America* (Wheeling, IL: Harlan Davidson, 2009), 311; LeoGrande, *Our Own Backyard,* 239.

25. The other key components were the National Campaign Plan and the Woerner report. Michael Childress, *The Effectiveness of U.S. Training Efforts in Internal Defense and Development: The Cases of El Salvador and Honduras* (Santa Monica, CA: RAND, 1995), 3–5.

26. Benjamin Schwartz, *American Counterinsurgency Doctrine and El Salvador: The Frustrations of Reform and the Illusions of Nation Building* (Santa Monica, CA: RAND, 1991), 11.

27. US Congress, *The Role of the U.S. Southern Command in Central America,* August 1, 1984 (Washington: US Government Printing Office, 1984).

28. Quoted in LeoGrande, *Our Own Backyard,* 259.

29. Central Intelligence Agency (CIA), "El Salvador: The Role of Roberto D'Aubuisson," March 4, 1981, CIA Freedom of Information Act website, https://www.cia.gov/library/readingroom/docs/DOC_0000654925.pdf. For the amount spent by the United States, see Walter LaFeber, *Inevitable Revolutions: The United States in Central America* (New York: Norton, 1993), 318.

30. Kenneth Sharpe, "U.S. Policy toward Central America: The Post-Vietnam Formula under Siege," in *Crisis in Central America: Regional Dynamics and U.S. Policy in the 1980s,* ed. Nora Hamilton (Boulder, CO: Westview, 1988), 23.

31. Martin Diskin, *The Impact of U.S. Policy in El Salvador, 1979–1985,* Institute of International Studies, Policy Papers in International Affairs no. 27 (Berkeley: University of California Press, 1986), 59.

32. Cynthia Arnson, *Crossroads: Congress, the President, and Central America, 1976–1993* (University Park: Pennsylvania State University Press, 1993), 149.

33. As LeoGrande argues, Duarte provided hope that he could transform El Salvador into something resembling a real democracy. Even for skeptical members, he still represented the lesser of two evils. LeoGrande, *Our Own Backyard,* 259.

34. Raúl Mijango, *Mi Guerra: Testimonio de toda una vida* (San Salvador: Laser Print, 2007), 256.

35. Herard von Santos, *Soldados de Elite en Centroamérica y México* (San Salvador: Imprenta Nacional, 2008), 139.

36. Ibid., 140. The term was used by members of the Fuerzas Armadas de Liberación (FAL) stationed at the Guazapa Volcano. Herard von Santos, email interview with the author, October 7, 2014.

37. John Fishel and Max Manwaring, *Uncomfortable Wars Revisited* (Norman: University of Oklahoma Press, 2006), 115.

38. Greg Walker, *At the Hurricane's Eye: U.S. Special Forces from Vietnam to Desert Storm* (New York: Ivy, 1994), 93.
39. Frank Smyth, "Secret Warriors: U.S. Advisers Have Taken Up Arms in El Salvador," *Village Voice,* August 11, 1987. He noted that the CIA had been active in providing training for PRAL units and used intelligence gathered from their missions to coordinate air strikes against FMLN detachments.
40. José Moroni Bracamonte and David Spencer, *Strategy and Tactics of the Salvadoran FMLN Guerrillas: Last Battle of the Cold War, Blueprint for Future Conflicts* (Westport, CT: Praeger, 1995), 159.
41. US General Accounting Office (GAO), *El Salvador: Military Assistance Has Helped Counter but Not Overcome the Insurgency* (Washington, DC: GAO, 1991).
42. Childress, *Effectiveness of U.S. Training Efforts in Internal Defense and Development,* 24.
43. John Waghelstein, interview by Colonel Charles Charlton Jr., transcript, Senior Officers Oral History Program, US Army Military History Institute, Carlisle Barracks, Pennsylvania, 66.
44. Quoted in William Meara, *Contra Cross: Insurgency and Tyranny in Central America, 1979–1989* (Annapolis, MD: Naval Institute Press, 2006), 60.
45. Ibid., 57.
46. "Status of the War," Security Assistance—Helicopters Folder (no. 1689), Box 13, El Salvador II Collection: Salvadoran Biographies to Security Assistance, NSA.
47. "Military Strategy of the FMLN," May–June 1985, Folder 3, Box 2, David E. Spencer Collection, Hoover Institution, Stanford University, Palo Alto, California.
48. Mijango, *Mi Guerra,* 257.
49. "Readecuacion Tactica del Ejercito: Un Nuevo Fracas," 1986, Folder 3.1, Box 3, Salvadoran Subject Collection, Hoover Institution, Stanford University, Palo Alto, California.
50. "Linea Militar: Fase Prepatoria de la Contraofensiva Estrategica," November 1986, Loose Collection Folder, Box 1, David E. Spencer Collection, Hoover Institution, Stanford University, Palo Alto, California.
51. Central Intelligence Agency (CIA), "El Salvador: A Net Assessment of the War," February 1986, CIA Freedom of Information Act website, https://www.cia.gov/library/readingroom/docs/CIA-RDP86T01017R000707070001-9.pdf.
52. Defense Intelligence Agency (DIA), "El Salvador: Domestic Troubles," December 11, 1985, El Salvador Folder, Box 1, Oliver North Files, Ronald Reagan Library, Simi Valley, California.
53. Hugh Byrnes, *El Salvador's Civil War: A Study of Revolution* (Boulder, CO: Lynne Rienner, 1996), 143.
54. Bracamonte and Spencer, *Strategy and Tactics of the Salvadoran FMLN Guerrillas,* 24.

55. LeoGrande, *Our Own Backyard,* 278.

56. Cynthia McClintock, *Revolutionary Movements in Latin America: El Salvador's FMLN and Peru's Shining Path* (Washington, DC: US Institute of Peace, 1998), 232.

57. Tom Barry and Deb Preusch, "The War in El Salvador: A Reassessment," *Monthly Review* 38 (April 1987): 30.

58. McClintock, *Revolutionary Movements in Latin America,* 232.

59. Duarte's successor went even further, dismantling state monopolies and privatizing the banking system, nationalized by the first junta. Alfredo Cristiani also began the process of reorganizing the farm cooperatives established under the various agrarian reform acts. Edwin Corr, "Societal Transformation for Peace in El Salvador," *Annals of the American Academy of Political and Social Science* 541 (September 1995): 152.

60. DIA, "El Salvador."

61. Mijango, *Mi Guerra,* 339.

62. Central Intelligence Agency (CIA), "El Salvador's Insurgents: Resurrecting an Urban Political Strategy," September 1986, CIA Freedom of Information Act website, https://www.cia.gov/library/readingroom/docs/CIA-RDP04T00794 R000100260001-0.pdf.

63. Ibid.

64. Unknown author, "JTIC Special Advisory 03-91—Salvadoran Insurgent Repopulation of Rear Guard Areas, Part II," March 1991, El Salvador Online Collections, NSA.

65. Ibid.

66. Todd, *Beyond Displacement,* 133.

67. Unknown author, "JTIC Special Advisory 03-91."

68. Ibid.

69. Sharpe, "El Salvador Revisited," 477.

70. According to one account, after the termination of the conflict, approximately 20,000 land mines threatened rural Salvadorans.

71. Central Intelligence Agency (CIA), "El Salvador: Guerrilla Use of Mine Warfare," June 1987, CIA Freedom of Information Act website, https://www.cia .gov/library/readingroom/docs/DOC_0000049319.pdf.

72. Ibid.

73. Charles Briscoe, "Los Artefactos Explosivos Improvisados: Spanish for IEDs," *Veritas* 2, no. 1 (2006): 52.

74. United Nations, *From Madness to Hope.*

75. CIA, "El Salvador: Guerrilla Use of Mine Warfare."

76. To cite such an example, a poster, "Innocent Victim of FMLN Mines," depicted a girl missing a leg, presumably injured by one of these weapons. Posters emblazoned with this image greeted international visitors at the Salvadoran airport, and as the CIA noted, this poster along with previous efforts had positive effects both in El Salvador and internationally. Supposedly, this

particular propaganda effort paid handsome dividends with human rights organizations—highly critical of the US and Salvadoran government—except
those "functioning as insurgent front groups." Ibid. There is a copy in the Library of Congress Salvadoran Human Rights Collection.

77. US Senate Arms Control and Foreign Policy Caucus, *Bankrolling Failure: The
United States Policy in El Salvador and the Urgent Need for Reform*, Novem-
ber 1987, Box 2, Salvadoran Subject Collection, Hoover Institution, Stanford
University, Palo Alto, California.

78. Bracamonte and Spencer, *Strategy and Tactics of the Salvadoran FMLN Guerrillas,* 32.

79. Meara, *Contra Cross,* 58.

80. William Pascasio (Comandante Memo), interview with author, August 20,
2013, San Salvador, El Salvador. Several other former *comandantes* interviewed
acknowledged the damage caused by this strategy; Todd, *Beyond Displacement,*
74.

81. Wendy Shaull, *Tortillas, Beans, and M16s: Behind the Lines in El Salvador*
(London: Pluto, 1990), 46.

82. Americas Watch Committee and the Lawyers Committee for International
Human Rights, *Free Fire,* 56.

83. Telegram, Conversation with UCA Rector Ellacuría, May 22, 1985, El Salvador
Online Collections, NSA.

84. Edwin Corr, interview with the author, April 11, 2014, Norman, Oklahoma.

85. Bracamonte and Spencer, *Strategy and Tactics of the Salvadoran FMLN Guerrillas,* 31.

86. "El Salvador Vencera: Hablan los comandantes del Frente Farabundo Martí
(San Salvador, 1982)," Folder 6, Universidad Centroamericana, San Salvador,
El Salvador.

87. Quoted in Byrnes, *El Salvador's Civil War,* 134.

88. Telegram, "A Mayor's Story," February 17, 1989, El Salvador Online Collections, NSA.

89. Central Intelligence Agency (CIA), "El Salvador: Rebels Target Mayors," February 1989, CIA Freedom of Information Act website, https://www.cia.gov
/library/readingroom/docs/DOC_0000049379.pdf.

90. Pablo Parada Andino, interview with the author, August 20, 2013, San Salvador,
El Salvador.

91. United Nations, *From Madness to Hope.*

92. Byrnes, *El Salvador's Civil War,* 141.

93. LeoGrande, *Our Own Backyard,* 262.

94. Sam Dillon and Juan Tamayo, "Salvadorans Will Keep Talking," *Miami Herald,*
October 16, 1984.

95. Alfonso Chardy, "La Palma Talks Are a Credit to Reagan Policy, Aides Say,"
Miami Herald, October 16, 1984.

96. Associated Press, "Salvador Rightist Leader Calls Peace Talks a Fraud," *Miami
Herald,* October 18, 1984.

97. Philip Taubman, "U.S. Aides Say Salvadoran Army Is Now on Top," *New York Times,* October 7, 1984.

98. Sharpe, "El Salvador Revisited," 482.

99. According to Edwin Corr, "The elements of a peace agreement had to include the FMLN's acceptance of the 1984 Constitution (with some amendments but not a re-write), free and fair elections with more than one political party, the rule of law, respect for human rights, civilian control over the military, etc. . . . We would not and did not accept the FMLN's proposals of a shared government in transition to some kind of future government yet to be defined." Corr interview, April 11, 2014.

100. Telegram, "Dialogue One Year after Ayagualo—No Movement with the FMLN; but Just Maybe with the FDR," December 1985, Folder 486, Box 9: Files—Economic Assistance-Guerrilla, NSA.

101. Byrnes, *El Salvador's Civil War,* 142.

102. Edwin Corr also emphasized the importance of improving human rights to his country team. Corr interview, April 11, 2014.

103. Quoted in John Waghelstein, "Military-to-Military Contacts: Personal Observations—the El Salvador Case," *Low Intensity Conflict and Law Enforcement* 10, no. 2 (Summer 2003): 22.

104. United Nations, *From Madness to Hope.*

105. US Department of State, "Vice President Bush Visits Latin America," February 1984.

106. William Deane Stanley, *The Protection Racket State: Elite Politics, Military Extortion, and Civil War in El Salvador* (Philadelphia, PA: Temple University Press, 1996), 263.

107. Schwartz, *American Counterinsurgency Doctrine and El Salvador,* 82.

108. Martha Doggett, *Underwriting Injustice: AID and El Salvador's Judicial Reform Program* (New York: Lawyers Committee for Human Rights, 1989).

109. CIA, "El Salvador: A Net Assessment of the War."

110. Schwartz, *American Counterinsurgency Doctrine and El Salvador,* 52.

111. CIA, "El Salvador: A Net Assessment of the War."

112. Philip J. Williams and Knut Walter, *Militarization and Demilitarization in El Salvador's Transition to Democracy* (Pittsburgh, PA: University of Pittsburgh Press, 1997), 120.

113. "Excerpt of Speech by Comandante Claudio Armijo," *Boletin Informativo* (June 1986), Folder 2.2, Salvadoran Subject Collection, Hoover Institution, Stanford University, Palo Alto, California.

114. "Poder Popular Doble Cara: Lineamientos de Organizacion," n.d., Box 1, David E. Spencer Collection, Hoover Institution, Stanford University, Palo Alto, California.

115. Ibid.

116. "Readecuacion Tactica del Ejercito."

117. "Linea Militar."

118. "Poder Popular Doble Cara."

119. Michael McClintock, *Instruments of Statecraft: U.S. Guerrilla Warfare, Counterinsurgency, and Counter-Terrorism, 1940–1990* (New York: Pantheon, 1992), 420.

120. Corr interview, April 11, 2014.

121. Scott W. Moore, "Purple, Not Gold: Lessons from USAID-USMILGP Cooperation in El Salvador, 1980–1992" (master's thesis, Naval Postgraduate School, 1997), 62.

122. US Senate Arms Control and Foreign Policy Caucus, *Bankrolling Failure*, 15.

123. Central Intelligence Agency (CIA) Directorate of Intelligence, "El Salvador: The Struggle for Rural Control—a Reference Aid," Folder 3.1, Box 3, Salvadoran Subject Collection, Hoover Institution, Stanford University, Palo Alto, California.

124. Moore, "Purple, Not Gold," 60.

125. Ibid., 59.

126. National Commission for the Restoration of Areas (CONARA), *Cabildos Abiertos: La Revolución Pacífica en El Salvador* (San Salvador: Publicidad Rumbo, n.d.). A copy is available at the Fundación Salvadoreña para el Desarrollo Económico y Social (FUSADES) library.

127. CIA Directorate of Intelligence, "El Salvador."

128. Moore, "Purple, Not Gold," 60.

129. CIA Directorate of Intelligence, "El Salvador."

130. Byrnes, *El Salvador's Civil War,* 149.

131. The White House also refused to close down the Contra camps. Roger Peace, *A Call to Conscience: The Anti-Contra War Campaign* (Amherst: University of Massachusetts Press, 2012), 25.

132. Rose J. Spalding, "From Low-Intensity War to Low-Intensity Peace: The Nicaragua Peace Process," in *Comparative Peace Processes in Latin America,* ed. Cynthia Arnson (Washington, DC: Woodrow Wilson Center, 1999), 33.

133. Stephen Kinzer, *Blood of Brothers: Life and War in Nicaragua* (New York: Putnam's, 1991), 347.

134. Ibid., 349.

135. Peace, *Call to Conscience,* 216.

136. Kinzer, *Blood of Brothers,* 353.

137. Telegram, Visit by Presidential Delegation Headed by Panamanians, March 22, 1986, DDRS.

138. Ibid.

139. Hal Brands, *Latin America's Cold War* (Cambridge, MA: Harvard University Press, 2010), 218.

140. Todd Greentree, *Crossroads of Intervention: Insurgency and Counterinsurgency Lessons from Central America* (Westport, CT: Praeger Security International, 2008), 150.

141. Byrnes, *El Salvador's Civil War,* 169.

142. United Nations, *From Madness to Hope.*

143. US Senate Arms Control and Foreign Policy Caucus, *Bankrolling Failure*, 1.
144. James Hallums, email interview with the author, March 5, 2014.
145. John Waghelstein, phone interview with the author, April 1, 2014. Colonel Hallums also acknowledged the reticence of the Salvadoran high command. Hallums interview, March 5, 2014.
146. The report noted that PRAL units had "achieved successes far out of proportion to their size." Apart from these units, "Salvadoran attempts to adopt small unit tactics have been ineffective." Andrew Bacevich, *American Military Policy in Small Wars: The Case of El Salvador* (Cambridge, UK: Pergamon Brassey's, 1988), 37.
147. Ibid., 40.
148. Hallums interview, March 5, 2014.
149. Quoted in Michael Massing, "The Stale, Small War in El Salvador," Alicia Patterson Foundation, http://aliciapatterson.org/stories/stale-small-war-el-salvador.
150. Tommie Sue Montgomery, "Fighting Guerrillas: The United States and Low-Intensity Conflict in El Salvador," *New Political Science* 9, no. 1 (Fall–Winter 1990): 21–53.
151. Ronald Reagan, "Remarks at the Welcoming Ceremony for President José Napoleón Duarte Fuentes of El Salvador," October 14, 1987, http://www.reagan.utexas.edu/search/speeches.
152. The document also attributed the failure of civilian institutions to bribery, incompetence, laziness, and lack of funds. Telegram, Post Reporting Plan: Governance—Generic Problems in the Functioning of Civilian Government Institutions, May 23, 1989, El Salvador Online Collections, NSA.
153. Bacevich, *American Military Policy in Small Wars*, vii.
154. Carollee Bengelsdorf, Margaret Cerullo, and Yogesh Chandrani, eds., *The Selected Writings of Eqbal Ahmad* (New York: Columbia University Press, 2006), 69.

5. TERMINATING THE BLOODLETTING, 1989–1992
   1. Walter LaFeber, *Inevitable Revolutions: The United States in Central America* (New York: Norton, 1993), 346.
   2. James A. Baker III, *The Politics of Diplomacy: Revolution, War, and Peace, 1989–1992* (New York: Putnam's, 1995), 42.
   3. William LeoGrande, "From Reagan to Bush: The Transition in U.S. Policy towards Central America," *Journal of Latin American Studies* 22, no. 3 (October 1990): 595.
   4. LaFeber, *Inevitable Revolutions*, 346.
   5. LeoGrande, "From Reagan to Bush," 620.
   6. Hugh Byrnes, *El Salvador's Civil War: A Study of Revolution* (Boulder, CO: Lynne Rienner, 1996), 177.
   7. Cynthia Arnson, *Crossroads: Congress, the President, and Central America, 1976–1993* (University Park: Pennsylvania State University Press, 1993), 228.

8. Hal Brands, "Reform, Democratization, and Counterinsurgency: Evaluating the US Experience in Cold War–Era Latin America," *Small Wars and Insurgencies* 22, no. 2 (May 2011): 310.

9. William Walker, interview with author, February 17, 2014, Washington, DC. According to the MILGP study, there was no way the FMLN would win. The Department of Defense and CIA made conclusions along similar lines but also believed that no stalemate existed. CIA, "El Salvador Government and Insurgent Prospects," February 1989, Salvadoran Human Rights, vol. 1, Library of Congress (LOC).

10. Todd Greentree, *Crossroads of Intervention: Insurgency and Counterinsurgency Lessons from Central America* (Westport, CT: Praeger Security International, 2008), 108.

11. Greg Grandin, *Empire's Workshop: Latin America, the United States, and the Rise of the New Imperialism* (New York: Metropolitan, 2006), 104.

12. William LeoGrande, *Our Own Backyard: The United States in Central America, 1977–1992* (Chapel Hill: University of North Carolina Press, 1998), 565.

13. Joaquín Villalobos, *The War in El Salvador: Current Situation and Outlook for the Future* (San Francisco: Solidarity, 1986), 21.

14. CIA, "Talking Points for DCI," January 11, 1989, El Salvador Online Collection, National Security Agency (hereafter NSA).

15. Byrnes, *El Salvador's Civil War*, 143.

16. James LeMoyne, "The Guns of El Salvador: Eight Long Years of Political Terror," *New York Times*, February 5, 1989.

17. Juan Orlando Zepeda, *Perfiles de la Guerra en El Salvador* (San Salvador: New Graphics, 2008), 242.

18. CIA, "Talking Points for DCI."

19. Over a period of several years, hundreds of FMLN combatants were murdered under the command of Mayo Sibrian, *el carnicero de paracentral*. Sibrian believed that the FMLN had been infiltrated by spies and the CIA. One study posits that his forces carried out 1,000 summary executions. These executions took place allegedly with the consent of Salvador Sánchez Cerén, Sibrian's boss and current president of El Salvador. These crimes were also never investigated by the UN Truth Commission after the conflict. See Marvin Galeas, "Grandeza y Miseria en una Guerrilla: Informe de una Matanza," *Reportaje Especial de Centroamérica 21*; "Le Pedí a Sánchez Cerén para Massacre," *El Diario de Hoy,* December 10, 2008, http://www.elsalvador.com/mwedh/nota/nota_completa.asp?idCat=6351&idArt=3118159.

20. Americas Watch, *A Year of Reckoning: El Salvador a Decade after the Assassination of Archbishop Romero* (Washington, DC: Human Rights Watch, 1990), 8. As the report noted, deaths from mines declined substantially during the second half of the year.

21. Douglas Farah, "El Salvador's Mayors Quit in Droves," *Washington Post*, January 8, 1989.

22. Telegram, Ambassador's Meeting with UCA Rector Ellacuría, April 5, 1989, El Salvador Online Collections, NSA.

23. Miguel Castellanos, *The Comandante Speaks: Memoirs of an El Salvadoran Guerrilla Leader* (Boulder, CO: Westview, 1991).

24. Telegram, Ambassador's Meeting with UCA Rector Ellacuría. The UN Truth Commission report noted that the murders of Castellanos, Peccorini, Alvarado, and Porth caused the FMLN considerable damage in public opinion.

25. Cynthia McClintock, *Revolutionary Movements in Latin America: El Salvador's FMLN and Peru's Shining Path* (Washington, DC: US Institute of Peace, 1998), 153.

26. Telegram, USG Response to Deterioration in Human Rights Situation in El Salvador, January 7, 1989, El Salvador Online Collections, NSA.

27. This was derived from a statement from Martha Doggett, who appeared before Congress. See El Salvador at the Crossroads: Peace or Another Decade of War, Hearings before the Subcommittees on Human Rights and International Organizations and on Western Hemisphere Affairs, 101st Congress, 2nd sess., January 24 and 31, 1990, and February 6, 1990, 110.

28. CIA, "Talking Points for DCI."

29. CIA, "El Salvador Government and Insurgent Prospects."

30. Ibid.

31. Quoted in Arnson, *Crossroads,* 230.

32. LeoGrande, "From Reagan to Bush," 607.

33. Jeffery M. Paige, *Coffee and Power: Revolution and the Rise of Democracy in Central America* (Cambridge, MA: Harvard University Press, 1997), 321.

34. Philip J. Williams and Knut Walter, *Militarization and Demilitarization in El Salvador's Transition to Democracy* (Pittsburgh, PA: University of Pittsburgh Press, 1997), 124.

35. Diana Villiers-Negroponte, *Seeking Peace in El Salvador: The Struggle to Reconstruct a Nation at the End of the Cold War* (New York: Palgrave Macmillan, 2012), 57.

36. Ibid., 58.

37. CIA, "El Salvador: Capital Tense," November 8, 1989, El Salvador Human Rights, LOC.

38. Zepeda, *Perfiles de la guerra en El Salvador,* 199.

39. Charles Armstrong, "Urban Combat: The FMLN's 'Final Offensive' of 1989," *Marine Corps Gazette* (November 1990): 53.

40. Tommie Sue Montgomery, *Revolution in El Salvador: From Civil Strife to Civil Peace* (Boulder, CO: Westview, 1995), 217.

41. Byrnes, *El Salvador's Civil War,* 152.

42. United Nations, *From Madness to Hope: The 12-Year War in El Salvador—Report of the Commission on the Truth for El Salvador,* http://www.usip.org/sites/default/files/file/ElSalvador-Report.pdf.

43. "Program Politica," 1989, David E. Spencer Collection, Folder 1, Box 2, Hoover Institution, Stanford University, Palo Alto, California.

44. Marta Harnecker, *Con la Mirada en Alto: Historia del FPL* (Chile: Ediciones Biblioteca Popular, 1991), 140.
45. Zepeda, *Perfiles de la guerra en El Salvador*, 204.
46. David Spencer, *From Vietnam to El Salvador: The Saga of the FMLN Sappers and Other Guerrilla Forces in Latin America* (Westport, CT: Praeger, 1996), 281–282.
47. Christopher Marquis, "Salvador Battle Hurt Talk Hopes," *Miami Herald*, November 16, 1989.
48. Mario Lungo, *El Salvador in the Eighties: Counterinsurgency and Revolution* (Philadelphia, PA: Temple University Press, 1996), 177–178.
49. Raúl Mijango, *Mi Guerra: Testimonio de toda una vida* (San Salvador: Laser Print, 2007), 320.
50. Walker interview, February 17, 2014.
51. These impressions were gathered from ibid.
52. LeMoyne, "Guns of El Salvador."
53. The individual was the former president of the Salvadoran airline, Taca, who relayed the story to Ambassador William Walker. Walker interview, February 17, 2014.
54. In one case, the Salvadoran Air Force dropped three 500-pound bombs on a guerrilla command outpost, which, according to one account killed one civilian, wounded another, and killed an indeterminate number of insurgents. *Miami Herald*, "Aircraft Strafe Salvadoran Capital," November 15, 1989.
55. Armstrong, "Urban Combat," 55.
56. This quotation was part of Aronson's testimony before Congress. El Salvador at the Crossroads: Peace or Another Decade of War, Hearings before the Subcommittees on Human Rights and International Organizations and on Western Hemisphere Affairs, 101st Cong., 2nd sess. (January 24 and 31, 1990, and February 6, 1990).
57. Quoted in Arnson, *Crossroads*, 246.
58. Quoted in William LeoGrande, "After the Battle of San Salvador," *World Policy Journal* 7, no. 2 (Spring 1990): 331.
59. "Ofensiva Terrorista bajo Control Dice Gobierno," *El Diario de Hoy*, November 14, 1989.
60. Christopher Marquis, "Salvador Sends Heavy Arms into Suburbs; Toll Tops 300," *Miami Herald*, November 14, 1989.
61. United Nations, *From Madness to Hope.*
62. James Hallums, email interview with author, March 5, 2013.
63. Inter-American Commission on Human Rights, Organization of American States, "Report 136/99," http://www.cidh.oas.org/annualrep/99eng/Merits/El Salvador10.488.htm; United Nations, *From Madness to Hope.*
64. Quoted in Byrnes, *El Salvador's Civil War*, 161.
65. Villiers-Negroponte, *Seeking Peace in El Salvador*, 52.
66. Telegram, Conversation with UCA Rector Ellacuría, February 22, 1985, El Salvador Online Collection, NSA.
67. United Nations, *From Madness to Hope.*

68. Zepeda, *Perfiles de la Guerra en El Salvador,* 217.

69. Arnson, *Crossroads,* 253.

70. US House Foreign Affairs Subcommittee Hearing on El Salvador, information memorandum, February 2, 1990, El Salvador Human Rights, OSD/RSA-IA, LOC.

71. US Senate Arms Control and Foreign Policy Caucus, *Barriers to Reform: A Profile of El Salvador's Military Leaders* (Washington, DC: US Congress, 1990), Caleb Rossiter Files, National Archives, Washington, DC.

72. LeoGrande, *Our Own Backyard,* 573.

73. CIA, "El Salvador: The FMLN after the November 1989 Offensive," January 26, 1990, El Salvadoran Human Rights, vol. 1, LOC.

74. Twelve Special Forces advisers and important international figures were staying at the hotel at the time of the crisis. Mijango, *Mi Guerra,* 241.

75. CIA, "El Salvador: The FMLN after the November 1989 Offensive."

76. José Moroni Bracamonte and David E. Spencer, *Strategy and Tactics of the Salvadoran FMLN Guerrillas: Last Battle of the Cold War, Blueprint for Future Conflicts* (Westport, CT: Praeger, 1995), 35.

77. CIA, "El Salvador: The FMLN after the November 1989 Offensive."

78. LeoGrande, *Our Own Backyard,* 571.

79. Benjamin Schwartz, "Dirty Hands," review of *Our Own Backyard: The United States in Central America, 1977–1992,* by William LeoGrande, *Atlantic Monthly* (December 1998): 114.

80. José Medrano, interview with author, August 22, 2013, San Salvador, El Salvador.

81. Raúl Mijango, interview with the author, August 22, 2013, San Salvador, El Salvador.

82. Medrano interview, August 22, 2013.

83. General William Westmoreland made this infamous remark in a speech he gave at the National Press Club in Washington, DC. The general had been asked to return to the United States by President Lyndon Baines Johnson to drum up domestic support for the war effort.

84. Michael Gordon, "General Says Salvador Can't Defeat Guerrillas," *New York Times,* February 9, 1990.

85. This view was confirmed by Ambassador William Walker. Walker interview, February 17, 2014.

86. Baker, *Politics of Diplomacy,* 603.

87. Ibid.

88. Arnson, *Crossroads,* 248.

89. See Bernard Aronson's testimony at the US House of Representatives, Subcommittee on Western Hemispheric Affairs, Committee on Foreign Affairs, January 24, 1990 (Washington: US Congress).

90. Walker interview, February 17, 2014.

91. Telegram, GOES-FMLN Negotiations: Where Do We Go from Here? September 22, 1989, El Salvador Online Collection, NSA.

92. Byrnes, *El Salvador's Civil War*, 173.
93. Telegram, GOES-FMLN Negotiations.
94. Hal Brands, *Latin America's Cold War* (Cambridge, MA: Harvard University Press, 2010), 217.
95. Quoted in Roger Peace, *A Call to Conscience: The Anti-Contra War Campaign* (Amherst: University of Massachusetts Press, 2012), 238.
96. Medrano interview, August 22, 2013; Comandante Balta, *Memorias de un Guerrillero* (San Salvador: New Graphics, 2006), 388.
97. Spencer, *From Vietnam to El Salvador,* 282; Medrano interview, August 22, 2013.
98. US State Department, Negotiations to End the War in El Salvador, memorandum, April 1990, El Salvador Online Collections, NSA.
99. James Corum, "The Air War in El Salvador," *Airpower Journal* (Summer 1998): 36.
100. Mijango, *Mi Guerra,* 349.
101. Quoted in Byrnes, *El Salvador's Civil War,* 184.
102. US intelligence operatives blamed Villalobos for the incident, a claim he has denied. For a description of the events, see United Nations, *From Madness to Hope.*
103. Telegram, El Salvador–Nicaragua: Anti-Aircraft Weapons, May 11, 1985, El Salvador Online Collections, NSA.
104. Corum, "Air War in El Salvador," 36.
105. CIA, "El Salvador: Assessing the Impact of Rebel Surface-to-Air Missiles," June 7, 1991, CIA Freedom of Information Act website, https://www.cia.gov/library/readingroom/docs/DOC_0000808523.pdf.
106. National Security Agency, "El Salvador Pol-Mil Situation as of 7 Jan. 1991," January 1991, El Salvador Online Collections, NSA.
107. Mijango, *Mi Guerra,* 349–351.
108. Villiers-Negroponte, *Seeking Peace in El Salvador,* 76.
109. Walker interview, February 17, 2014.
110. Ibid.
111. Villiers-Negroponte, *Seeking Peace in El Salvador,* 76.
112. Arnson, *Crossroads,* 261.
113. Douglas Farah, "Salvadoran Ex-Rebel, Key to Peace Pact, Tries Centrist Politics," *Washington Post,* November 12, 1992. This account was also confirmed during my interview with Walker.
114. Walker interview, February 17, 2014.
115. Arnson, *Crossroads,* 261.
116. For an excellent discussion of the various intrigues and how peace was achieved, Villiers-Negroponte's book *Seeking Peace in El Salvador* offers one of the most thorough accounts.
117. National Security Agency, "Negotiations to End the War in El Salvador," May 1991, El Salvador Online Collections, NSA.

118. LeoGrande, *Our Own Backyard,* 576.
119. Tracy Wilkinson, "Salvador Sánchez Cerén Wins El Salvador's Presidential Election," *Los Angeles Times,* March 13, 2014.
120. "Quijano Niega Haber Llamado a Fuerzas Armadas a Intervenir Elección," *El Diario,* March 12, 2014, http://diariolatino.net/index.php?option=com_content&view=article&id=15882:quijano-niega-haber-llamado-a-fuerzas-armadas-a-intervenir-eleccion&catid=34:nacionales&Itemid=53.
121. "Fuerza Armada Respectará Resultados de Elecciones Presidenciales," *La Prensa Grafica,* March 12, 2014, http://mediacenter.laprensagrafica.com/videos/v/fuerza-armada-respetar-resultados-de-elecciones-presidenciales.
122. Kyle Longley, *In the Eagle's Shadow: The United States and Latin America* (Wheeling, IL: Harlan Davidson, 2009), 324.
123. Quoted in David Spencer, "External Resource Mobilization and Successful Insurgency in Cuba, Nicaragua, and El Salvador, 1959–1992" (PhD diss., George Washington University, 2002), 242.
124. Facundo Guardado, interview with author, August 22, 2013, San Salvador, El Salvador.
125. Medrano interview, August 22, 2013.
126. Balta, *Memorias de un Guerrillero,* 404.
127. Williams and Walter, *Militarization and Demilitarization in El Salvador's Transition to Democracy,* 163, 169.
128. James LeMoyne, "Salvadorans Stream into U.S., Fleeing Poverty and Civil War," *New York Times,* April 13, 1987.
129. Elliot Abrams, "Drug Traffickers Threaten Central America's Democratic Gains," *Washington Post,* January 3, 2014.
130. US Army and Marine Corps, *FM 3-24.*
131. Jules Witcover, "Should We Continue to Be the Indispensable Nation?" *Chicago Tribune,* September 28, 2013.

CODA: "THE SALVADORAN OPTION" IN IRAQ

1. *USA Today,* "Rumsfeld Blames Iraq Problems on Pockets of 'Dead-Enders,'" June 18, 2003.
2. Roland Watson, "El Salvador 'Death Squads' to Be Employed by U.S. against Iraqi Militants," *Times of London,* January 10, 2005, Overseas News.
3. Quoted in David Pedersen, *American Value: Migrants, Money, and Meaning in El Salvador and the United States* (Chicago: University of Chicago Press, 2013), 237.
4. Todd R. Greentree, *Crossroads of Intervention: Insurgency and Counterinsurgency Lessons from Central America* (Westport, CT: Praeger Security International, 2008); Mark Peceny and William D. Stanley, "Counterinsurgency in El Salvador," *Politics and Society* 38, no. 1 (2010): 38–67.
5. *Nation,* "Death Squads—They're Back!" January 31, 2005.
6. Christopher Dickey, "Death-Squad Democracy," *Newsweek,* January 11, 2005.

7. Jonathan D. Tepperman, "Salvador in Iraq: Flashback," *New Republic*, April 5, 2005.

8. Quoted in Pedersen, *American Value*, 239.

9. Robert Dreyfuss, "Phoenix Rising," *American Prospect*, December 10, 2003.

10. Peter Maas, "The Salvadorization of Iraq?" *New York Times Magazine*, May 1, 2005. David Corbett also makes this point on his website. See "The Salvadoran Option (Part 3): Lending Money to the Gambler," June 18, 2007, http://www .davidcorbett.com/commentaries/commentary_salvador_option3.php.

11. Negroponte's tenure as US ambassador to Honduras in the middle of the 1980s was marred by disappearances and death-squad killings. Jeremy Scahill, *Blackwater: The Rise of the World's Most Powerful Mercenary Army* (New York: Nation, 2007), 283; Dahr Jamail, "Managing Escalation: Negroponte and Bush's New Iraq Team," January 9, 2007, http://www.antiwar.com/jamail /?articleid=10289. Jamail's account is derived from the Honduras Commission on Human Rights report.

12. Duncan Campbell, "Bush Hands Key Post to Veteran of Dirty Wars: Written Off by Many after his Role in Central America, John Negroponte's Revived Career Hits a New High," *Guardian*, February 18, 2005.

13. During Casteel's hunt for Escobar, the DEA also allegedly collaborated with the paramilitary organization *Los Pepes,* which later transformed into the Autodefensas Unidas de Colombia (AUC). The AUC is a right-wing paramilitary force that has links to the Colombian military and is heavily involved in drug trafficking. Max Fuller, "For Iraq, 'The Salvadoran Option' Becomes Reality," June 2, 2005, http://globalresearch.ca/articles/FUL506A.html.

14. *Guardian*, "James Steele: America's Mystery Man," http://www.theguardian .com/world/video/2013/mar/06/james-steele-america-iraq-video. The *Guardian*'s documentary used classified information provided by Wikileaks as well as interviews to highlight Steele's important role. The documentary also strongly argues that this particular segment of US policy contributed to ethnic cleansing and sectarian war. According to an account published in Pedersen's *American Value*, Paul Wolfowitz initially had suggested the deployment of Steele to Iraq not because of his military background but because of his experiences as president and CEO of TM Power Ventures, based out of Houston, Texas. Wolfowitz believed Steele's electrical power and energy-development credentials would be useful in Iraq (240).

15. Maas, "Salvadorization of Iraq?"

16. In 2006, National Security Adviser Stephan Hadley prepared a memo for Bush administration officials. In the document, Hadley assessed Nouri al-Maliki's tenure as Iraqi prime minister. One of Hadley's recommendations included shaking "up his cabinet by appointing nonsectarian, capable technocrats in key service and (security) ministries." US military commanders had heavily criticized Maliki's performance, including his commitment to reconciliation. Throughout the rest of the US occupation of Iraq, policy makers continued

to pressure Maliki to broach the sectarian divide—with limited results. See "Stephen Hadley, Iraq Memo, November 8, 2006," in *The Iraq Papers,* ed. John Ehrenberg, J. Patrice McSherry, Jose Ramon Sanchez, and Caroleen Marji Sayej (Oxford, UK: Oxford University Press, 2010), 243.

17. Mona Mahmood, Maggie O'Kane, Chavala Madlena, and Teresa Smith, "Exclusive: General David Petraeus and 'Dirty Wars' Veteran behind Commando Units Implicated in Detainee Abuse," *Guardian,* March 6, 2013, http://m.guar diannews.com/world/2013/mar/06/pentagon-iraqi-torture-centres-link.

18. Quoted in Andrew Cockburn, *Kill Chain: The Rise of the High-Tech Assassins* (New York: Henry Holt, 2015), 88.

19. Whether in Afghanistan, Colombia, or Iraq, the US infatuation with assassinating insurgent leadership has failed to produce dividends. See ibid., 149–150 and 246–247.

20. Greg Grandin and Gilbert M. Joseph's edited volume on terror and COIN violence in Latin America barely mentions the two superpowers and instead focuses more on Latin American actors. As chapters in Grandin and Joseph's book demonstrate, the various insurgent and revolutionary movements threatened the power and structure of the elites in the region. The brutal violence employed by the region's governments was not simply a response to the perfidy and ideological extremism of the rebels; the fact that the rebels attracted support threatened the elites' interests and prerogatives. Grandin and Joseph, eds., *A Century of Revolution: Insurgent and Counterinsurgent Violence during Latin America's Long Cold War* (Durham, NC: Duke University Press, 2010).

21. Quoted in McClintock, *Instruments of Statecraft: U.S. Guerrilla Warfare, Counterinsurgency, and Counter-Terrorism, 1940–1990* (New York: Pantheon, 1992), 429.

22. Benjamin Schwartz, *American Counterinsurgency Doctrine and El Salvador: The Frustrations of Reform and the Illusions of Nation Building* (Santa Monica, CA: RAND, 1991), 79.

23. Jonah Goldberg, "Going El Salvador," *National Review Online,* January 13, 2005, http://www.nationalreview.com/articles/213371/going-el-salvador/jonah -goldberg.

24. As Douglas Feith claimed before the US House International Relations Committee on May 15, 2003, "Some Iranian influence groups have called for a theocracy on the Tehran model. But it appears that popular support for clerical rule is narrow, even among the Shia population. The Shiite tradition does not favor clerical rule—the Khomeini'ites in Iran were innovators in this regard. . . . The Iranian model's appeal in Iraq is further reduced by the cultural divide between Persians and Arabs." Quoted in Peter W. Galbraith, *The End of Iraq: How American Incompetence Created a War without End* (New York: Simon and Schuster, 2006), 89.

25. Erik Schmitt, "U.S. Envoy's Cables Show Worries on Afghan Plans," *New York Times,* January 25, 2010.

26. Mark Landler and Michael R. Gordon, "U.S. to Send up to 300 Military Advisers to Iraq," *New York Times*, June 19, 2014.

27. Juan Ramón Medrano, interview with author, August 19, 2013.

28. For several years, El Salvador had the highest murder rate in the world. Recently, Honduras supplanted El Salvador with this dubious honor. For recent statistics, see the UN Office on Drugs and Crime, "Global Study on Homicide 2013," https://www.unodc.org/documents/data-and-analysis/statistics /GSH2013/2014_GLOBAL_HOMICIDE_BOOK_web.pdf.

29. The mediator of the truce, former guerrilla Raúl Mijango, was arrested in May 2016 for allegations of bringing banned items into prisons and associating with gang members. Joshua Partlow, "El Salvador Arrests People Who Pushed for Peace in Gang War," *Washington Post,* May 5, 2016; Nelson Renteria, "Murders in El Salvador Spike to Record High for May," Reuters, May 26, 2014.

Archives

UNITED STATES

Hoover Institution, Stanford University, Palo Alto, California
    Council for Inter-American Security Records
    Díaz, Nidia, Collection
    Lansdale, Edward, Papers
    Salvadoran Subject Collection
    Spencer, David E., Collection
    SWORD Collection
Jimmy Carter Presidential Library, Atlanta, Georgia
    Brzezinski, Zbigniew, Collection
    Central Intelligence Agency Records Search Tool (CREST) RAC Files
    Pastor, Robert, Country Files
Library of Congress, Washington, DC
    El Salvador Human Rights Collection (Hispanic Reading Room)
    Rossiter, Caleb, Files
National Archives and Records Administration (NARA), College Park, Maryland
    Agency of International Development (AID), Record Group 286
    Central Intelligence Agency Records Search Tool (CREST)
    Department of State, General Records, Record Group 59
    El Salvador Human Rights Collection
National Security Archives, Washington, DC
    El Salvador Human Rights Collection (Archival)
    El Salvador: The Making of U.S. Policy, 1977–1984 (El Salvador 1977–1984)
    War, Peace, and Human Rights: 1980–1994 (El Salvador 1980–1994)
Ronald Reagan Presidential Library, Simi Valley, California
    Fontaine, Roger, Files
    Latin America Directorate, National Security Council
    Lilac, Robert, Files
    Meese, Edwin, Files
    Menges, Constantine, Files
    National Security Council Executive Secretariat: Meeting Files
    North, Oliver, Files
    Tillman, Jacqueline, Files
    White House Office of Records Management (WHORM) Files
    Wigg, David, Files

EL SALVADOR

Fundación Salvadoreña para el Desarrollo Económico y Social (FUSADES)
Universidad Centroamericana (UCA)

Newspapers
Boston Globe
Diario de Hoy, El (San Salvador)
Miami Herald
New York Times
Prensa Grafica, La (San Salvador)
Village Voice
Washington Post

Email Interviews
Bacevich, Andrew
Birtle, Andrew
Gosse, Van
Hallums, James
von Santos, Herard

Oral Interviews
Andino, Pablo Parada
Corr, Edwin
Fishel, John T.
Guardado, Facundo
Krauss, Clifford
Medrano, José
Medrano, Juan Ramón
Mijango, Raúl
Pascasio, William
Waghelstein, John
Walker, William
Woerner, Fred

Government Publications
US Congress. *Central American Migration to the United States.* Hearing before the Subcommittee on Immigration and Refugee Affairs of the Committee on the Judiciary, US Senate, 101st Congress, 1st session (June 21, 1989).
———. *El Salvador at the Crossroads: Peace or Another Decade of War?* Hearings before the Subcommittees on Human Rights and International Organizations, and on Western Hemisphere Affairs of the Committee on Foreign Affairs, House of Representatives, 101st Congress, 2nd session (January 24 and 31, 1990, and February 6, 1990) (see testimony of Bernard Aronson).
———. *El Salvador: The United States in the Middle of a Maelstrom—a Report to the Committee on Foreign Relations, U.S. Senate, and the Committee on Appropriations, U.S. Senate.* Washington, DC: US Government Printing Office, 1982.
———. *Presidential Certification on El Salvador.* Vol. 1. Hearings before the Subcommittee on Inter-American Affairs of the Committee on Foreign Affairs,

House of Representatives, 97th Congress, 2nd session (February 2, 23, and 25, 1982, and March 2, 1982).

———. *The Role of Southern Command in Central America.* Hearings before the Subcommittee on Western Affairs of the Committee on Foreign Affairs, House of Representatives, 98th Congress, 2nd session (August 1, 1984).

———. *The Situation in El Salvador.* Hearings before the Committee on Foreign Relations, US Senate, 97th Congress, 1st session (March 18, 1981, and April 9, 1981).

———. *The Situation in El Salvador.* Hearings before the Subcommittees on Human Rights and International Organizations and on Western Hemisphere Affairs of the Committee on Foreign Relations, House of Representatives, 98th Congress, 2nd session (January 26, 1984, and February 6, 1984).

US General Accounting Office (GAO). *El Salvador: Extent of U.S. Military Personnel in Country.* Washington, DC: General Accounting Office, 1990.

———. *El Salvador: Military Assistance Has Helped Counter but Not Overcome the Insurgency.* Washington, DC: General Accounting Office, 1991.

Articles, Books, and Other Secondary Sources

Ahern, Thomas L. *Vietnam Declassified: The CIA and Counterinsurgency.* Lexington: University Press of Kentucky, 2010.

Almeida, Paul. *Waves of Protest: Popular Struggle in El Salvador, 1925–2005.* Minneapolis: University of Minnesota Press, 2008.

Americas Watch. *A Year of Reckoning: El Salvador a Decade after the Assassination of Archbishop Romero.* Washington, DC: Human Rights Watch, 1990.

Americas Watch Committee/Lawyers Committee for International Human Rights. *Free Fire: A Report on Human Rights in El Salvador, August 1984.* New York: Americas Watch Committee, 1984.

Anderson, Thomas P. *La Matanza: El Salvador's Communist Revolt of 1932.* Lincoln: University of Nebraska Press, 1971.

Andrade, Dale. *Ashes to Ashes: The Phoenix Program and the Vietnam War.* Lexington, MA: Lexington, 1990.

———. "Westmoreland Was Right: Learning the Wrong Lessons from the Vietnam War." *Small Wars and Insurgencies* 19, no. 2 (June 2008): 145–181.

Armony, Ariel C. *Argentina, the United States, and the Anti-Communist Crusade in Central America, 1977–1984.* Athens: Ohio University Press, 1997.

Armony, Ariel, and Thomas W. Walker, eds. *Repression, Resistance, and Democratic Transition in Central America.* Wilmington, DE: Scholarly Resources, 2000.

Armstrong, Charles. "Urban Combat: The FMLN's 'Final Offensive' of 1989." *Marine Corps Gazette* 74, no. 11 (Spring 1990): 52–57.

Arnold, James R. *Jungle of Snakes: A Century of Counterinsurgency Warfare from the Philippines to Iraq.* New York: Bloomsbury, 2009.

Arnson, Cynthia. *Crossroads: Congress, the President, and Central America, 1976–1993.* University Park: Pennsylvania State University Press, 1993.

Asprey, Robert B. *War in the Shadows: The Guerrilla in History.* New York: William Morrow, 1994.

Aussaresses, Paul. *The Battle of the Casbah: Terrorism and Counter-Terrorism in Algeria, 1955–1957.* New York: Enigma, 2002.

Baker, James, III. *The Politics of Diplomacy: Revolution, War, and Peace, 1989–1992.* New York: Putnam's, 1995.

Baloyra, Enrique A. *El Salvador in Transition.* Chapel Hill: University of North Carolina Press, 1982.

———. "Salvaging El Salvador." *Journal of Democracy* 3, no. 2 (April 1992): 70–80.

Balta, Comandante. *Memorias de un Guerrillero.* San Salvador: New Graphic, 2006.

Barber, William Foster, and C. Neale Ronning. *Internal Security and Military Power: Counterinsurgency and Civic Action in Latin America.* Columbus: Ohio State University Press, 1966.

Bell, Aaron. "Transnational Conservative Activism and the Transformation of the Salvadoran Right, 1967–1982." PhD diss., American University, January 2016.

Bengelsdorf, Carollee, Margaret Cerullo, and Yogesh Chandari, eds. *The Selected Writings of Eqbal Ahmad.* New York: Columbia University Press, 2006.

Bennett, Huw. *Fighting the Mau Mau: The British Army and Counter-Insurgency in the Kenya Emergency.* Cambridge, UK: Cambridge University Press, 2013.

Bickel, Keith B. *Mars Learning: The Marine Corps Development of Small Wars Doctrine, 1915–1940.* Boulder, CO: Westview, 2001.

Birtle, Andrew. *U.S. Army Counterinsurgency and Contingency Operations Doctrine, 1860–1941.* Washington, DC: Center of Military History, 1998.

———. *U.S. Army Counterinsurgency and Contingency Operations Doctrine, 1942–1976.* Washington, DC: Center of Military History, 2006.

Blasier, Cole. *The Hovering Giant: U.S. Responses to Revolutionary Change in Latin America, 1910–1985.* Pittsburgh, PA: University of Pittsburgh Press, 1985.

Blaufarb, Douglas S. *The Counterinsurgency Era: U.S. Doctrine and Performance, 1950 to the Present.* New York: Free Press, 1977.

Blum, William. *Killing Hope: U.S. Military and CIA Interventions since World War II.* Monroe, ME: Common Courage Press, 1995.

Bonner, Raymond. *Weakness and Deceit: U.S. Policy and El Salvador.* New York: Times, 1984.

Branch, Daniel. *Defeating Mau Mau, Creating Kenya: Counterinsurgency, Civil War, and Decolonization.* New York: Cambridge University Press, 2009.

Brands, Hal. *Latin America's Cold War.* Cambridge, MA: Harvard University Press, 2010.

———. "Reform, Democratization, and Counterinsurgency: Evaluating the US Experience in Cold War–Era Latin America." *Small Wars and Insurgencies* 22, no. 2 (May 2011): 290–321.

Briscoe, Charles. "Los Artefactos Explosivos Improvisados: Spanish for IEDs." *Veritas* 2, no. 1 (2006): 47–53.

Brogan, Michael Patrick. "The Impact of the Vietnam Analogy on American Policy in El Salvador from 1979–1984." Master's thesis, US Army Command and General Staff College, 1994.

Brooks, David C. "U.S. Marines, Miskitos, and the Hunt for Sandino: The Río Coco Patrol in 1928." *Journal of Latin American Studies* 21, no. 2 (May 1989): 311–342.

Burbach, Roger, and Patricia Flynn, eds. *The Politics of Intervention: The United States in Central America.* New York: Monthly Review, 1984.

Byrne, Hugh. *El Salvador's Civil War: A Study of Revolution.* Boulder, CO: Lynne Rienner, 1996.

Cale, Paul. "The United States Military Advisory Group in El Salvador, 1979–1992." 1996, www.smallwarsjournal.com/documents/cale.pdf.

Campell, Bruce, and Arthur David, eds. *Death Squads in Global Perspective: Murder with Deniability.* New York: St. Martin's, 2000.

Carlson, Freedom. "Violence in Counterinsurgency: The Case of El Salvador." Master's thesis, US Marine Corps Command Staff College, 2009.

Cassidy, Robert M. *Counterinsurgency and the Global War on Terror: Military Culture and Irregular War.* Westport, CT: Praeger Security International, 2006.

Castellanos, Miguel. *The Comandante Speaks: Memoirs of an El Salvadoran Guerrilla Leader.* Boulder, CO: Westview Press, 1991.

Chávez, Joaquín. "The Pedagogy of Revolution: Popular Intellectuals and the Origins of the Salvadoran Insurgency, 1960–1980." PhD diss., New York University, 2010.

Childress, Michael. *The Effectiveness of U.S. Training Efforts in Internal Defense and Development: The Cases of El Salvador and Honduras.* Santa Monica, CA: RAND, 1995.

Choharis, P., and J. Gavrilis. "Counterinsurgency 3.0." *Parameters* 40, no. 1 (Spring 2010): 34.

Cienfuegos, Fermán. *Veredas de Audacia: Historia del FMLN.* San Salvador: CIAZO, 1993.

Clayton, Anthony. *The Wars of French Decolonization.* London: Longman, 1994.

Clements, Charles. *Witness to War: An American Doctor in El Salvador.* Toronto: Bantam, 1984.

Clutterbuck, Richard. *The Long, Long War: Counterinsurgency in Malaya and Vietnam.* New York: Praeger, 1966.

Coatsworth, John H. *Central America and the United States: The Clients and the Colossus.* New York: Twayne, 1994.

Cockburn, Alexander. *Kill Chain: The Rise of the High-Tech Assassins.* New York: Henry Holt, 2015.

Coffey, Ross. "Revisiting CORDS: The Need for Unity of Effort to Secure Victory in Iraq." *Military Review* (October 2006): 92.

Connelly, Matthew. *A Diplomatic Revolution: Algeria's Fight for Independence and the Origins of the Post-Cold War Era.* Oxford, UK: Oxford University Press, 2002.

Corr, Edwin, and Stephen Sloan, eds. *Low-Intensity Conflict: Old Threats in a New World.* Boulder, CO: Westview Press, 1992.

Corum, James S. "The Air War in El Salvador." *Airpower Power Journal* 12, no. 2 (Summer 1998): 27–44.

———. *Fighting the War on Terror: A Counterinsurgency Strategy.* St. Paul, MN: Zenith, 2007.

Cox, Ronald. *Power and Profits: U.S. Policy in Central America.* Lexington: University Press of Kentucky, 1994.

Craddock, Christopher, and M. L. R. Smith. "'No Fixed Values': A Reinterpretation of the Theory of Guerre Révolutionnaire and the Battle of Algiers, 1956–1957." *Journal of Cold War Studies* 9, no. 4 (Fall 2007): 68–105.

Dalton, Roque. *Miguel Mármol.* Translated by Kathleen Ross and Richard Schaaf. Willimantic, CT: Curbstone, 1987.

Danner, Mark. *The Massacre at El Mozote: A Parable of the Cold War.* New York: Vintage, 1994.

Davison, W. P. *Some Observations on Viet Cong Operations in the Villages.* Santa Monica, CA: RAND, 1968.

Demarest, Geoff. "Let's Take the French Experience in Algeria out of U.S. Counterinsurgency Doctrine." *Military Review* 90, no. 4 (July 2010): 19–24.

Dickey, Christopher. "Behind the Death Squads: Who They Are, How They Work, and Why No One Can Stop Them." *New Republic,* December 26, 1983.

DiMarco, Lou. "Losing the Moral Compass: Torture and Guerre Révolutionnaire in the Algerian War." *Parameters* 36, no. 2 (Summer 2006): 63–76.

Diskin, Martin. *The Impact of U.S. Policy in El Salvador, 1979–1985.* Berkeley: University of California Press, 1986.

Doggett, Margaret. *Underwriting Injustice: AID and El Salvador's Judicial Reform Program.* New York: Lawyers Committee for Human Rights, 1989.

Downie, Richard Duncan. *Learning from Conflict: The U.S. Military in Vietnam, El Salvador, and the Drug War.* Westport, CT: Praeger, 1998.

Dunkerley, James. *The Long War: Dictatorship and Revolution in El Salvador.* London: Junction, 1982.

Echevarria, Antulio. *Fourth Generation Warfare and Other Myths.* Carlisle, PA: Strategic Studies Institute, 2005.

Ellis, John. *A Short History of Guerrilla Warfare.* New York: St. Martin's, 1976.

Erisman, H. Michael, ed. *The Caribbean Challenge: U.S. Policy in a Volatile Region.* Boulder, CO: Westview, 1984.

Etchinson, Don L. *The United States and Militarism in Central America.* New York: Praeger, 1975.

Fall, Bernard. *Street without Joy.* New York: Schocken, 1964.

———. *Two Viet-Nams: A Political and Military Analysis.* New York: Praeger, 1967.

Fishel, John T., and Max Manwaring. *Uncomfortable Wars Revisited.* Norman: University of Oklahoma Press, 2006.

Fitzgerald, David. "Learning to Forget? The U.S. Army and Counterinsurgency Doctrine and Practice from Vietnam to Iraq." PhD diss., University College Cork, 2010.

Fitzgerald, Frances. *Fire in the Lake: The Vietnamese and the Americans in Vietnam.* Boston: Little, Brown, 2002.

French, David. *The British Way in Counterinsurgency, 1945–1967.* Oxford, UK: Oxford University Press, 2011.

———. "Nasty Not Nice: British Counterinsurgency Doctrine and Practice, 1945–1967." *Small Wars and Insurgencies* 23, nos. 4–5 (October–December 2012): 744–761.

Galula, David. *Counterinsurgency Warfare: Theory and Practice.* New York: Praeger, 1964.

———. *Pacification in Algeria, 1956–1958.* Santa Monica, CA: RAND, 1963.

Gates, John M. "Indians and Insurrectos." *Parameters* 13, no. 1 (May 1983): 59–68.

———. *Schoolbooks and Krags: The United States Army in the Philippines, 1898–1902.* Westport, CT: Praeger, 1973.

Gentile, Gian. "Let's Build an Army to Win All Wars." *Joint Forces Quarterly* 52 (First Quarter 2009): 27–33.

———. *Wrong Turn: America's Deadly Embrace of Counterinsurgency.* New York: New Press, 2013.

Gettleman, Marvin, ed. *El Salvador: Central America in the New Cold War.* New York: Grove, 1987.

Gill, Leslie. *The School of the Americas: Military Training and Political Violence in Americas.* Durham, NC: Duke University Press, 2004.

Gortzak, Yoav. "Using Indigenous Forces in Counterinsurgency Operations: The French in Algeria, 1954–1962." *Journal of Strategic Studies* 32, no. 2 (April 2009): 307–333.

Grandin, Greg. *Empire's Workshop: Latin America, the United States, and the Rise of the New Imperialism.* New York: Metropolitan, 2006.

Grandin, Greg, and Gilbert M. Joseph, eds. *A Century of Revolution: Insurgent and Counterinsurgent Violence during Latin America's Long Cold War.* Durham, NC: Duke University, 2010.

Greenberg, Lawrence M. *The Hukbalahap Insurrection: A Case Study of a Successful Anti-Insurgency Operation in the Philippines, 1946–1955.* Washington, DC: US Army Center of Military History, 1987.

Greentree, Todd R. *Crossroads of Intervention: Insurgency and Counterinsurgency Lessons from Central America.* Westport: Praeger Security International, 2008.

Grenier, Yvon. *The Emergence of Insurgency in El Salvador: Ideology and Political Will.* Pittsburgh, PA: University of Pittsburgh Press, 1999.

Grieb, Kenneth. "The United States and the Rise of General Maximilian Hernandez Martinez." *Journal of Latin American Studies* 3, no. 2 (November 1971): 151–172.

Grinter, Lawrence E., and Peter M. Dunn, eds. *American War in Vietnam: Lessons, Legacies, and Implications for Future Conflicts.* Westport, CT: Greenwood, 1987.

Guevara, Ernesto. *Guerrilla Warfare.* New York: Monthly Review, 1961.

Gurman, Hannah, ed. *Hearts and Minds: A People's History of Counterinsurgency.* New York: New Press, 2013.

Haines, David R. "COIN in the Real World." *Parameters* 38, no 4 (Winter 2008): 43–59.

Hamilton, Donald W. *The Art of Insurgency: American Military Policy and the Failure of Strategy in Southeast Asia.* Westport, CT: Praeger, 1998.

Hamilton, Nora, ed. *Crisis in Central America: Regional Dynamics and U.S. Policy in the 1980s.* Boulder, CO: Westview Press, 1988.

Hammes, Thomas X. *The Sling and the Stone: On War in the 21st Century.* St. Paul, MN: Zenith, 2006.

Harnecker, Marta. *Con la Mirada en Alto: Historia del FPL.* San Salvador: UCA Editores, 1993.

Hashim, Ahmed. *Insurgency and Counter-Insurgency in Iraq.* Ithaca, NY: Cornell University Press, 2006.

Hayden, H. "Revolutionary Warfare: El Salvador and Vietnam—A Comparison." *Marine Corps Gazette* (1991): 50–54.

Herring, George C. *America's Longest War: The United States and Vietnam, 1950–1975.* Boston: McGraw-Hill, 2002.

———. "Vietnam, El Salvador, and the Uses of History." In *The Central American*

Crisis: Sources of Conflict and the Failure of U.S. Policy. Edited by George Herring and Kenneth M. Coleman. Wilmington, DE: Scholarly Resources, 1985, 97–110.

Hilsman, Roger. "Internal War: The New Communist Tactic." *Marine Corps Gazette* 47, no. 1 (January 1963): 50–54.

———. *To Move a Nation: The Politics of Foreign Policy in the Administration of John F. Kennedy.* Garden City, NJ: Doubleday, 1967.

Holden, Robert H. *Armies without Nations: Public Violence and State Formation in Central America, 1821–1960.* Oxford, UK: Oxford University Press, 2004.

Horne, Alistair. *A Savage War of Peace: Algeria, 1954–1962.* New York: New York Review of Books, 2006.

Huggins, Martha K. *Political Policing: The United States and Latin America.* Durham, NC: Duke University Press, 1998.

———. "U.S. Supported State Terror: A History of Police Training in Latin America." In *Vigilantism and the State in Modern Latin America: Essays on Extralegal Violence.* Edited by Martha Huggins. New York: Praeger, 1991, 219–242.

Human Rights Watch. *Landmines: A Deadly Legacy.* New York: Human Rights Watch, 1993.

Hunt, Richard A. *Pacification: The American Struggle for Vietnam's Hearts and Minds.* Boulder, CO: Westview Press, 1995.

Joes, Anthony James. *Resisting Rebellion: The History and Politics of Counterinsurgency.* Lexington: University Press of Kentucky, 2004.

———. *Urban Guerrilla Warfare.* Lexington: University Press of Kentucky, 2007.

Joseph, G. M., and Daniela Spenser, eds. *In from the Cold: Latin America's New Encounter with the Cold War.* Durham, NC: Duke University Press, 2008.

Karnow, Stanley. *In Our Image: America's Empire in the Philippines.* London: Century, 1990.

Kelly, George Armstrong. *Lost Soldiers: The French Army and Empire in Crisis, 1947–1962.* Cambridge: Massachusetts Institute of Technology Press, 1965.

———. "Revolutionary War and Psychological Action." *Military Review* (October 1960): 4–13.

Kilcullen, David. *The Accidental Guerrilla: Fighting Small Wars in the Midst of a Big One.* Oxford, UK: Oxford University Press, 2009.

Kinzer, Stephen. *Blood of Brothers: Life and War in Nicaragua.* New York: Putnam's, 1991.

Kirkpatrick, Jeanne. "U.S. Security and Latin America." *Commentary* 71, no. 1 (1981): 29–40.

Klare, Michael, and Cynthia Arnson. *Supplying Repression: U.S. Support for Authoritarian Regimes Abroad.* Washington, DC: Institute for Policy Studies, 1977.

Klare, Michael, and Peter Kornbluh. "The New Interventionism: Low-Intensity Warfare in the 1980s and Beyond." In *Low-Intensity Warfare: Counterinsurgency, Proinsurgency, and Antiterrorism in the Eighties.* Edited by Michael Klare and Peter Kornbluh. New York: Pantheon, 1988, 3–20.

Kramer, Paul A. *The Blood of Government: Race, Empire, the United States, and the Philippines.* Chapel Hill: University of North Carolina Press, 2006.

Krepinevich, Andrew F. *The Army and Vietnam*. Baltimore, MD: Johns Hopkins University Press, 1988.

Kuzmarov, Jeremy. "Modernizing Repression: Police Training, Political Violence, and Nation-Building in the 'American Century.'" *Diplomatic History* 33, no. 2 (April 2009): 191–221.

LaFeber, Walter. *Inevitable Revolutions: The United States in Central America*. New York: Norton, 1993.

Langguth, A. J. *Hidden Terrors*. New York: Pantheon, 1978.

Lawrence, T. E. *Seven Pillars of Wisdom: A Triumph*. Garden City, NJ: Doubleday, 1935.

Leites, Nathan, and Charles Wolf. *Rebellion and Authority: An Analytic Essay on Insurgent Conflicts*. Chicago, IL: Markham, 1970.

LeoGrande, William M. "After the Battle of San Salvador." *World Policy Journal* 7, no. 2 (Spring 1990): 331–356.

———. "From Reagan to Bush: The Transition in U.S. Policy towards Central America." *Journal of Latin American Studies* 22, no. 3 (October 1990): 595–621.

———. *Our Own Backyard: The United States in Central America, 1977–1992*. Chapel Hill: University of North Carolina Press, 1998.

———. "A Splendid Little War: Drawing the Line in El Salvador." *International Security* 6, no. 1 (Summer 1981): 27–52.

Lindo-Fuentes, Héctor, and Erik Ching. *Modernizing Minds in El Salvador: Education Reform and the Cold War, 1960–1980*. Albuquerque: University of New Mexico Press, 2012.

Lindo-Fuentes, Héctor, Rafael Lara Martinez, and Erik Ching. *Remembering a Massacre in El Salvador: The Insurrection of 1932, Roque Dalton, and the Politics of Historical Memory*. Albuquerque: University of New Mexico Press, 2007.

Linn, Brian McAllister. *The Philippine War, 1899–1902*. Lawrence: University Press of Kansas, 2000.

———. *The U.S. Army and Counterinsurgency in the Philippine War, 1899–1902*. Chapel Hill: University of North Carolina Press, 1989.

Longley, Kyle. *Grunts: The American Soldier in Vietnam*. Armonk, NY: M. E. Sharpe, 2008.

———. *In the Eagle's Shadow: The United States and Latin America*. Wheeling, IL: Harlan Davidson, 2002.

Lungo, Mario. *El Salvador in the Eighties: Counterinsurgency and Revolution*. Philadelphia, PA: Temple University Press, 1996.

Luttwak, Edward. "Dead End: Counterinsurgency Warfare as Military Malpractice." *Harper's* (February 2007).

Manwaring, Max, and Courtney Prisk, eds. *El Salvador at War: An Oral History of Conflict from the 1979 Insurrection to the Present*. Washington, DC: National Defense University Press, 1988.

Markel, Wade. "Draining the Swamp: The British Strategy of Population Control." *Parameters* 36, no. 1 (Spring 2006): 35–48.

Marlowe, Ann. *David Galula: His Life and Intellectual Context*. Carlisle, PA: Strategic Studies Institute, 2010.

Marshall, Alex. "Imperial Nostalgia, the Liberal Lie, and the Perils of Post-Modern Counterinsurgency." *Small Wars and Insurgencies* 21, no. 2 (2010): 233–258.

May, Glenn. "A Filipino Resistance to American Occupation: Batangas, 1899–1902." *Pacific Historical Review* 48, no. 4 (November 1979): 531–556.

Mazzei, Julie. *Death Squads or Self-Defense Forces? How Paramilitary Groups Emerge and Challenge Democracy in Latin America.* Chapel Hill: University of North Carolina Press, 2009.

McClintock, Cynthia. *Revolutionary Movements in Latin America: El Salvador's FMLN and Peru's Shining Path.* Washington, DC: US Institute of Peace, 1998.

McClintock, Michael. *The American Connection: State Terror and Popular Resistance in El Salvador.* London: Zed, 1985.

———. *Instruments of Statecraft: U.S. Guerrilla Warfare, Counterinsurgency, and Counter-Terrorism, 1940–1990.* New York: Pantheon, 1992.

McPherson, Alan L. *Intimate Ties, Bitter Struggles: The United States and Latin America since 1945.* Washington, DC: Potomac, 2006.

———. *The Invaded: How Latin Americans and Their Allies Fought and Ended U.S. Occupations.* Oxford, UK: Oxford University Press, 2014.

McSherry, J. Patrice. *Predatory States: Operation Condor and Covert War in Latin America.* Lanham, MD: Rowman and Littlefield, 2005.

Meara, William. *Contra Cross: Insurgency and Tyranny in Central America, 1979–1989.* Annapolis, MD: Naval Institute Press, 2006.

Mijango, Raúl. *Mi Guerra: Testimonio de Toda Una Vida.* San Salvador: Laser Print, 2007.

Millet, Richard. *Searching for Stability: The U.S. Development of Constabulary Forces in Latin America and the Philippines.* Fort Leavenworth, KS: Combat Studies Institute, 2006.

Montgomery, Tommie Sue. "Fighting Guerrillas: The United States and Low-Intensity Conflict in El Salvador." *New Political Science* 9, no. 1 (Fall–Winter 1990): 21–53.

———. *Revolution in El Salvador: From Civil Strife to Civil Peace.* Boulder, CO: Westview Press, 1995.

———. *Revolution in El Salvador: Origins and Evolution.* Boulder, CO: Westview, 1982.

Moore, Scott W. "Purple, Not Gold: Lessons from USAID-USMILGP Cooperation in El Salvador, 1980–1992." Master's thesis, Naval Postgraduate School, 1997.

Moroni Bracamonte, José Angel. *Strategy and Tactics of the Salvadoran FMLN Guerrillas: Last Battle of the Cold War, Blueprint for Future Conflicts.* Westport, CT: Praeger, 1995.

Moyar, Mark. *Phoenix and the Birds of Prey: Counterinsurgency and Counterterrorism in Vietnam.* Annapolis, MD: Naval Institute Press, 1997.

———. *A Question of Command: Counterinsurgency from the Civil War to Iraq.* New Haven, CT: Yale University Press, 2009.

———. *Triumph Forsaken: The Vietnam War, 1954–1965.* Cambridge, UK: Cambridge University Press, 2006.

Nagl, John A. *Counterinsurgency Lessons from Malaya and Vietnam: Learning to Eat Soup with a Knife.* Westport, CT: Praeger, 2002.

Nairn, Allan. "Behind the Death Squads: An Exclusive Report on the U.S. Role in El Salvador's Official Terror." *Progressive* (May 1984).

Nashel, Jonathan. *Edward Lansdale's Cold War: Culture, Politics, and the Cold War.* Amherst: University of Massachusetts Press, 2005.

Norton, Jason. "The French-Algerian War and *FM 3-24*, Counterinsurgency: A Comparison." Master's thesis, US Army Command and General Staff College, 2007.

O'Neill, Bard E. *Insurgency and Terrorism: From Revolution to Apocalypse.* Washington, DC: Potomac, 2005.

Paige, Jeffery M. *Coffee and Power: Revolution and the Rise of Democracy in Central America.* Cambridge, MA: Harvard University Press, 1997.

Paret, Peter. *French Revolutionary Warfare from Indochina to Algeria: The Analysis of a Political and Military Doctrine.* New York: Praeger, 1964.

Paterson, Thomas, ed. *Kennedy's Quest for Victory: American Foreign Policy, 1961–1963.* Oxford, UK: Oxford University Press, 1989.

Peace, Roger. *A Call to Conscience: The Anti-Contra War Campaign.* Amherst: University of Massachusetts Press, 2012.

Pearce, Jenny. *Promised Land: Peasant Rebellion in Chalatenango, El Salvador.* London: Latin America Bureau, 1986.

Peters, Ralph. "New Counterinsurgency Manual Cheats on the History Exam." *Armed Forces Journal* (February 2007). http://www.armedforcesjournal.com /2007/02/2456854.

Peterson, Michael E. *The Combined Action Platoons: The U.S. Marines' Other War in Vietnam.* New York: Praeger, 1989.

Petras, James. "The Anatomy of State Terror: Chile, El Salvador, and Brazil." *Science and Society* 51, no. 3 (Fall 1987): 314–338.

Phares, Matthew. "Combating Insurgency: Can Lessons from the Huk Rebellion Apply to Iraq?" Master's thesis, US Marine Corps Command and Staff College, 2008.

Pike, Douglas. *The Viet-Cong Strategy of Terror.* Saigon: US Mission Vietnam, 1970.

Polk, William Roe. *Violent Politics: A History of Insurgency, Terrorism, and Guerrilla War from the American Revolution to Iraq.* New York: HarperCollins, 2007.

Porch, Douglas. *Counterinsurgency: Exposing the Myths of the New Way of War.* Cambridge, UK: Cambridge University Press, 2013.

———. "The Dangerous Myths and Dubious Promise of COIN." *Small Wars and Insurgencies* 22, no. 2 (May 2011): 239–257.

Porter, Gareth. *Perils of Dominance: Imbalance of Power and the Road to War in Vietnam.* Berkeley: University of California Press, 2005.

Prados, John. *The Hidden History of the Vietnam War.* Chicago: Ivan R. Dee, 1995.

———. *Vietnam: The History of an Unwinnable War, 1945–1975.* Lawrence: University Press of Kansas, 2009.

Price, David H. *Weaponizing Anthropology: Social Science in the Service of the Militarized State.* Oakland, CA: Counterpunch and AK Press, 2011.

Pye, Lucien. "Armies in the Process of Political Modernization." In *The Role of the Military in Underdeveloped Countries.* Edited by John J. Johnson. Princeton, NJ: Princeton University Press, 1962, 69–91.

Rabasa, Angel, Lesley Anne Warner, Peter Chalk, Ivan Kihilko, and Paraag Shukla. *Money in the Bank: Lessons Learned from Past Counterinsurgency Operations.* Santa Monica, CA: RAND, 2007.

Rabe, Stephen G. "Controlling Revolutions: Latin America, the Alliance for Progress, and Cold War Anti-Communism." In *Kennedy's Quest for Victory: American Foreign Policy, 1961–1963.* Edited by Thomas G. Paterson. New York: Oxford University Press, 1989, 105–122.

———. *Killing Zone: The United States Wages Cold War in Latin America.* New York: Oxford University Press, 2011.

———. *The Most Dangerous Area in the World: John F. Kennedy Confronts Communist Revolution in Latin America.* Chapel Hill: University of North Carolina Press, 1999.

Race, Jeffrey. *War Comes to Long An: Revolutionary Conflict in a Vietnamese Province.* Berkeley: University of California Press, 2010.

Radu, Michael, and Vladimir Tismaneanu. *Latin American Revolutionaries: Groups, Goals, Methods.* Washington, DC: Pergamon-Brassey's International Defense, 1990.

Ramsey, Robert, III. *Advising Indigenous Forces: American Advisors in Korea, Vietnam, and El Salvador.* Fort Leavenworth, KS: Combat Studies Institute, 2010.

Record, Jeffrey. *Beating Goliath: Why Insurgencies Win.* Washington, DC: Potomac, 2007.

Reis, Bruno C. "The Myth of British Minimum Force in Counterinsurgency Campaigns during Decolonisation, 1945–1970." *Journal of Strategic Studies* 34, no. 2 (April 2011): 245–277.

Rempe, Dennis M. "An American Trojan Horse? Eisenhower, Latin America, and the Development of U.S. Internal Security Policy, 1954–1960." *Small Wars and Insurgencies* 10, no. 1 (Spring 1999): 34–64.

Renda, Mary A. *Taking Haiti: Military Occupation and the Culture of U.S. Imperialism, 1915–1940.* Chapel Hill: University of North Carolina Press, 2001.

Ricks, Thomas E. *Fiasco: The American Military Adventure in Iraq.* New York: Penguin Press, 2006.

Rid, Thomas. "The Nineteenth-Century Origins of Counterinsurgency Doctrine." *Journal of Strategic Studies* 33, no. 5 (October 2010): 727–758.

Rodríguez, Néstor, and Cecilia Menjivar, eds. *When States Kill: Latin America, the U.S., and Technologies of Terror.* Austin: University of Texas Press, 2005.

Rosello, Victor. "Lessons from El Salvador." *Parameters* (Winter 1993–1994): 100–108.

Rosenau, William. "The Kennedy Administration, U.S. Foreign Internal Security Assistance and the Challenge of 'Subterranean Warfare,' 1961–1963." *Small Wars and Insurgencies* 14, no. 3 (Autumn 2003): 65–99.

Rosenau, William, and Austin Long. *The Phoenix Program and Contemporary Counterinsurgency.* Santa Monica, CA: RAND, 2009.

Roser, Stephen. "The War in El Salvador: Is U.S. Military Strategy Working?" Master's thesis, National War College, 2005.

Rostow, Walt. "Guerrilla Warfare in Underdeveloped Areas." *Marine Corps Gazette* 46, no. 1 (January 1962): 46–49.

Rothstein, Hy S. *Afghanistan and the Troubled Future of Unconventional Warfare.* Annapolis, MD: Naval Institute Press, 2006.

———. "Less Is More: The Problematic Future of Irregular Warfare in an Era of Collapsing States." *Third World Quarterly* 28, no. 2 (2007): 275–294.

Sarkesian, Sam, ed. *Revolutionary Guerrilla Warfare.* Chicago: Precedent, 1975.

Schlesinger, Arthur, Jr. *A Thousand Days: JFK in the White House.* New York: Mariner, 2002.

Schmitz, David. *Thank God They're on Our Side: The United States and Right-Wing Dictatorships, 1921–1965.* Chapel Hill: University of North Carolina Press, 1999.

Schoultz, Lars. *Beneath the United States: A History of U.S. Policy toward Latin America.* Cambridge, MA: Harvard University Press, 1998.

Schroeder, Michael J. "The Sandino Rebellion Revisited: Civil War, Imperialism, Popular Nationalism, and State Formation Muddied Up Together in the Segovias of Nicaragua, 1926–1934." In *Close Encounters of Empire: Writing the Cultural History of U.S.–Latin American Relations.* Edited by Gilbert Joseph, Catherine LeGrand, and Ricardo Salvatore. Durham, NC: Duke University Press, 1998, 208–268.

———. "Social Memory and Tactical Doctrine: The Air War in Nicaragua during the Sandino Rebellion, 1927–1932." *International History Review* 29, no. 3 (September 2007): 508–549.

Schwartz, Benjamin. *American Counterinsurgency Doctrine and El Salvador: The Frustrations of Reform and the Illusions of Nation Building.* Santa Monica, CA: RAND, 1991.

Sepp, Kalev. "Best Practices in Counterinsurgency." *Military Review* (May–June 2005): 8–12.

Shackley, Theodore. *The Third Option: An American View of Counterinsurgency Operations.* Boston: McGraw-Hill, 1981.

Shafer, D. Michael. *Deadly Paradigms: The Failure of U.S. Counterinsurgency Policy.* Princeton, NJ: Princeton University Press, 1988.

Sharpe, Kenneth. "El Salvador Revisited: Why Duarte Is in Trouble." *World Policy Journal* 3, no. 3 (Summer 1986): 473–494.

Shaull, Wendy. *Tortillas, Beans, and M16s: Behind the Lines in El Salvador.* London: Pluto, 1990.

Shultz, Richard H. *Insurgents, Terrorists, and Militias: The Warriors of Contemporary Combat.* New York: Columbia University Press, 2006.

Skocpol, Theda. *States and Social Revolutions: A Comparative Analysis of France, Russia, and China.* New York: Cambridge University Press, 1979.

Smith, Rupert. *The Utility of Force: The Art of War in the Modern World.* New York: Knopf, 2007.

Spencer, David E. "External Resource Mobilization and Successful Insurgency in Cuba, Nicaragua, and El Salvador, 1959–1992." PhD diss., George Washington University, 2002.

———. *From Vietnam to El Salvador: The Saga of the FMLN Sappers and Other Guerrilla Forces in Latin America.* Westport, CT: Praeger, 1996.

Spenser, Daniela. "Revolutions and Revolutionaries in Latin America and the Cold War." *Latin American Research Review* 40, no. 3 (2005): 377–389.

Stanley, William Deane. *The Protection Racket State: Elite Politics, Military Extortion, and Civil War in El Salvador.* Philadelphia, PA: Temple University Press, 1996.

Stanley, William, and Mark Peceny. "Counterinsurgency in El Salvador." *Politics and Society* 38, no. 1 (2010): 67–94.

Stewart, Richard, gen. ed. *American Military History.* Vol. 2: *The United States Army in a Global Era, 1917–2003.* Washington, DC: US Army Center of Military History, 2009.

Stone, Oliver, and Peter Kuznick. *The Untold History of the United States.* New York: Gallery, 2012.

Sussman, Michael. *AIFLD: U.S. Trojan Horse in Latin America and the Caribbean.* Washington, DC: Ecumenical Program in Central America and the Caribbean (EPICA), 1983.

Taber, Robert. *The War of the Flea: A Study of Guerrilla Warfare Theory and Practice.* New York: L. Stuart, 1965.

Terzian, John. "SF Advisers in El Salvador: The Attack of El Paraíso." *Special Warfare* 14, no. 2 (Spring 2001): 18–25.

Thompson, Robert Grainger Ker. *Defeating Communist Insurgency: Experiences from Malaya and Vietnam.* London: Chatto and Windus, 1966.

Thornton, Skip. *Thinking about the Tactics of Modern War: The Salvadoran Example.* Fort Leavenworth, KS: Command and General Staff College, 1989.

Tierney, John J. *Chasing Ghosts: Unconventional Warfare in American History.* Washington, DC: Potomac, 2006.

Trinquier, Roger. *Modern Warfare: A French View of Counterinsurgency.* New York: Praeger, 1964.

Ucko, David. "Innovation or Inertia: The U.S. Military and the Learning of Counterinsurgency." *Orbis* 52, no. 2 (2008): 290–310.

United Nations. *From Madness to Hope: The 12-Year War in El Salvador—Report of the Commission on the Truth for El Salvador.* http://www.usip.org/files/file/ElSalvador-Report.pdf.

US Army. *Field Manual 100-20: Military Operations in Low-Intensity Conflict.* Washington DC: US Department of the Army, 1990.

US Army and Marine Corps. *FM 3-24, Counterinsurgency.* Washington, DC: US Department of the Army, December 2006.

US Marine Corps. *Small Wars Manual.* Washington, DC: US Government Printing Office, 1940.

Valentine, Douglas. *The Phoenix Program.* New York: William Morrow, 1990.

Valeriano, Napoleon D. *Counter-Guerrilla Operations: The Philippine Experience.* New York: Praeger, 1962.

Vanden, H. E. "Terrorism, Law, and State Policy in Central America: The Eighties." *New Political Science* 18 (Fall–Winter, 1990): 314–338.

Vanden, H. E., and Robert Taylor. "Defining Terrorism in El Salvador: La Matanza." *Annals of the American Academy of Political and Social Science* 463 (September 1982): 106–118.

Villalobos, Joaquín. *The War in El Salvador: Current Situation and Outlook for the Future.* San Francisco, CA: Solidarity, 1986.

Villiers-Negroponte, Diana. *Seeking Peace in El Salvador: The Struggle to Reconstruct a Nation at the End of the Cold War.* New York: Palgrave Macmillan, 2012.

Vö, Nguyen Giáp. *People's War, People's Army: The Viet Công Insurrection Manual for Underdeveloped Countries.* New York: Praeger, 1962.

Wade, Christine. *Captured Peace: Elites and Peacebuilding in El Salvador.* Athens: Ohio University Press, 2016.

Waghelstein, John. "El Salvador and the Press: A Personal Account." *Parameters* 15, no. 3 (1985).

———. "Military-to-Military Contacts: Personal Observations—the El Salvador Case." *Low-Intensity Conflict and Law Enforcement* 10, no. 2 (Summer 2003).

———. "Ruminations of a Pachyderm, or What I Learned in the Counterinsurgency Business." *Small Wars and Insurgencies* 5, no. 3 (1994): 360–378.

Walker, Greg. *At the Hurricane's Eye: U.S. Special Forces from Vietnam to Desert Storm.* New York: Ivy, 1994.

Welch, Richard E. "American Atrocities in the Philippines: The Indictment and the Response." *Pacific Historical Review* 43, no. 2 (May 1974): 233–253.

White, Richard Alan. *The Morass: United States' Intervention in Central America.* New York: Harper and Row, 1984.

Williams, Philip J., and Knut Walters. *Militarization and Demilitarization in El Salvador's Transition to Democracy.* Pittsburgh, PA: University of Pittsburgh Press, 1997.

Williams, Walter L. "United States Indian Policy and the Debate over the Philippine Annexation: Implications for the Origins of American Imperialism." *Journal of American History* 66, no. 4 (March 1980): 810–883.

Wood, Elisabeth Jean. *Insurgent Collective Action and Civil War in El Salvador.* Cambridge, UK: Cambridge University Press, 2003.

Ximenes [nom de plume]. "Revolutionary War." *Military Review* (August 1957): 103–108.

Young, Marilyn. *The Vietnam Wars, 1945–1990.* New York: HarperCollins, 1991.

Zasloff, Joseph Jermiah. *Rural Resettlement in Vietnam: An Agroville in Development.* Saigon: Michigan State University, Vietnam Advisory Group, 1961.

Zedong, Mao. *On Guerrilla Warfare.* New York: Praeger, 1961.

Zepeda, Juan Orlando. *Perfiles de la Guerra en El Salvador.* San Salvador: New Graphics, 2008.

INDEX

Abizaid, John, 170
Abrams, Elliot, 80, 102, 130, 164
Afghanistan, 8, 37–38, 62, 91, 167, 170, 174, 177, 180, 229n19
AFL-CIO, 84
Agencia Nacional de Seguridad de El Salvador (ANSESAL), 48, 55, 72
Aguinaldo, Emilio, 16–17, 186n9
  capture of, 19
Ahuachapán, 86
Albright, Madeleine, 168
Algeria, 15, 25–28, 37, 176, 191n65, 192n70, 209n60
Alianza Republicana Nacionalista (ARENA), 83, 140–141, 144–145, 156, 161, 164, 180–181
al-Madrid, Abu Ayyub, 174
al-Maliki, Nouri, 177
Alvarado, José Roberto García, 142, 223n24
al-Zarqawi, Abu Musab, 174
American Institute for Free Labor Development (AIFLD), 56, 84, 86
Americas Watch, 101, 117
Andino, Pablo Parada, 78
Arias, Oscar, 130–131
  Peace Plan, 130
Aronson, Bernard, 148, 151, 154–155, 159
Atlacatl Battalion, 72–73, 80
Ayagualo, 120–121

Baker, James, III, 138–139, 148, 154, 159
Balangiga, 19
Baloyra, Enrique, 53
Balta, Comandante (Juan Ramón Medrano), 83, 157, 209n58
Barrientos, René, 29
Batista, Fulgencio, 39
Battle of Algiers, 26
Bell, David, 46
Bell, J. Franklin, 18
Berlin Wall, 146, 156
Bins, Jack R., 172
Boer War, 36
Bolivia, 9, 28–30
Bonner, Raymond, 86

Brígada Rafael Arce Zablah (BRAZ), 78
Brzezinski, Zbigniew, 61
Buenos Aires, 113
Bush, George H. W., 2, 124, 138–140, 148, 150–151, 154, 157, 159
Bush, George W., 14, 83, 169–171, 176–179
Bushnell, John, 69

Caldwell, John, 4
Candaba, 23
Carpio, Salvador Cayetano, 53, 75, 204n109, 208n55
Carranza, Nicholás, 48
Carter, Jimmy, 12, 41, 54–62, 65, 84, 94, 211n97
Casteel, Steven, 172
Castellanos, Miguel, 142, 223n24
Castro, Fidel, 49, 59, 165
Central American Refugee Center, 98
Central Intelligence Agency (CIA), 197n26
  in El Salvador, 50, 69, 74, 83–84, 89, 92, 104–105, 112, 119, 140–144, 152, 158, 181, 216n39, 217n76, 222n9, 222n19
  in Nicaragua, 5, 130
  in Vietnam, 34, 188n41
Cerén, Salvador Sánchez, 78, 164, 222n19
Cerron Grande Dam, 116
Chaffee, Adna, 19
Chalatenango, 68, 78, 100
Chamorro, Violeta, 156
Chapultepec Peace Accords, 72, 138, 144, 161
Chechnya, 37
Cheek, James, 56
Cheney, Dick, 83, 170
Chile, 43, 77
Christ, Hans, 56
Christopher, Warren, 59
Cienfuegos, Fermán, 60
Civil Operations and Rural Development Support (CORDS), 34, 90
Clark, William, 124
Clausewitz, Carl, 77, 209n61
Clinton, Hillary, 168
Coffman, James H., 173

....p 5 longest U.S. nation-building effort between
Vietnam and Iraq.
73 Hopkins: CRER
98 400,000 Salvadorans came to U.S.
101 forced draft urbanization
[Re US spent a huge amount — and failed]